Jewish Writers, German Literature

Jewish Writers, German Literature

The Uneasy Examples of Nelly Sachs and Walter Benjamin

Edited by

Timothy Bahti and Marilyn Sibley Fries

Ann Arbor

THE UNIVERSITY OF MICHIGAN PRESS

1998   1997   1996   1995   4   3   2   1

A CIP catalog record for this book is available from the British Library.

Library of Congress Cataloging-in-Publication Data

Jewish Writers, German Literature.
        p.   cm.
    ISBN 0-472-10621-X
    1. German literature—20th century—History and criticism.
    2. German literature—Jewish authors—History and criticism.
    3. Sachs, Nelly. 4. Benjamin, Walter, 1892–1940. 5. Authors,
    German—20th century—Biography. 6. Authors, Jewish—Germany—
    Biography.
    PT405.J49 1996
    830.9′8924—dc20   95-25355
                                                                  CIP

Contents

Acknowledgments

This volume took its inception in a conference we organized at the University of Michigan in February 1992, bringing together many of our contributors for several days of critical exchange. This would not have been possible without support from many quarters, and we wish to acknowledge the University of Michigan's Horace H. Rackham School of Graduate Studies, the University Council on International Academic Affairs, the Office of the Vice President for Research, the Dean's Office of the College of Literature, Science, and the Arts, the Department of Germanic Languages and Literatures, and the Program in Comparative Literature. We likewise gratefully acknowledge the generous support of the German Academic Exchange Service (DAAD), the Helmut Stern Foundation, and the Winkelman Foundation.

Bengt Holmqvist's care for the person and texts of Nelly Sachs enabled much of the attention that she has merited and begun to receive. He intended to join our gathering, illness kept him back, and he died shortly afterward. We wish to acknowledge, especially in absentia, his contribution to our own efforts.

Peter Blickle, Ph.D. candidate in the Department of Germanic Languages and Literatures at Michigan, has provided invaluable assistance to the editors in the final preparation of this manuscript. To him, and to Susan Whitlock, our editor at the University of Michigan Press, our special thanks.

Marilyn Sibley Fries, co-editor of this volume, died shortly before its completion. Her inspiration and continued labor made the book possible. It stands as part of her legacy to humane understanding.

Editors' Notes

Works by Walter Benjamin and Nelly Sachs are cited in parentheses throughout this volume according to the following abbreviations and notations:

Benjamin, Walter. *Gesammelte Schriften*. Ed. Rolf Tiedemann and Hermann Schweppenhäuser. 7 vols. Frankfurt am Main: Suhrkamp, 1972–89. Citations show roman volume number, followed by page number.

Benjamin, Walter. *Illuminations*. Trans. Harry Zohn. Ed. Hannah Arendt. New York: Schocken, 1968. Cited as *Illuminations*.

Benjamin, Walter. *Reflections: Essays, Aphorisms, Autobiographical Writings*. Trans. Edmund Jephcott. Ed. Peter Demetz. New York: Schocken, 1978. Cited as *Reflections*.

Sachs, Nelly. *Briefe der Nelly Sachs*. Ed. Ruth Dinesen and Helmut Müssener. Frankfurt am Main: Suhrkamp, 1984. Cited as *Briefe*.

Sachs, Nelly. *Fahrt ins Staublose: Die Gedichte der Nelly Sachs*. Frankfurt am Main: Suhrkamp, 1961. Commonly referred to as *Gedichte I*; cited as I.

Sachs, Nelly. *O the Chimneys: Selected Poems, Including the Verse Play, Eli*. Trans. Michael Hamburger, Christopher Holme, Ruth Mead, Matthew Mead, and Michael Roloff. New York: Farrar, Straus and Giroux, 1967. Cited as *Chimneys*.

Sachs, Nelly. *The Seeker and Other Poems*. Trans. Ruth Mead, Matthew Mead, and Michael Hamburger. New York: Farrar, Straus and Giroux, 1970. Cited as *Seeker*.

Sachs, Nelly. *Suche nach Lebenden: Die Gedichte der Nelly Sachs*. Vol. 2. Frankfurt am Main: Suhrkamp, 1971. Known as *Gedichte II*; cited as II.

Sachs, Nelly. *Zeichen im Sand: Die szenischen Dichtungen der Nelly*

Sachs. Frankfurt am Main: Suhrkamp, 1962. Referred to in Sachs scholarship, and here, as III.

Works not available in published English translation have been translated by editors and/or contributors unless otherwise noted.

Chapter 1

Introduction

Timothy Bahti and Marilyn Sibley Fries

Nelly Sachs and Walter Benjamin are associated by the contingency of their nearly contemporaneous centenaries. But more deeply, the time for such association is now, not as a time that honors one hundred years' passage, but as a time that is coming true. ("Lang ist die Zeit, / Es ereignet sich aber / Das Wahre," a line of Hölderlin's to which Benjamin alludes in his *Origin of the German Trauerspiel*.)[1] What is coming true is the massive revision of German-Jewish literary and cultural work in the light of today's changes and the decisions of the whole last century—the same hundred years since Benjamin's and Sachs's births. Not the least of today's changes is the decisive rejection of Marxism in a (consequently, if awkwardly) reunified Germany and a (still emerging) Central Europe that had, both of them, been condemned to an extended, apparently endless occupation by and preoccupation with this discourse of power. And surely the most demonstrative and horrific of this century's decisions— the cuts that separate and judge—was the cutting off of Jews from Germany and Central Europe, from earth and life. That eastern Germany is—barely—surviving nearly a half a century of Marxism is both dramatic in the achievement and pathetic in its means; that Nelly Sachs— barely, physically if not psychically—survived the Holocaust is perhaps to no one's benefit more than to those who deserve it the least: Germans as the housers of her tongue. That Benjamin will yet survive his own preoccupation with and occupation by Marxism—of nearly seventy years running by now—is as fateful and true as was his death at the Spanish-French border, a threshold between the land of the first expulsion of European Jews (another centenary, times five) and the lands of the new expulsion by the Nazis.

The essays in this collection represent a variety of scholarly treatments of Nelly Sachs and Walter Benjamin—various in their methods, their focus on biography, genre, or motif, their specificity or scope—but they collect around a central and enduring paradox represented by the two authors. As Jewish writers of German citizenship, they were made to suffer to the point of madness and death. Nonetheless surviving in the form of their writings, Sachs and Benjamin reconfronted German literature with an uneasy set of options. To celebrate Sachs as Jewish, as a Holocaust poet, was to avoid treating her as a German writer—a writer, after all, of and in German—while draping this avoidance in the cloak of regret and atonement. Benjamin could be categorized in turn as an émigré writer and a New Left or Frankfurt school writer, and as he then emerged as a German philosopher and critic of the first order, the Jewish themes and motifs of his work could be studiously avoided. The paradox, then, is that Jewishness and Germanness cohabit no better in the receptions of their work than they did in the treatments of their lives; nor do their individualities as distinctive *writers* and their places within the *collective* tradition of German literature. The authors in this collection of essays reconfront and restage this difficulty: the contact and conflict between Jewish writers and German literature, both brought about by, and productive of, specific historical, cultural, and philosophical issues. The scholarly treatment of Sachs and Benjamin in this volume can elucidate these issues from many perspectives, but it can neither explain nor explain away the entanglement of Jewish roots and German letters. Jewish writing and German literature are always already in an uneasy relationship. The brilliant and stubborn individuality of Sachs and Benjamin makes their exemplarity as Jewish writers in German literature that much more uneasy.

"There are many different ways of dispatching a poet," Werner Weber noted in his "Laudatio" for Nelly Sachs in 1965. "The friendliest—admittedly also the most insidious—is this: one applauds the poet under any and all circumstances, but most preferably under celebratory ones."[2] Weber could not have known how prophetic his words would prove to be. After living and writing in exile in Sweden since 1940, publishing her first volumes of German poetry not in the democratic western part of Germany, but rather in the Soviet occupied zone and in the Netherlands;[3] after almost two decades of deliberate nonrecognition by German readers and critics, Nelly Sachs seemed to be experiencing a change of fortune, to be assuming her deserved position in twentieth-century German literature. The German Publishing Industry named her recipient of its Peace Prize in 1965, following her recognition by various other organizations.[4] In 1966, Nelly Sachs was awarded the Nobel Prize for Literature, together with the Israeli writer Samuel Josef Agnon. In a final and ironic act of reclamation, the City of Berlin named Nelly Sachs, a German born in Berlin in 1891, an honorary citizen in 1967.

But all this acclaim was to be her undoing—personally and professionally; it was to dispatch the person to extended sojourns in the nether realms of persecution mania, her oeuvre to the prison of classification. As "poet of the Jewish fate" [Dichterin jüdischen Schicksals],[5] she would be claimed by well-meaning as well as self-serving critics as a voice of historical reconciliation. It is tempting to read this as a posthumous murder of the creature with which Nelly Sachs identified and which constitutes her work's chief image; this butterfly is dead, unjustly pinned in the glass showcase. Her vital central metaphors—the living butterfly in flight (another ambiguous word) and metamorphosis; the desert sands where the footprints' traces are constantly re-covered; the air in which epitaphs are inscribed (and dissipate); the silent language—which refuse permanence and point beyond themselves to nonimagistic and nonlinguistic fields of reference, are here brought to a standstill, made to stand for something fixed and supposedly finished.

Recognition is an ambiguous term, and Nelly Sachs's recognition—as a Jewish poet—ultimately served the recognizers better than it did the object of their re-cognition, who had throughout her career increasingly withdrawn to a position deliberately obscured by the transmissive, other-voiced features of her work. The retraction of her persona for the sake of her poetry was, after all, not only her way of confirming the universal aspect of that work and her belief in its externally inspired production; it was also a way of hiding a vulnerable self, of protecting against that kind of recognition which had been so dangerous during eight years under Hitler in Germany, of avoiding exposure as a Jew. But the 1960s in Germany marked a time of public and political "German-Jewish reconciliation," and Nelly Sachs was forced to function as representative for that impetus, conveniently reclaimed as an alibi of German goodwill and understanding. By locking her into this representative role, Germany could avoid close encounters with her poetry—with its difficult medium as well as its condemnatory message—and could once again elude that exercise known as "coming to terms with the past." As her admiring fellow-poet and correspondent Hilde Domin noted in 1977, it seemed as though "German postwar society, with its deferential honoring of this representative of insurmountable, unarticulable and yet articulated suffering, had freed itself from the obligation to *live* with such poems, that is, the necessity of reading and loving them."[6] Paradoxically, an oeuvre turned almost exclusively toward that past and its remembrance was made to issue in a putatively new and friendlier future. More than twenty-five years later, that future has yet to arrive, and Nelly Sachs remains boxed in the category that prescribes attention to the Holocaust as a precondition for an interest in her work.

Critics echoing earlier critics and employing the same epithets again and again keep the doors closed to a more fruitful analysis. Such analysis, begun particularly in monographs by Ehrhard Bahr and Ruth Dinesen, and extended in this volume, has the potential of discovering that Sachs's work, while propelled by and alluding to the Holocaust, does not always reside thematically within this field of reference.[7] Indeed, Sachs saw herself as a poet of suffering, her life as a process of dying, her creative gift the result of overwhelming inspiration that required her to give voice to suffering peoples everywhere. Especially her perception of herself as a mouthpiece links her with such German Romantic poets as Novalis and Hölderlin, while the form and content of her verse remind scholars of modernists like Trakl and Rilke. However, her whole enterprise, embracing both form and content, most often locates her in the contextual tradition of her fellow Jews, Kafka and Celan.

The tendency to such great suffering may inhere in the emotional receptivity of the writer. This was surely the case with Sachs, whose historical positioning amplified her pain and grief and ultimately produced her greatest works but did not constitute their sole foundation. Indeed, as Ruth Dinesen points out, Sachs's path of suffering leads through several different moments in her life. Her own particular fate (*Schicksal*—her word), the initial and very personal impulse of her writing, was her intense love at age seventeen for a man with whom she could not be joined, and who was subsequently transported to a death camp.[8] The genocide of "her people" (whose definition can and should be extended beyond the Jews) undeniably occupies a central position in her major works, but toward the end of her life, the realm of suffering shifted from the Nazi genocide and the Diaspora to the lost souls of hospital mental wards.

Her themes, motifs, images, and metaphors, her favored figure of synecdoche—all are infinitely expandable within the realm of the suffering. That most arise from her intense preoccupation with the Old Testament, the Kabala, and with various Hasidic tales should not confine our reception of her. Indeed, her central challenge and question, for which she finds articulation in the Zohar, concerns the birth of the alphabet, naming, and language. In attempting to find expression for the inexpressible, Nelly Sachs not only suggests the viability of *Gestus* as the sole possible indicator of a truth that cannot be named,[9] she also positions herself very much (if unconsciously) within this century's traditions of language skepticism, reminding us that such questioning not only has ancient roots, but that it may also spring from sources other than the theoretical and philosophical writings of the day.

Because Sachs worked in virtual isolation from all manner of tradition (read: the canons of German poetry and the ideas of modernity), her poetry is frequently viewed as hermetic, generated by and in the realm of profound personal pain and grief and understandable chiefly with reference to its own semantic field and historical positioning. But she situates herself otherwise, and her allusions to biblical and Hasidic traditions and tales demand familiarity with these sources—especially where they treat the emergence of names and letters—if, indeed, they eventually return us to mysticism. Her writings are ultimately readable by taking the meaning of *hermetic* quite literally, even as we qualify it by insisting on the equal importance of *music* and *sense:* "obscure, difficult poetry in which the language and imagery are subjective and in which the 'music' and the suggestive power of the words are of as great an importance (if not greater) as the sense."[10] While none of the contributors to this volume uses the word hermetic, most share the perspective suggested by this definition: they focus on the subjectivity of language and imagery, on music, and particularly on the words' suggestive power. In so doing, none seeks to diminish the sense of the senselessness of historical brutality recorded in her words; but all acknowledge—some, like Bahr, most explicitly; others more obliquely—the limits of poetic metaphor as well as the damage done to both suggestion and sense by attempts to back-translate her metaphor into everyday speech.[11]

If Benjamin's goal was to be the greatest literary critic in German, Nelly Sachs held—at first glance—no comparable hubristic aims. Indeed, during most of the period in which she produced what she termed her "valid" works, she lived outside any context against which she might have calculated her stature. Calculation, in fact, plays no part in Sachs's enterprise; a poet of modernity who may be said to have anticipated many postmodern questions, especially in her "scenic poems," she holds a place in the most ancient of traditions: that which regards the poet as vehicle or mouthpiece of an external power, and the process of writing as one that takes place via inspiration, that is, the internalization and expression of a breath or spirit from outside the mind and body of the writer. The writing artist in this condition is at once inside and outside herself, simultaneously in control and controlled by an external force. The tradition through which the individual is reduced to a mouthpiece of spirit contains saints, martyrs, and mystics—the receptacles of the voice of God—and it includes poets, painters, composers, and others for whom the artist's calling comes from the beyond.

Sachs aligns herself with these traditions. But during and after the German genocide, when she discovers many of her central themes and metaphors in biblical and Hasidic tales formerly unknown to her, she cannot be as sure of her God as her mystical and lyrical predecessors might have been. In his poem "for Nelly Sachs" following their first meeting in Zurich (Ascension Day, 1960), Paul Celan writes:

Of your God was our talk, I spoke
against him . . .
. . . .
Your eye looked on, looked away,
your mouth
spoke its way to the eye, and I heard:

We
don't know, you know,
we
don't know, do we?,
what
counts.[12]

[Von deinem Gott war die Rede, ich sprach
gegen ihn . . .
. . . .
Dein Aug sah mir zu, sah hinweg,
dein Mund
sprach sich dem Aug zu, ich hörte:

Wir
wissen ja nicht, weißt du,
wir

wissen ja nicht,
was
gilt.][13]

Ceding the foreground to her poetic work, Sachs effaced her own person, refusing to leave much more than scant autobiographical traces and insisting on the inconsequentiality of her individual experience. Frustrated biographers and critics, eager to understand her work in the context of her life, frequently quote with some irony her dismissive remark: "I live in Sweden and write German. That should be enough for you."[14] Sachs's reluctance to detail her own life lay primarily in what she perceived as its representative character: as assimilated Jew from upper-class Berlin, robbed of her German identity and sheathed in an unfamiliar Jewish one, forced into exile and isolation by Nazism, she is no different than thousands of others. This position guarantees her membership in the *Gemeinschaft der Leidenden* (community of sufferers) defined, over the course of her career, first as the Jews of the Diaspora and ultimately as all sufferers. In a sense, Sachs could herself be regarded as an instance of the rhetorical figure of which she is so fond: she sees herself as synecdoche, her own intense suffering suggesting its universal manifestation.

The horrible commonality of Sachs's history is demonstrated by its superficial parallels with Benjamin's: born in Berlin a mere seven months apart (she on 10 December 1891, he on 15 July 1892), each grew up in the relative wealth, comfort, and culture of an assimilated Jewish home. As a "sickly" girl, Sachs briefly attended public and private school, received considerable home tutoring, and, at the age of seventeen, finished school with no practical preparation for future life. Benjamin, in contrast, read extensively, explored the city of Berlin, and was deeply involved in the intellectual circles and discussions of his day. In 1933, Benjamin fled into exile in France; Sachs remained in Berlin with her mother and managed their real-estate holdings. For both, the decisive year was 1940: on 16 May, Sachs and her mother escaped the clutches of the Gestapo (they had already been summoned for "transport" to a concentration camp) to Sweden; on 27 September, Benjamin despaired in his attempt to flee across the Franco-Spanish border from the same satanic forces and took his life. Both stood on the threshold of their fiftieth birthdays; Sachs would live in Sweden for another thirty years, until her death there in 1970—the same year in which Paul Celan committed suicide. In the postwar years, each would be appropriated and celebrated by such groups and forces and political ideologists as saw fit to do this; neither would or could be integrated or reintegrated into "mainstream" German letters and literature, although this was perhaps more the case for Sachs, "poet of the Holocaust," "poet of the Jewish fate," than for Benjamin, whose Jewishness could be suppressed by the focus on his literary-critical activities and, above all and for several decades, by his association with the Frankfurt school around Horkheimer and Adorno. Further, the "exportability" as well as the currency of Benjamin's thought and writings have produced far more critical activity around and familiarity with his work than Nelly Sachs has ever enjoyed. The evident reasons for this have to do with the difficulties of lyric poetry in general, and her poetry in particular; they have to do with the fact that the people in whose language she wrote were not prepared to accept her—could not approach her oeuvre with anything close to "objectivity"—and with the focus, in the always-problematic translations, on the works surrounding the Holocaust theme.[15]

But most crucially, Nelly Sachs's reception is complicated by its displacement: as a German author, she has been read and analyzed far more frequently outside Germany than within it. Her major critics are Swedes, Danes, Americans—and Germans who do not live in that country. Despite a relative flurry of activity on the part of the first postwar generation in Germany, despite a great deal of sympathetic reception on the part of several women poets and critics in Germany (most notably Ingeborg Bachmann, Elisabeth Borchers, Hilde Domin, Käte Hamburger, Ilse Aichinger, and Marie Luise Kaschnitz), the bulk of research even today seems to issue from elsewhere. Hence, perhaps, the particular representation of voices in this volume, about which some brief comments seem in order here. In the process of organizing the conference on which this collection of essays is based, we sought out those individuals in Germany known to have concerned themselves deeply with Nelly Sachs and her work. We received a very polite but declining letter from Hans Magnus Enzensberger, perhaps the most judicious of all her German readers; Hilde Domin, at first inclined to participate, later had to withdraw for personal reasons. In contrast, the response from scholars from Sweden (Bengt Holmqvist), from Switzerland (Johannes Anderegg), from Denmark (Ruth Dinesen), and from the United States (Ehrhard Bahr, Dorothee Ostmeier, and Elisabeth Strenger) was overwhelmingly positive, particularly because these several scholars had done most of their work in their separate places and were excited about having the opportunity to spend several days in discussion with each other at the first symposium ever to devote a full day to Nelly Sachs. The results of this discussion lie, in part, in the contrasts that emerge between the rigorously imagistic-communicative analysis of one poem by Anderegg and the formal-biographical schema provided by Dinesen, between the historical-contextual discussion of Sachs's metaphorics by Bahr and the literary-historical situating of Sachs's epitaphic voice by West. Such contrasts mark this collection as part of the enlargement of scholarly attention to Sachs's work.

At the centenary of Benjamin and Sachs, we are faced first with two different tasks in revisiting their works in their German/Jewish contexts. Benjamin's life work was cut short, if not incomplete at his death in 1940; Sachs's, although she had published a few poems in Berlin in the 1920s and 1930s, did not really begin until she heard the first reports of genocide in 1942 and wrote her first collection, *In den Wohnungen des Todes,* published in 1947, notably in East Berlin (where, presumably, the Holocaust theme was tolerable because of the Soviet socialist leaders' disavowal of any national socialist legacy). Although in both cases our efforts at reading are a matter of revision, in the case of Benjamin the body to be reviewed is extensive and established, covering, as it does, more than fifty years since his death; in Sachs's case, as Ehrhard Bahr notes, there is hardly a mentionable "Sachs literature," and that which does exist refers almost exclusively to her early writings:

> A few exceptions notwithstanding, the work of the Nobel Prize recipient Nelly Sachs is just as unknown today as it was in 1966. Again and again mention is made only of her two early works from the 1940s: the poetry collection *In den Wohnungen des Todes* and the scenic poem *Eli. A Mystery Play of the Sufferings of Israel.* Neither literary criticism nor literary scholarship seems to have any clear idea of her conception of a total theater of mime, language, and music; or of her later scenic poems as well as her late lyric poetry, which will surely form the basis of her lasting importance in the future.[16]

The phrase "at first glance" above suggests another aspect of Sachs's life as poet that forces reconsideration of her apparent modesty. The reference is to her notion of being called, of regarding herself as a receptor of external inspiration and as a mouthpiece for the suffering people to whose community she belongs. Her challenge was to give voice to the sufferers and to the dead, to discover ways of indicating that for which there seemed to be no usable language. The path toward such discovery, initially undertaken in virtual isolation from any schools of thought or artistic circles, would lead Sachs back in time to prealphabetic eras—to her own as well as to those biblical and Hasidic-Kabalistic myths referred to above; its results would rehearse and anticipate aesthetic-theoretical problems and topics with which we have hardly begun to come to terms, but to which current trends in literary theory and scholarship offer some possible inroads. These give us the freedom to follow the signs Sachs provides, without feeling compelled to declare their "meaning"; they allow us to acknowledge the borders of language, the suggestive function of the mystical and transcendent, and, above all, the importance of gesture as a key component in her work. They permit us to grapple with her *Rätsel* (enigmas) without having to find their "solution."

The story of Benjamin's suicide on the Spanish-French border in 1940, alluded to several times already, is both widely and poorly known, for its moving details—the absent transit visa, the overdose of morphine, the repentant guard—obscure the structure of what may be as deep as a fatality and as shallow as a misunderstood request for a bribe. From this undisentangled crux, this noncrossing, comes, not a knowledge of Benjamin's death as a locus of narrative authority preinscribed by himself for nearly a decade (through allusions, anticipations, perhaps even suicide attempts), but the fact of its occurrence as the occasion for a martyring reception: martyrdom as interpretation.[17] Death by the fascists—albeit via his own hands—played into his afterlife at the hands of the Marxists as symmetrically as do the well-known theses that conclude his "Work of Art in the Age of Mechanical Reproduction": the aestheticization of politics, responded to by the politicization of aesthetics.

As Marxists used to say when they used to be Marxists, "It cannot be an accident that . . ."—in this case, an accident that an end of interest in Marxism is concurrent with a renascent interest in the Jewishness of German letters and culture. The false universalisms of Marxist ideology, such as feudal, bourgeois, and communist epochs, or, in the later, swishier versions, postcapitalist, even postrevolutionary epochs—false because universal before any specificity—block the particulars of *this* woman, *this* group, *this* place. The blockage of anti-Jewish hatred in Eastern Europe by Communist regimes (in some cases, only its discrete control and manipulation) may still occasionally look like a good thing as one confronts the present alternatives. But the blindness to the obvious—German letters in this century are, massively, Jewish letters—must lift at least a bit as the European continent's historicopolitical struggles are reunderstood as national, ethnic, even racial, and not determined by class or means of production. Instead of blocking out a century in terms of fascism, antifascism, emigration, and Marxist and Communist revisionisms and alternatives, the categories of assimilation, counterassimilation, repression, annihilation, survival, and the utterances of the last—the last laugh, the last word—are the more accurate ones for describing the contours of a culture. The end of the cold war (the fall of the Wall, "1989," and so on)—a cliché, but like them all, having its truth—is the revival of hot ethnicity, including German hatred of the foreigner (the Jew, the Turk, the gypsy) within.[18] Within this German, if not always this Germany, is where Nelly Sachs and Walter Benjamin always were, even when displaced. It is not they who are to be re-placed, but our attention and scholarship.

We have seen that Nelly Sachs's typification as "the poet of the Jewish fate" made her a prisoner of classification, reghettoized by the preeminence of the Holocaust, incarcerated *from* the readings that now reach toward her texts and contexts. It is one of the several ironies of the crossings and reversals that inform the conjunction of Nelly Sachs and Walter Benjamin that his typification as a "Marxist critic" very nearly turned him into a non-Jew, and that today the Jewishness of his German letters can be attended to as if anew.

This happens before our eyes, before our gaze upon this volume's contributions. The supersession of a Marxist vocabulary is the signal scholarly development for Benjamin studies at the present time. France, as it often does, got there first, from Pierre Missac's early commentaries upon Benjamin, to Jacques Derrida's philosophic probings of Benjamin on language.[19] The first large American intervention that could consider Benjamin as a philosopher and writer, and not a Marxist, was Rainer Nägele's anthology of essays, *Benjamin's Ground*.[20] After Bettine Menke's magisterial *Sprachfiguren*,[21] German Benjamin scholarship will be unable any longer to attend to him with the partial, ideologically determined instruments that dominated it for the past two and a half decades. The most recent international colloquium on Benjamin, held in Lausanne in 1993 (its proceedings to be published by Suhrkamp), scarcely heard the syllables *marxistisch* uttered.[22]

If all this is welcome news to scholarship, and contemporaneous with the liberation, however fitful, of the extrascholarly regions of European culture from Marxist consequences, there is also something uncannily familiar—but precisely, because uncanny, still unknown—about the procedure. Gershom Scholem argued, with Benjamin himself, against Marxist influences and consequences throughout the 1920s and 1930s.[23] His coeditorship of Benjamin's collected works and letters with Theodor W. Adorno reflected an uneasy alliance in a triangulated militarized zone—the other coordinate was Bertolt Brecht during Benjamin's lifetime, Marxism afterward—the atmosphere of which is captured by the title of Irving Wohlfarth's forthcoming English-language study: *No Man's Land*.[24] For an American audience, the most relevant signpost of a Yogi Berraesque "déjà vu all over again" will be Hannah Arendt's fifty-five-page introduction to the first English translation of Benjamin's writings in 1968 (originally a *New Yorker* article).[25] This was the first major discussion of Benjamin in English. Arendt was scrupulously fair (as well as customarily informed) in presenting the many aspects of Benjamin's personality, life, and work. But who remembers—where were the consequences?—that the long second section of her essay brought Benjamin closest not to Brecht, not to Adorno, not to anyone else in the Frankfurt school (Marcuse, for example, having his heyday in America at the time of Arendt's commentary), but to Kafka—and did so by explicitly (re)raising "the Jewish question."

Kafka and Benjamin: the greatest prose fiction writer and the greatest literary critic in this century's German, gathered together twenty-five years ago in what is still the finest single piece of English on Benjamin. What was not being seen, then and for a long time since? For one thing, that the list could be extended: Freud and psychoanalysis, Wittgenstein and Husserl and philosophy, Celan and poetry—in each case the century's best in German is Jewish. This *could not* be seen, let alone said, in postwar, that is, post-Holocaust Germany, for the combination of repression, self-revulsion, and guilt denied would have gagged at such possible identifications (easier, as we have seen, to have Nelly Sachs just be "Jewish," far away from Germany, or to have Celan be "just" the poet of "Todesfuge"). It was without interest to the easy internationalisms of Marxist analysis. And American Germanists and Marxists, pale versions of their continental relatives, saw and spoke things no differently.

The opportunity, now as then, is not to *cherchez le juif,* but to bring into as forceful a collision as possible the two sets of facts: that, at its highest levels, twentieth-century German (literature, culture) is Jewish, and that twentieth-century "Germany" (its murderous policies from

1919 to 1945, but also its scholarly disciplines and discourses, national as well as international) has tried to repress, expel, or annihilate this other within.[26] In the cases of Benjamin and Sachs, surprises await such supercollisions. To continue where we have lingered already, Benjamin's relation to Adorno—arguably the most important philosopher in post-war Germany—will no longer be accessible through such terms as commodity, or class, but through those of truth content, allegory, name, idea, happiness, and constellation. (And a text like Adorno's 1931 inaugural lecture at Frankfurt, "The Actuality of Philosophy," which reads like a crib sheet for a discussion of Benjamin's *Origin of the German Trauerspiel*, will assume its importance for the first time, as will his last work, *Aesthetic Theory*, Benjaminian from first page to last.) Once they are put together differently, Benjamin and Adorno will yield a vector pointing not toward Marxist horizons, but in redemptive and nonredemptive directions, toward Rosenzweig and Kafka. Similarly, the pairing of Benjamin and Brecht—the darlings of the 1960s and 1970s—appears far more contrived today than it ever did, even to Scholem and Adorno, in the 1930s. While Brecht may be the only world-class writer who will, to an extent, justify a continuing interest in Marxist aesthetics—if only to help one understand aspects of his texts, as one learns some Thomistic aesthetics the better to understand parts of Dante—Benjamin will reward Marxist poetics or hermeneutics not at all. Instead, Benjamin's literary affinities will properly (which is to say, allegorically) stretch from Kafka, Karl Kraus, and Joseph Roth to Goethe, Jean Paul, Schlegel, and Hamann. Who will care about Korsch, Tretiakov, and Tucholsky when there is Proust, or Fernando Pessoa, to compare? The new associations of Nelly Sachs, within but also without German poetry (as William West shows with Greek, English, and American verse in his remarkable essay in this volume), will surely be as fruitful as they are unexpected.

Several of the authors who treat Nelly Sachs in the present collection may well be familiar with Hans Magnus Enzensberger's open-ended introduction to *O the Chimneys*. Sachs's work, he writes, "demands of the reader not cleverness so much as humility: the work does not want to be made concrete or transformed, but experienced, patiently and with exactness. Therefore, it should not be said what the work means; at most we can allow ourselves allusions, suggestions to show the reader the way—one possible way" (*Chimneys*, vi). The authors' willingness to be led by the work and its subjectivity has, remarkably, resulted in an unforeseeable congruence among the several essays on Sachs, although each establishes its own context of analysis. Ruth Dinesen brings her exacting knowledge and inimitable familiarity with Sachs's life and work to bear as she insists on the equal weight of five identity-altering moments in that life; to her essay we owe the necessary recognition that Sachs's suffering and grief were mutable, if constant, and that we misread if we focus exclusively on the Third Reich and the Holocaust. Ehrhard Bahr's essay revisits the problematic addressed in his earlier book and by many other scholars— a question applicable not only to Sachs, but also to any author for whom the unimaginable and unimageable Nazi genocide is a point of reference: can/should the horrible be aestheticized? Bahr moves from the general question to a reading of a poem initially suppressed by the poet herself, most likely because she recognized the dangers of its appropriation, its potential to exculpate individuals by blaming "the world" the poem addresses for the fiery deaths of children. Bahr suggests that a later poem attempts to correct this miscalculated (and subsequently much-abused) earlier work and suggests that such revisions by Sachs may be frequent and are deserving of further attention.

Johannes Anderegg's reading of the poem "The Dancer" takes Enzensberger's advice quite literally and understands Sachs's poetry as if it were hermetic. Remaining almost exclusively within the realm of Sachs's semantic field—her imagistic universe as established in her oeuvre—Anderegg follows the gesture of the poem (and the dancer) to the edge of its signifying potential. Ultimately, the poem (or poetry in general) is an epitaph—for Anderegg the form of language in transformation, on the boundary between the transcendent and quotidian reality. Also concerned with epitaph—with its insufficiencies—William West explores Nelly Sachs's "Epitaphs Written into the Air" in the large historical-theoretical context of the epitaph as subgenre.

Elisabeth Strenger and Dorothee Ostmeier focus on the much-neglected scenic poems of Sachs, on which she worked throughout her life and which, in their attempt to combine mime, music, and other elements on the stage to circumvent and move beyond the restrictions of verbal and scenic representation, anticipate much of modern theater's experimentation. While Ostmeier argues convincingly for a theoretical connection between Benjamin's writings on drama and Nelly Sachs's theatrical works, Strenger, focusing on the same work as Ostmeier *(Der magische Tänzer),* explores it within the contexts of Hasidic tradition and German romanticism, especially in the link established to Kleist by the allusive marionette of Sachs's dramatic scene. Strenger concentrates on dance as the central figure and motif, as a motion of the body that permits transcendence beyond that body, as an ancient vehicle for the universal expression of ecstasy. Viewing this as a primary gesture of Sachs's work, Strenger brings us full circle, in a sense. Like several of the other authors, Strenger refers to an often-quoted letter by Nelly Sachs in which the poet writes of her own dancing to the piano playing of her father at a very young age. Sachs maintains that dance was her primary and essential (preverbal) means of expression until her "fate" forced her to move from dance to word. This letter and its suggestive contents run throughout the several essays almost as a leitmotif; the insistence on gesture, dance, mime, and music as the ultimate means of expressing realities for which language is insufficient is revealed as the key insight that joins these essays—all of them moving toward a fuller comprehension of Sachs's work—into a whole.

The contributions on Benjamin in this volume are distinguished by their calibre and their focus. Two of the world's leading Germanists have here two of their first appearances in English. Stéphane Mosès, himself a refugee from Germany in the 1930s and now, after a distinguished career in France, the first professor of German literature in post-Holocaust Israel, has for years been bringing German literature (Goethe, Jean Paul, Thomas Mann) and Jewish writers—Kafka, Rosenzweig, Celan—closer to one another. In "Benjamin's Metaphors of Origin," the motifs of names, ideas, and stars are traced from the earliest key texts such as "On Language as Such and on the Language of Man" and the *Origin of the German Trauerspiel* to the late projects of the Baudelaire studies and the *Arcades* work. That the earlier writings depart from reflections on Genesis and on Adamic and postlapsarian languages is well known; that the latter ones sustain and develop the very motifs is a compelling intervention into otherwise familiar, even stale accounts of Benjamin's work from the late 1930s. Benjamin's theory of allegory in the Baudelaire studies, for example, is the unfolding of his theory of allegory in the *Trauerspiel* book—and the Marxist rhetoric is precisely the allegorical display of its literal masking. The *Arcades Project,* scarcely translated and hence scarcely known to English readers, is now, with Mosès's introduction, available for a proper (that is, allegorical) contextualization within Benjamin's deepest concerns, and not a misleading location on some social-historical fringe.

Winfried Menninghaus, since 1980 with his *Walter Benjamins Theorie der Sprachmagie* one of the first and best to appreciate the constancy of linguistic models and projects throughout Benjamin's work, here explores the peculiar and powerful status of the *imageless* in Benjamin's thought and writing. Drawing upon Kant and early Romantic doctrines of the sublime—texts Benjamin knew intimately from the early days of his doctoral dissertation, "The Concept of Art Critique in German Romanticism"—Menninghaus both points back toward a Western tradition of aesthetics that at once privileges and limits the image and points forward to Benjamin's famous study of Goethe's novel *Die Wahlverwandtschaften,* with its strange, hardly imaginable character of Ottilie, and to other contemporaneous writings on the body, vision, and imagery. Behind these topics lies, of course, the Jewish prohibition of imagery, associated since Kant and Hegel with the sublime and now, with Menninghaus, with a dominant strain in much of Benjamin's work—precisely as the inverse, the determining other of his more well-known emphasis upon the dialectical or historical *image (Bild).*

The two other contributions on Benjamin in this volume dovetail quite productively. Both are interested in the *dramatic* in Benjamin, although not in the perhaps expected senses of the dramaturgical or the genre of drama. Rather, Dorothee Ostmeier—in what may be the world's first scholarly comparison of Benjamin and Sachs—investigates writings from Benjamin's early years, including the *Origin of the German Trauerspiel* but also the lesser-known essays on tragedy and *Trauerspiel,* and draws from them his understanding of drama as a linguistic enactment and confrontation of "figures." As he himself had then done with the German *Trauerspiel*—studying characters, plots, and monologues as the dark dramas of a language, even an allegorical structure, of mourning—Ostmeier draws "the drama of language" into the interpretation of Sachs's dramatic scenes and poems. Where in the *Trauerspiel* book Benjamin's Judaic sources and impulses had mostly remained submerged (or hidden in footnotes) behind the manifest Protestant and Catholic topoi of the study, Ostmeier's linking of Sachs to Benjamin allows the poet's Jewish themes to shed light upon the critic as the critic was used to provide access to the poet. Patricia Simpson, in a brilliant collocation of Benjamin, Brecht, and Kafka, also seizes upon the dramatic, specifically upon the gestus or gesture as a sign of language and its violences. In the strongly genitive sense of "a sign of language," gesture is not only a means for language but a kind that defines it as a member might its set; as a locus where the body and its worlds enter the codes, genres, and tropes of language, gesture (like voice, one might add) partakes of a violence that at once cuts off and inscribes. Brecht, with his theories and practices of the theatrical and world stages, becomes, in Simpson's reading of Benjamin's readings, a Kafkaesque creation, a sign among Kafka's gesticular and caricatural humanscapes. In Benjamin's understanding of Kafka, these creatures and creations recall, across historical amnesia, a *Vorgeschichte* that, of course, has nothing to do with Brechtian or otherwise Marxist historical developmentalisms, and everything to do with an *urgeschichtliche,* that is, *ursprüngliche* or original display of the violence of the signifier, of what, perhaps, precisely cannot be named in and by language.

The designation offered above of Benjamin as the greatest literary critic in German in this century is none other than the one aspired to by Benjamin himself. But he expressed this goal, in a letter of 20 January 1930 from Paris to Scholem in Jerusalem, not in German but in French: "Le but que je m'avais proposé . . . c'est d'être considéré comme le premier critique de la littérature allemande."[27] He preceded this admission by calling attention to his writing Scholem in "cette façon d'alibi qu'est pour moi le français." An alibi makes an excuse, perhaps an exculpation—true or false—certainly a claim to be *else-where, alius.* Where could these German Jews, writing in 1930, about but not in German and Germany, be but elsewhere? And where is "elsewhere" but both around and also within German and Germany—be this the Francophone and Francophile Rhineland, or the Jews of late-nineteenth-century Berlin and Central Europe, or the Jews of twentieth-century German literature and culture, the others within (even as Nelly Sachs's "acceptance" as a mark—a scar?—of "German-Jewish reconciliation" is, in the mot juste, an *alibi* that leaves both her and Germans elsewhere and avoids close encounters with her poetry)? As the century ends and the centenaries return, Benjamin the Jew speaking in French to German letters appears almost like an emblematic figure from the gallery of emblems in his book on German mourning, or from his book *Einbahnstraße* (One-way street). Two of its prose fragments appear divided and yet connected by their titles. First, banally, "Flag—":

How much more easily the leave-taker is loved! For the flame burns more purely for the one who vanishes in the distance, fueled by the fleeting scrap of material waving from the ship or railway window. Separation penetrates the disappearing person like a pigment and steeps him in gentle radiance. (I, 94)

The pathos is almost cloying, and something of its sticky sweetness infects every martyrdom and historicism that would attach itself to Walter Benjamin. But the next fragment, as distant in style as it is proximate in title, clears the air:

—At Half-Mast

If a person very close to us is dying, there is in the months to come something that we dimly apprehend—much as we should have liked to share it with him—could only unfold through his absence. We greet him at the last *(zuletzt)* in a language that he already *(schon)* no longer understands. (IV, 94)

In the first fragment, the perspective was from the harbor or train station; it is that of the one who does not leave. In this second fragment, the perspective is only deceptively the same; in fact, the focus is intenser, so intense that the perspective stays fixed on and with the very object that disappears, as it disappears. This "dying" one is greeted in his very absenting, his dying into death, in a language that utters itself into incomprehensibility: *zuletzt* means *schon, schon* means *zuletzt*. This dying one was for Benjamin German, and he spoke French to it, in a love letter that professed the wish to be its greatest lover. Benjamin wrote of Baudelaire that he was not a pessimist because he did not believe in a future (I, 657). Nor was Benjamin a pessimist in this sense. But looking back, seeing the death of German with the distance of Judaism and French and the intimacy of love, Benjamin sees a past unfold up to his very German lips: it and they yield the utterance of the incomprehensible. The moment of Sachs and Benjamin, German Jews and German literature, was when their vanishing present became the future, the destiny, now the past, that is twentieth-century German(y). Its incomprehensibility lies at our doorstep.

NOTES

1. For reasons discussed in Dorothee Ostmeier's essay in this volume, we retain the term *Trauerspiel* in translating the title of *Der Ursprung des deutschen Trauerspiels*.

2. "Laudatio anläßlich der Verleihung des Friedenspreises des deutschen Buchhandels an Nelly Sachs, im Oktober 1965," in Suhrkamp Verlag, ed., *Nelly Sachs zu Ehren: Zum 75. Geburtstag am 10. Dezember 1966: Gedichte, Beiträge, Bibliographie* (Frankfurt am Main: Suhrkamp, 1966), 33; Fries's translation.

3. *In den Wohnungen des Todes* (Berlin: Aufbau, 1947); *Sternverdunkelung: Gedichte* (Amsterdam: Berman-Fischer, Querido, 1949).

4. Lyrikpreis des Kulturkreises im Bundesverband der Deutschen Industrie, 1959; Meersburger Droste-Preis für Dichterinnen, 1960; first recipient of the Nelly-Sachs-Preis of the city of Dortmund, 1961; corresponding member of the Freie Akadamie der Künste, Hamburg, 1961; corresponding member of the Bayerische Akademie der schönen Künste, Munich, 1963.

5. Cf. Walter Berendsohn, *Nelly Sachs: Einführung in das Werk der Dichterin jüdischen Schicksals* (Darmstadt: Agora, 1974).

6. "Nachwort," in Nelly Sachs, *Gedichte* (Frankfurt am Main: Suhrkamp, 1977), 105; Fries's translation.

7. See Ehrhard Bahr, *Nelly Sachs* (Munich: Beck, 1980); Ruth Dinesen, *Nelly Sachs: Eine Biographie,* trans. Gabriele Gerecke (Frankfurt am Main: Suhrkamp, 1992).

8. See Dinesen's essay in this volume, as well as her *Nelly Sachs.*

9. See Patricia Anne Simpson, "In Citing Violence: Gestus in Benjamin, Brecht, and Kafka," in this volume.

10. J. A. Cuddon, *A Dictionary of Literary Terms and Literary Theory,* 3d ed. (Oxford: Blackwell, 1991), 406.

11. See Johannes Anderegg, "Nelly Sachs: The Poem and Transformation," in this volume.

12. "Zürich, The Stork Inn," *Poems of Paul Celan,* trans. Michael Hamburger (New York: Persea, 1988), 157.

13. Paul Celan, "Zürich, zum Storchen," *Gesammelte Werke* (Frankfurt am Main: Suhrkamp, 1983), 1:214.

14. Quoted by Ruth Dinesen in this volume, p. 35; no source given.

15. The two English-language translations of Sachs's works, published by Farrar, Straus, and Giroux in the wake of her receipt of the Nobel Prize (*O the Chimneys: Selected Poems, Including the Verse Play, Eli,* [New York: 1967], published in Great Britain as *Selected Poems: Including the Verse Play, Eli* [London: Jonathan Cape, 1968]), and *The Seeker and Other Poems,* 1970) provide well-crafted renderings of the works contained, but limit the English-speaker's knowledge of Sachs to a particular orientation and omit references to her ongoing and

intense activity with the scenic dramas (except for the early *Eli*), a lifelong preoccupation to which too little attention has been paid.

16. Bahr, *Nelly Sachs*, 9–10.

17. Compare the tone and vocabulary of the last strophe of Bertolt Brecht's poem, "Zum Freitod des Flüchtlings W.B.": "So liegt die Zukunft in Finsternis und die guten Kräfte / Sind schwach. All das sahst du / Als du den quälbaren Leib zerstörtest." *Ausgewählte Gedichte* (Frankfurt am Main: Suhrkamp, 1964), 62.

18. Jane Kramer reports in "Letter from Europe: Neo-Nazis: A Chaos in Hand" (*New Yorker* 14 June 1993), that, prior to a brutal burning in the village of Hünxe, skinheads said they were looking "for Jews, for anybody not German" (61) (they burned a Lebanese family instead). Even as the ethnicity of the victims has changed over fifty years, their typology—that the Jew is the *type* for the other within Germany—has not.

19. See Missac's *Passage de Walter Benjamin* (Paris: Seuil, 1987), which draws upon his conversations with Benjamin in the 1930s, his translations of Benjamin in the 1940s, and his publications from the 1960s onward, and Derrida's "Des tours de Babel" (1980), *Psyché: Inventions de l'autre* (Paris: Galilée, 1987), 203–35.

20. *Benjamin's Ground: New Readings of Walter Benjamin*, ed. Rainer Nägele (Detroit: Wayne State University Press, 1988), originally published as a special issue of *Studies in Twentieth Century Literature* 11, no. 1 (fall 1986). How different the European reception was is indicated by the 1965 publication of Rolf Tiedemann's *Studien zur Philosophie Walter Benjamins*, well *before* any noteworthy Marxist interpretations.

21. Bettine Menke, *Sprachfiguren: Name, Allegorie, Bild nach Benjamin* (Munich: Fink, 1991).

22. *Übersetzen: Walter Benjamin,* ed. Christiaan Hart Nibbrig (Frankfurt am Main: Suhrkamp, forthcoming 1996).

23. This is amply documented in Scholem's memoir, *Walter Benjamin—die Geschichte einer Freundschaft* (Frankfurt am Main: Suhrkamp, 1975) and the later letters exchanged between the two, *Walter Benjamin/Gershom Scholem, Briefwechsel 1933–1940,* ed. Gershom Scholem (Frankfurt am Main: Suhrkamp, 1980).

24. Irving Wahlforth, *No Man's Land* (Baltimore: Johns Hopkins University Press, forthcoming).

25. Walter Benjamin, *Illuminations*, ed. Hannah Arendt, trans. Harry Zohn (New York: Harcourt, Brace and World, 1968), 1–55.

26. This overstatement should be qualified by noting two salutary developments: the volume *Juden in der deutschen Literatur: Ein deutsch-israelisches Symposion,* ed. Stéphane Mosès and Albrecht Schöne (Frankfurt am Main: Suhrkamp, 1986), and the series *Conditio Judaica,* under the sponsorship of the

Werner-Reimers-Stiftung and the editorship of Hans Otto Horch, appearing since 1988 at the distinguished publishing house Max Niemeyer Verlag, Tübingen.

27. Walter Benjamin, *Briefe,* ed. Gershom Scholem and Theodor W. Adorno (Frankfurt am Main: Suhrkamp, 1966), 2:505.

Chapter 2

The Search for Identity:
Nelly Sachs's Jewishness

Ruth Dinesen

Some time ago, a Danish colleague of mine wrote a history of Eastern Jewry. She was working intensely on this project and told me a lot about it when I met her the first time. In the course of the conversation I asked her, "Are you perhaps yourself a Jew?" to which she answered, briefly, "No," and the conversation continued. This was nothing remarkable; I also worked on a Jewish topic without being a Jew—nevertheless the emphasis on the word "No" stuck with me.

After several years we met again. Her book had been published and had been followed by another. I knew that she had gone through a serious illness. Talking about it, she told me suddenly that she had just converted to Judaism. Still remembering the previous "No," I asked her for her reason. I was told a long story about the discovery of a Jewish identity. This story is on the one hand quite personal; on the other it seems to me typical enough to serve as the introduction to my topic.

The chances for recovery were slim; she looked death in the eye and thought about where she wanted to be buried and about burial rites. At this boundary she felt unexpectedly alien in her familiar environment, like one who did not belong; she sought her burial place at a Jewish cemetery. She is completely irreligious; no faith guided her. She had grown up without the least knowledge of a Jewish culture, had never before called herself a Jew, and certainly not a Zionist; therefore her decision was not political. Then why? She called this her "ethnic identity"— a designation to which I could not relate.

Then she told her story, starting with her Jewish orthodox grandparents, who had fled Russia, persecuted by a pogrom, and had eventually landed in Vienna. There their children—my colleague's parents—distanced themselves from their Jewish upbringing; atheistic and politically

23

active, they raised their own children to be completely assimilated. The militant anti-Semitism in Vienna caught the family unprepared. Expelled from Austria like unwelcome strangers, they were viewed in England as possible enemies, and after the beginning of the war they were temporarily interned there. This twice-estranged woman went to Denmark, lived as a Dane, was married in the church, had her children christened—but she remained a foreigner, marked already by her use of the language, which betrayed her at once.

On death's threshold the feeling of foreignness overwhelmed her. She looked for a place from which she could not be expelled. Through her history, discovered in long talks with her maternal grandmother, she found her way back to her Jewish identity, and thus to a sense of groundedness that made it possible for her to die. She did not find a perfect world, a religion, a cultural or political system; she found a community of foreigners in the world—not of course the community of all foreigners and expellees, but rather the singular foreignness of the Jews in the Diaspora: an "ethnic alienation" that returned to her the identity she had lost, the identity of a Jew.

Her story is unique—but I have listened to other unique stories of numerous other Jews. Everyone has his or her own inimitable history, but it is remarkable how Jewish identity inscribes itself into a biography's record. Identity comes into being and is captured in the narration of a human life.

The biography of Nelly Sachs leads repeatedly to the boundary of death. As a poet she sought this border position and gleaned her poems each time from this closeness to death. These poems functioned for her simultaneously as breathing exercises at the threshold of destruction, and as the search for the possibility for life after the loss of identity. Here I suggest tentatively five stages in her search for identity:

> *The first stage,* when a partnership with a beloved man was forbidden to the sixteen-year-old girl;
> *The second stage,* when the forty-year-old woman was denied her German identity;
> *The third stage,* when the refugee found herself rescued but totally isolated in Stockholm;
> *The fourth stage,* when the last remaining beloved person, her mother, died;

The fifth and last stage, the loss of any orientation and of any shelter through mental disorder.

This, then, is a narration of five stages in a human development, each of them a crisis whose working through brought the poet face-to-face with death, but which in every instance led to a new level of self-understanding.

The "Jewish component" of this life can only be described against the background of its complete absence during the first stage.

The unhappy love of the very young girl must be taken seriously as resulting in the loss and gain of identity, although this experience might seem insignificant to a later observer. It was, indeed, life threatening due to her refusal of food; and the poet herself regarded it up to her death as her *Schicksal* (fate) and as the primary source of her work.[1]

The love crisis led Nelly Sachs to the word; earlier she had expressed her feelings in a child's free dance, which accompanied her father's piano playing. She dealt in her poetic attempts with the painful love experience and found a path toward a new self-understanding. The prose collection *Legenden und Erzählungen* (1921) includes some texts about the renunciation of love; but here I prefer to discuss the sonnets that date from that period. This early cycle appeared for a long time to be lost; in 1959 Nelly Sachs searched for it in vain.[2]

After my visit in Jerusalem in January 1986 with Eva Steinthal, who belonged to the early circle of Nelly Sachs's friends, Steinthal gave me a handwritten copy of these poems,[3] which she had prepared, "in 1923 at the latest," for the pleasure of her lifelong friend Friedl Meier. The cycle, which includes twenty-four poems, celebrates a lost beloved; the "I" mourns its unhappy fate and seeks partners in misfortune, referred to as "sisters," with whom to identify. In addition to classical examples, one finds the Madonna in a prominent position among these sisters. The Mother of God is also praised in other poems over the years—but there are definite indications that this meek servant did not quite suffice as a model for the poet.

The Nelly Sachs Archive in Stockholm maintains the library of the poet as it existed at the time of her death. Here one finds the *Fioretti* twice: *Die Blümlein des heiligen Franziskus von Assisi* and *Die schönsten Legenden des heiligen Franz,*[4] the latter with a dedication "to the celebration of love 1920," and the former with a Francis manuscript by Nelly Sachs as enclosure. In St. Francis's "Song of the Sun" we read:

Praised be thou, Lord,
by our brother, Death of the body.

In her third sonnet, Nelly Sachs likewise calls death "brother":

Death, my brother, thou once burntest in me

But the "I" is hindered by "a cherub" from acting according to its death drive, and the fourth sonnet consequently begins with the question: "Where to turn with this love?" whereupon the "I" answers itself: "By giving in meekness, I can fulfill myself."

The "I" defines meekness as a life spent in service to the poor and the orphans, but also in loving nature—"blossom and leaf and every animal"—which is "born mute and deaf to the word." Obvious here, although he remains unnamed, is the inspiration of St. Francis, whose legend tells not only of his preaching to the birds and the flowers but also of his liberation of captured wildlife or fish.

This cycle is followed by four sonnets titled "Franz von Assisi." From the very beginning Francis is called "the hero," a "king of gestures." In this cycle of sonnets, the most important sign of his paradigmatic and heroic characteristics is the *Inbrunst* (ardor) that climaxes in his vision of God. The fire of his love illuminates earth's hidden agonies: the tearless suffering of Nature—"dust, animal, and plant"—under its own laws. This is a singular concept, and it captivated the poet: here it is angels who bow beneath earth's yoke; in her later work, nature's ardor, born of suffering, opens the Godly eye so that it weeps.[5] Francis assumes a central position in the sensibilities of the poet. In 1959, for example, she writes to two young German friends: "Your pictures, photos, are all around me in the cabin at Lake Mälar together with my other loved ones. St. Francis is on the new bookshelf."[6]

Betrayed by love, the young girl turned to religion. She sought this not in the form of a community of faith;[7] her independence and own assumptions led her, rather, to search for herself in religious models. In keeping with the values of the times, these were more likely to be Catholic saints than, for example, Protestant or Jewish mystics. She seeks, on the one hand, an antithesis to her death drive, a balance that is masked as a longing for heaven, as a burning desire for God; here and in her later works, she calls this yearning *Inbrunst* (ardor). On the other hand, her religiosity is characterized by her close relationship—her connectedness—to nature, which again echoes contemporary sensibilities by prescribing the poet's task: to give voice to a mute and tearless nature, and to translate creation's sighs into poetic expression.

At this point, we may recall Rilke's speech on modern poetry of 1898, which contains the following definition:

> Art seems to me to be an individual's attempt to seek—beyond the narrow and the dark—an understanding with all things, with the smallest as well as with the largest, and to come closer to the ultimate and quiet sources of all life through such consistent conversations. The secrets of things merge in his inner being with his own deepest sensitivities and become for him loud, as if they were his own desires.[8]

Although in later years Nelly Sachs did not want to be reduced to any influences and therefore denied all knowledge of Rilke,[9] she had long owned *Die Aufzeichnungen des Malte Laurids Brigge* and *Das Stundenbuch*,[10] as well as Rilke's translation of the *Vierundzwanzig Sonette der Louïze Labé*,[11] which may be seen as a model for Sachs's own cycle of sonnets. After the death of her mother, she seems again to have sought consolation in Rilke: "How I look forward to The Duino Elegies . . . I own the Book of Hours and also The Sonnets to Orpheus," she writes to Gudrun Dähnert in 1950.[12]

But I am anticipating myself. Through her poetic work, Nelly Sachs worked through the loss of her identity as a loving woman. Gradually, she comes to think of herself as a writer—as a German author, to be sure, without the smallest Jewish component; this is clear, for example, in her first publication *Legenden und Erzählungen* (Legends and stories) from 1921.[13] The religiosity that dominates this collection is distinguished by the ardor and connectedness with nature, for which St. Francis provided the model; the poetic task that she conceives in many ways resembles Rilke's poetic enterprise.[14]

Nelly Sachs was as unprepared as other assimilated German Jews to cope with the denial of her identity as a German by the National Socialist rulers. Leo Hirsch, the cultural editor of the *Berliner Tagesblatt* until this newspaper was suspended by the Nazis, describes the modern Jewish German author's situation in 1938 as follows:

> It is, in truth, also very difficult for the writer. No matter what he wrote before the change, it was hardly "Jewish." Now he is expected—and expects himself—to bring about the renaissance of Jewish culture. How does one do that? . . . Whoever writes about graveyards must at least also be able to decipher the Hebrew epitaphs. Most Jewish authors suffer from this lack of knowledge: they can read only German. As a result, the Jewish world remains almost closed to them. They take another look at the Bible, but only the Luther translation is halfway accessible. But because one is dependent on such materials in order to remain alive, one gives oneself a Jewish orientation as easily as possible, secondhand. Since one cannot get at the biblical sources, Auerbach's *Wüste und Gelobtes Land* has to suffice; history is acquired by way of Graetz and Dubnow, and Hasidism via Buber's little Schocken volume. None of this would be worth speaking of if it concerned only a few individuals in this country who have been identified, *nolens volens,* as Jewish authors; but it is the difficult problem of Jews in all countries who have been cast out of their old customs. They have unlearned the Jewish way of thinking; thus they are incapable of Jewish writing.[15]

Hirsch had published three poems by Nelly Sachs in the *Berliner Tagesblatt* in 1933;[16] he also enabled her last publication in Berlin, on April 4, 1939, in the *Monatsblätter* of the Jewish Cultural Society (Jüdischer Kulturbund).[17] Immediately after her escape to Sweden, Nelly Sachs enlisted the help of Swedish refugee workers in an attempt to get Hirsch and his wife out of Berlin as well.[18] She did not succeed.

Hirsch's analysis of the situation of the Jewish author fits Nelly Sachs exactly. *Der Umschwung* (the change)—as the Jewish newspapers called Hitler's assumption of power, with all its evil consequences—had cast her out of the German community and into a group of persecuted people who were forced to think of themselves as Jews, and to make the best of it. This could not be achieved through external force alone; it was necessary to construct a quasi-Jewish identity—an inner attitude that would provide some kind of counterpressure. In accord with Hirsch's comment, she was expected and expected herself to produce Jewish poems; but she had not unlearned Jewish thinking—she had never learned it and thus had to make do with brief introductory essays.

The Luther Bible in the Stockholm collection does not seem to come from Berlin;[19] it is full of marginal notes and bookmarks, and there is also an envelope with notes on the Bible. The marginal comments concern the biblical story of Samson, which Nelly Sachs used as model for her scenic poem *Simson fällt durch Jahrtausende* (Simson falls through millennia) in 1958. Most of the notes are dated after the death of her mother in 1950. As far as can be determined, no mark or note originates from the time before the escape to Stockholm. This corresponds well to the assumption of Margit Sahlin (the daughter of Enar Sahlin, who was Nelly Sachs's friend during the first refugee years); Margit Sahlin reports that her father was astonished to discover that the two Jewish ladies (Sachs and her mother) did not own a Bible and demonstrated only a vague understanding of biblical tradition, whereupon he provided a Bible and read to them from it.

Although Nelly Sachs's insight into the biblical stories was scant, in the opinion of this Swedish mentor, who was well versed in the Scriptures, the tales nevertheless provided material for the "newly Jewish" poet in her renewed search for identity. Twelve poems under the title "Melodien der Bibel" exist in the Lagerlöf bequest as enclosures to a letter from 26 November 1938.[20] The only biblical or Jewish elements in these "Melodies of the Bible" are what Kurt Pinthus calls "Jewish decorations and motifs . . . in which a poem is wrapped," but which do not, in his opinion, make a poem "Jewish."[21] The "Jewish feeling and Jewish perspective" that are necessary for this are not yet discernible in Nelly Sachs's writing. This is most evident in a small poem in folk-song rhyme earlier titled "Hirtenlied" (Shepherd's song), which is later recast as a biblical poem and renamed "Jakob und Rahel"—without any further alteration in the poem's language.

A few of these poems speak nonetheless to the situation of the times; they are songs of the flight and the Diaspora: "Eine Mutter singt in der Wüste ihr Kind in den Schlaf" (A mother sings her child to sleep in the desert), "Lied eines Mädchens aus Babylonischer Gefangenschaft" (Song of a girl from Babylonian imprisonment), "Esther geht zum König" (Esther goes to the king).

Nelly Sachs remained in Berlin long enough to receive the obligatory name "Sara" in January 1939.[22] In these extreme circumstances, Jewish identity remained for her only an outer shell imposed upon her, without any significant content.

In his *Versuch einer Charakterisierung des Jüdischen: Juden—Christen—Deutsche* of 1961, H. G. Adler concludes: "'To be a Jew' means, therefore, to belong to a certain community of destiny";[23] Simon N. Herman formulated the same view in 1977 as follows:

> The feeling of interdependence, of a common fate, represents the widest minimal basis, the common denominator, of Jewish belonging in our times. . . . A Jew anywhere is what he is because of the centuries of Diaspora existence experienced by his people.[24]

Rescued from Berlin, Nelly Sachs experienced the essence of Jewish identity in Stockholm much in the sense of these words; in exile she experiences the full implications of the Diaspora. From this time on she declares herself to be a part of the suffering and persecuted European Jewry; she accepts the community of destiny and places her own destiny and herself as poet in the service of the Jewish people as she has come to understand it.

She looks back to Germany, observes and absorbs everything that happens to the chosen people, suffers immensely from her nightly visions; but she has no religious or artistic idiom to work through the experiences until she becomes absorbed in Buber's adaptations of the Hasidic stories.

In her unpublished memoirs, Gudrun Dähnert says that the friends talked about the legend of the Ba'al Shem[25] in the years of persecution:

> During this threatening time, around 1937, Lichen [little Nelly] gave me Martin Buber's legend of Ba'al Shem. Anneliese also read this wonderful book. It generated warm conversations among the three of us.[26]

I do not know whether the Schocken volume, mentioned by Hirsch, was actually available to these friends at the time. It cannot be located in the Nelly Sachs library. It would have been almost too fitting to Hirsch's description of a newly Jewish author.

These "warm conversations" were followed, in the solitude of her exile in Stockholm, by Nelly Sachs's decisive discovery of a possible means of identification. In Martin Buber's Hasidic tales and in his introduction she found the sketch of a people that satisfied her religious, psychological, and poetic needs. In the sense of this description, her self-perception became that of a Jew.

Buber asserts that the particularity of Jewish mysticism resides in the "way" and the "fate of the people, out of which it grew." In the post-Hitler era, we seize up at the mention of anything that sounds like racist teaching. Buber's emphasis on a special Jewish character therefore makes us uneasy. It is said that the Jew has a special propensity toward mysticism; extreme contrasts release new energies in the Jew. According to Buber, devotion to a boundless mystery may thus originate in a poor and restricted existence; indeed, it borrows its strength precisely from these limitations. He suggests that pathos arises from this and stretches its arms out to embrace the boundless.[27]

If this describes a Jewish characteristic, then one can indeed maintain that Nelly Sachs lived the Jewish way, especially in her first years of exile: closeted in a small, dark, and cold room with her sick mother, she exhibited the pathetic will, understood in the Buberian sense, to embrace the boundlessness of the tragedy and of the divine. Her own statements about the Hasidim are not determined psychologically, but rather by content. They refer to central images and to the kind of world understanding that these represent.

According to Martin Buber's interpretation, the basis of Hasidic teaching lies in the recognition that the relationship between God and his creation is a linguistic one. God is seen concretely as the one who speaks; the formation of things constitutes the answer. In this creative dialogue, all things and all living beings find themselves face-to-face with God, addressed by God, addressing God and receiving response. The dialogue between God and his people takes place in the world, but the world is also the medium of the dialogue. Buber speaks about "Gegenstand" [object], but he does not mean thereby that the dialogue concerns the world, rather that it takes place between the human being and the parts of the world that the human being encounters. "God speaks to humans through the things and beings that he sends into their lives; human beings answer through their actions toward these things and beings."[28] The similarity to Rilke's description of the relationship between humans and things as "dialogue/conversation" is striking.

This poetic comprehension of the world must have been immensely fascinating for Nelly Sachs as author. Since her St. Francis period, she had tried to define the poetic task given her by God as service to things; now, feeling herself chosen to give voice to a dead people, she encounters

Buber's Hasidism. Here she finally finds a weltanschauung that contains essential elements of her own religiosity. At the same time, precisely this view of life and this missionary sense are described as specifically Jewish. She identifies with this people described by Buber—with the suffering and ecstatic people of the prophets and mystics. This explains her unqualified support for Israel in these years of persecution as well as her subsequently hesitant attitude toward the state of Israel; it explains her later expansion of this community to include all suffering and persecuted human beings.

Nelly Sachs wrote her "Jewish" poetry during and after the war: the poems of the books *In den Wohnungen des Todes* and *Sternverdunkelung,* the former published in 1947 by the Aufbau-Verlag, the latter in 1949 by the Berman-Fischer Verlag. Sounding a dirge for European Jewry, the poems of this period arose from her sense of Jewish identity. But the mystery play *Eli: Ein Mysterienspiel vom Leiden Israels*[29] is most clearly related to Hasidic motifs. Describing its completion to a Swedish friend,[30] Nelly Sachs quotes Martin Buber extensively; the text itself includes images, figures, tales, and liturgical elements from the Hasidic books. A Hasidic farm boy, who blew his shepherd's pipe out of pure religious exuberance or ardor during the feast of atonement, stands model for the eight-year-old shepherd boy Eli, who sounds his pipe to God when his parents are being chased down an alley by Nazi executioners. The Hasidic boy of the tale broke the curse and drove anger from the face of the earth, says the Ba'al Shem; but the Heavens remain closed to Eli, the Polish boy, who is murdered by a young soldier.[31]

Eli is a unique interweaving, on the one hand, of memories and of reports of painful events that actually took place before the eyes of the world, and, on the other, of the ethnic and religious self-image that Nelly Sachs found in Martin Buber's Hasidic tales. With this complex poetic expression there emerges as well a new concept of the poet's function. A poet who speaks for an entire people has to give precedence to their statement: the "I" of the author has to disappear from the work of art.

Religious consciousness also influences the image of the poet. The poet is not a craftsperson who works in her shop with collected linguistic materials; she is a mystic who perceives secret things. Just as the assignment to serve as mouthpiece for others demands an objectivity of poetic expression, so mystical vision demands the meekness of a mystic. This subservient poetic attitude toward the mystery gives rise to the unique pathetic style that is evident in Sachs's poems of the succeeding years.

This stylistic pathos appears in *Eli* as a "rhythm that makes Hasidic-mystical ardor visible to the actor, even in mime," as Nelly Sachs writes in the comments to *Zeichen im Sand* (III, 345). In *Eli,* she does not portray only Hasidic views and a scene of Jewish life. She carries her own destiny, her poetics, and her personality as poet with her as she enters this ethnic and religious Jewish community and represents it through her art.

Her loss of identity as a German, her personal experience of the closeness of death, her grieving participation in the dying and death of her loved ones and of the many people unknown to her renew Nelly Sachs's complete isolation and loss of orientation in her Stockholm exile, a situation from which she rescues herself only by accepting a Jewish identity. She embraces the biblical myth, the history of the Diaspora, and considers herself, in Buber's sense, a part of the dispersed and persecuted Jewish people, who are entrusted with a special God-given task.

On 7 February 1950, Margarethe Sachs died and left her daughter in uncomprehending grief. Nelly Sachs had accompanied her mother to the boundary of death. Indeed, it seemed to her at times as if she had accompanied her beyond it; she did not want to return. In mind and spirit, she had already left life behind her, and she was reluctant to learn it again. To learn solitude, no longer to perceive oneself as daughter, to develop a new self-image: it is once again a matter of the loss of self at the threshold of death and of the search for a new identity. What she finds is a strengthened consciousness of her vocation as poet, a further development of the concept—reached by way of Rilke and Buber—that sees the poet in the image of creator.

On 25 October 1950,[32] Nelly Sachs finds Ernst Müller's book *Der Sohar und seine Lehre*[33] in the library of the Jewish congregation in Stockholm. This book signals the start of a deeper absorption in the verbal mysticism of the Zohar. Among her books in Stockholm is Gershom Scholem's translation of the first chapter of the Zohar, *Die Geheimnisse der Schöpfung,* with handwritten notes in text and margins, and pressed flowers and bookmarks still between the pages today.[34]

Here one really cannot agree with Leo Hirsch when he says that one can look at the books published by Schocken for a quick and easy introduction to the unfamiliar Jewish spiritual life. This Zohar text, as it is presented in Scholem's translation, cannot be read quickly and easily. Again and again the text changes abruptly: from an apparent description of the external events of creation to a description of the form and context of the letters. The juxtaposition of created world and individual segments of language, a combination entirely unmediated by thought, provokes an intuitive experience that sees language contained in the individual parts of the world, and the world in language.

On the first page of Scholem's introduction, Nelly Sachs underlines the words "Wort" [word] and "geheime Wirklichkeit" [secret reality]. These two underscorings can be seen as headings for her entire engagement with the Kabala. This is the core of the Zohar and the core of her own work with poetic expression: the duality of the secret reality of mysticism and the word's unique creative power.[35]

The notion of the poem as epiphany connects Nelly Sachs directly to the modern poets of the early twentieth century and assigns her a central position in that period's search for linguistic expression. In her view, mysticism and a modernist conception of language belong inseparably together.

The newly acquired identity of the poet becomes evident in her Zohar cycle of April 1952. The description of the Zohar writer in the poems is objective; Nelly Sachs does not forget to include him in the text as the writing "I." She has him represent—assert, in fact—the reciprocal dependence of word and reality; nothing exists before it is given a name. She has him create a universe from his letters, and in so doing presents him as the poet per se. This poet, who groups words together and forms linguistic structures, who simultaneously heals and recreates the cosmos, also creates structure in chaos, a place for the encounter between the divine and the created world.

Language and religiosity, mysticism and modern poetry join to form an ideal image for the work of the poet. In this image, Nelly Sachs finds her new identity as a poet—successor to the Zohar writer, as she understands him.

The final period, with its closeness to death and increased sense of identity, is more complicated and more difficult for the distressed poet. For several years following the death of her mother, Nelly Sachs lived according to her new self-understanding of being called to heal the world through the poetic word. The message of reconciliation among human beings, of humanity and nature, of cosmos and God, was entrusted to her. Many poems emerged, but her voice was not heard. Her first volume of poems was out of print, the remaining copies of *Sternverdunkelung* were destroyed, and no one had the courage to publish the newly written poems. Added to this was the struggle for existence under conditions of extreme poverty, which forced her to accept charity and gifts from friends. Finally, in 1957, Heinrich Ellermann published a large and heterogeneous collection of poems under the title *Und niemand weiß weiter;* Alfred Andersch printed poems in his journal *Texte und Zeichen,*[36] and the literary public of West Germany embraced them.

It is as if the wall against which she had pounded so long had now fallen—but the poet falls as well. The relief and joy sweep over her, and she lacks the stamina to endure this. She begins to complain of headaches; the poems of the new cycle *Flucht und Verwandlung*[37] appear, young friends come to visit, she is celebrated—but the anxieties of the years of persecution return. In her exposed position as literary-prize winner,[38] as the saint of the movement to compensate the war victims, she becomes the target of anti-Semitic invective and threats—a target both real and imagined. Her persecution mania needs treatment; her three-year stay in the mental sanitorium Beckomberga is interrupted only rarely. She perceives herself as a Jew who is once again persecuted, as representative of all persecuted Jews; and she intercedes on Adolf Eichmann's behalf[39]—as a gesture of reconciliation, but also out of fear of retaliatory measures. Worried to death, she steadfastly sees death as a way to salvation.

At Beckomberga she reformulates her religious message. She retains her earlier belief in an undogmatic faith with Christian nuances and remains true to her Kabalistic mysticism, now enlivened by new inspirations from the mysticism of all peoples: Native American,[40] Indian, and Tibetan,[41] among others. She speaks as a poet of nothingness,[42] no longer of the God of a positive religion, and she perceives herself as a citizen of the world. After accepting the Nobel Prize in 1966, she no longer wished to discuss the sources of her metaphors, her poetic language. She could reject all conjectures very abruptly: "I live in Sweden and write German; that should be enough for you."

It became increasingly important to her to deny speculations about the literary sources of her work and the circumstances of her life. Two letters to Bengt Holmqvist from February and March 1968[43] occupy a special position in Nelly Sachs's oeuvre, because she expressed her views only rarely in discursive prose. Both letters are written from the same solemn perspective, as recorded testaments to which the receiver could refer after her death. The content is a summary of her lifelong topic: religion or the religious way of life.

Religions are not opinions or systems, but lived life, an inner dimension, a burning commitment: "Since childhood, I have lived only in the precise moment that burned." The moment burns, and she burns as well. This is the Franciscan "burning," which she had called *Inbrunst* (ardor) since her earliest poetry.

She had never been theoretically concerned with matters of faith; rather she had always, and with her whole being, striven to move beyond preconceived boundaries. This endeavor to cross all boundaries, which is articulated in her poems as stretching over the edge of life, as bending over into the ocean from the furthest point of land, was designated *Sehnsucht* (longing) from her earliest poetry on. In these late formulations, Nelly Sachs retains the inner core of her being, that which constitutes her repeatedly renewed identity. The religious personality exists, prior to dogma, in a nonmediated relation to life and is filled with an ardent longing to cross life's boundaries.

During the deepest humiliation, in moments of the most extreme desperation, the Hasidic mysticism of Martin Buber's adaptations touches her sensibilities as something to which she can relate inwardly. Nevertheless, she claims that it would be a misunderstanding to speak of a Kabalistic influence on her work. World mysticism, religious mysticism in general, her own life, and her fate are determining factors for her poetry. In the sanitorium, lost in the hell of persecution mania, she perceives the living flame of postbiblical Jewish mysticism as her beckoning companion. This deepest humiliation seems to her, "at the edge of insanity," to be the necessary precondition for an existence in the spirit of Jewish mysticism, not as theory but as an option for life. But precisely at this point she ceases to regard the Jewish people as sole representatives of suffering humanity. Those chosen to suffer are not only Jews; Sachs finds her people, the people of suffering, all over the world. She thus expands her religious mysticism from Kabalistic Hasidism to what she calls "world mysticism."

She points to her "Baalschem-Francis-poem" as characteristic of her efforts at unification rather than separation. This poem unites Ba'al Shem and St. Francis of Assisi with Christ in the garden of Gethsemane, when he screamed to God in fear:

On the utmost tip of the spit of land
curfew

abyss threatens addicted gravity
St. Francis—Baalshem, overstep the holy feast
shining in nothing—
The Mount of Olives prays with the single cry
which tore the stone's heart
music of agony
in the ear of the universe
that which is stigmatized by worlds
ignites its own colloquial language—

(*Seeker*, 343)

[Auf der äußersten Spitze der Landzunge
Ausgangsverbot
Abgrund droht süchtiger Schwerkraft
Franziskus—Baalschem übersteigen heiliges Fasten
glänzen im Nichts—
Der Ölberg betet mit dem einzigen Schrei
der dem Stein ein Herz zerriß
Musik der Agonie
ins Ohr des Universums
das mit Welten Stigmatisierte
entzündet seine Umgangssprache—

(I, 353)][44]

Nelly Sachs's self-conception is now finally grounded in a religiosity without dogma, in a mysticism of suffering and redemption that breaks with the Jewish tradition and finds resonance in all other religious paradigms.

Just in time for the acceptance of the Nobel Prize for Literature on 10 December 1966, Nelly Sachs received permission from the Swedish office of personal records to erase the fear-instilling name Sara from her registry. Thus freed from the externally imposed marking as a Jew, she concluded her acceptance speech as she had often done at festive events—with a reading of the following poem from *Flucht und Verwandlung* (1959):

Fleeing,
what a great reception

on the way—
. . . .
This stone
with the fly's inscription
gave itself into my hand—
I hold instead of a homeland
the metamorphoses of the world—

(*Chimneys*, 145)

[In der Flucht
welch großer Empfang
unterwegs—
. . . .
Dieser Stein
mit der Inschrift der Fliege
hat sich mir in die Hand gegeben—
An Stelle von Heimat
halte ich die Verwandlungen der Welt—

(I, 262)]

This poem records Sachs's identity as that of a stranger in the world, her poetic enterprise as one that aims to be a mouthpiece for the mute and suffering creature: Diaspora and poetic priesthood, the word's redeeming service to the world as the task of one who is nowhere at home.

Translated by Dorothee Ostmeier and Marilyn Sibley Fries

NOTES

1. Ruth Dinesen, *Nelly Sachs: Eine Biographie*, trans. Gabriele Gerecke (Frankfurt am Main: Suhrkamp, 1992), 9 and 48ff.; henceforth cited as *Biographie*.

2. Cf. Sachs's letter to Walter A. Berendsohn, 4 February 1959, *Briefe*, 205.

3. The literary bequest of Selma Lagerlöf, which was opened in 1991 at the Royal Library Stockholm, contains another copy of the sonnets with the following handwritten note on the title page: "Nelly Sachs, Berlin, Siegmundshof 16," as well as a note from another hand: "received Falun 11.24.1923." This typewritten copy of the cycle includes only twenty-two poems; the cycle in this copy

is followed by the Francis of Assisi sonnets. Two sonnets of the Lagerlöf bequest are not contained in the Steinthal copy. The total production amounts to twenty-six sonnets about love and four sonnets on Francis of Assisi.

4. Both volumes were translated into German by Rudolf G. Binding. The first appeared in Leipzig, 1919; the second in the Insel Bücherei series, no. 70, n.d.

5. From the poem "Halleluja bei der Geburt eines Felsens" (I, 291–92).

6. Letter to Elisabeth Borchers and Peter Hamm, 16 January 1959. Original letter privately owned; references are to photocopy located in the Deutsches Literaturarchiv, Marbach.

7. Olof Lagercrantz, *Versuch über die Lyrik der Nelly Sachs,* trans. Helene Ritzerfeld (Frankfurt am Main: Suhrkamp, 1967), 40–41: "In her youth Nelly Sachs had been taught by a Jewish rabbi in Jewish religion and had decided that Judaism was too rational and respectful of laws."

8. Rainer Maria Rilke, *Sämtliche Werke* (Frankfurt am Main: Insel, 1976), 10, 365.

9. Cf. *Das Buch der Nelly Sachs,* ed. Bengt Holmqvist (Frankfurt am Main: Suhrkamp, 1977), 34: "The young Nelly Sachs, however, never read Rilke." Holmqvist's essay, which he quotes here, was reviewed several times by Nelly Sachs and finally "authorized" by her (unpublished letter to Holmqvist from 25 February 1968).

10. This with a dedication from 28 June 1920.

11. First published in 1918, here without year.

12. 30 August 1950, *Briefe,* 120.

13. Nelly Sachs presented this book to Selma Lagerlöf with the following dedication: "This book brings heartfelt greetings from Germany to Selma Lagerlöf on her birthday. It is written by a young German who honors the great Swedish poet as her shining model" (*Briefe,* 17).

Fritz J. Raddatz's rejection of this oeuvre is based on the criticism of this early work as

> epigonic prose by a daughter of the educated bourgeoisie, a writing exercise, extremely distant not only from contemporary modern literature . . . but also from reality . . . [I]nstead of that: Jacob Böhme, mysticism, and pious, legendary Christianity. An absurd process, to be forced from that to pious Judaism.

Fritz J. Raddatz, *Verwerfungen: Sechs literarische Essays* (Frankfurt am Main: Suhrkamp, 1972), 45. Raddatz sees the "daughter of the educated bourgeoisie" at work in the later poems as well; he does not recognize her fundamental religious attitude but instead rejects this as "Umdeutung" [reinterpretation] and "Verklärung" [transfiguration] (45–46); from this position one can understand his final statement: "Nelly Sachs has a black subject. . . . It overwhelmed the sheltered bourgeois girl from Berlin's West with the music room and the bibliophile education: she did not overcome it" (51).

14. She seems to connect to a different Rilkean train of thought, as Kurt Pinthus attests on the occasion of Rilke's sixtieth birthday: "From his earliest to his last letters, Rilke repeatedly praises this receptiveness, this drawing closer to living things, in order to plumb their essence through ardent comprehension. . . . Whoever has had the opportunity to read the poetic endeavors of young Jews over the last several years knows how strong Rilke's influence on Jewish youth was and still is. . . . Here one could find something for which many Jews also longed: Rilke's passion to transport the worldly into the transcendental. One found a concept of a God who could be approached directly, without a mediator." Kurt Pinthus, "Rilkes 'Briefe aus Muzot': Zu Rilkes 60. Geburtstag: 4 December 1935," *C.-V.-Zeitung* (Berlin) 49 (3d supplement), 5 December 1935. This essay also contains a quotation later used by Nelly Sachs: "We are the bees of the invisible" (cf. letter to Gudrun Harlan, 6 June 1947: "I once read Rilke's 'Muzot-letters' and knew this sentence about the bees of the invisible" [*Briefe,* 77]).

15. Leo Hirsch, "Die Kehrseite der Konjunktur," *Der Morgen* (Berlin) 5, no. 14 (1938): 163–68.

16. "Die Rehe" (The deer), 26 February, "Das Vogelnest" (The bird's nest), 9 July, "Schlummerreise" (The slumber journey), 21 December 1933.

17. "Nachtlied" (Nightsong), with the author's (Jewish) name: Nelly Sara Sachs.

18. Unpublished letter to Gunhild Tegen, 22 August 1944 (Manuscript Department of the University Library, Uppsala).

19. *Die Bibel oder die ganze Heilige Schrift des Alten und Neuen Testaments, nach der deutschen Übersetzung Martin Luthers.* The volume examined for this essay, published in Berlin, 1913, contains Nelly Sachs's signature.

It is probable that Nelly Sachs already owned the *Kleine Schul- und Hausbibel* (Small Bible for school and home) at that time; it contained "stories and devotional texts from the Holy Scriptures of the Israelites, in addition to a selection from the Apocrypha and aphorisms from the postbiblical period"; edited by Jakob Auerbach, 17th ed., pt. 1 (Berlin, 1928); the pages contain neither markings nor signature. She further owned the Buber-Rosenzweig translation of the book Isaiah: *Die Troestung Israels: Aus Jeschajahu, Kapitel 40 bis 55,* German by Martin Buber and Franz Rosenzweig (Berlin: Schocken, 1933). But she discovers the material for her first attempts with Jewish poetry in Johann Gottfried Herder, *Blätter der Vorzeit: Dichtungen aus der morgenländischen Sage (Jüdische Dichtungen und Fabeln)* (Berlin: Schocken, 1936). The book in Stockholm has bookmarks at the legend of Abraham's childhood, which was the starting point for the Abram poetry of the first years in Stockholm; but the Berlin poem "David und Jonathan" found its paradigm here as well. Cf. Ruth Dinesen, *"Und Leben hat immer wie Abschied geschmeckt": Frühe Gedichte und Prosa der Nelly Sachs* (Stuttgart: Heinz Akademischer Verlag, 1987), 83–84.

20. The cycle in the Lagerlöf bequest includes the following poems: "Brunnenlied," "Jakob's Traum," "Hagar und der Engel," "Jacob und Rahel," "Eine Mutter singt in der Wüste ihr Kind in den Schlaf," "Kleines Lied um das Mosekörbchen," "Bileam's Eselin," "David spielt vor Saul," "David und Jonathan," "Abendlieder der Ruth," "Lied eines Mädchens aus Babylonischer Gefangenschaft," "Esther geht zum König."

21. Kurt Pinthus, "Jüdische Lyrik der Zeit," *C.-V.-Zeitung* (Berlin) 15 (2d supplement), 9 April 1936: "It has been debated among the Jews whether Jewish poems are at all possible in the German language. I think a Jewish poem is possible in every language. . . . Furthermore, it is not the Jewish subject matter that makes a poem Jewish. . . . It is not a matter of the Jewish decorations and motifs in which a poem is wrapped, but rather of the Jewish feeling and Jewish perspective from which it necessarily derives, although feeling and perspective certainly do not always have to be traced back to a historical Jewish tradition. If one wants to talk about a 'Jewish poem' at all, then it is not entirely incorrect to entertain the notion of a Jewish component that would determine whether a poem can be considered 'Jewish.'" The small anthology of Jewish poems that follows this introduction includes, among others, Nelly Sachs's poem "Die Rehe" (The deer).

22. According to the second decree on the enforcement of the law concerning the alteration of surnames and first names of 17 August 1938: "Article 2: To the extent that Jews have different first names from those permitted according to Article 1, they must, as of January 1, 1939, assume an additional first name: male persons the first name Israel, female persons the first name Sara."

23. H. G. Adler, *Versuch einer Charakterisierung des Jüdischen: Juden— Christen—Deutsche*, ed. Hans Jürgen Schultz, 3d ed. (Stuttgart: Kreuz Verlag/Olten; Freiburg: Walter-Verlag, 1961), 54.

24. Simon N. Herman, *Jewish Identity: A Social Psychological Perspective*, Sage Library of Social Research, vol. 48 (Beverly Hills, Calif.: Sage, 1977), 43 and 47.

25. Martin Buber, *Die Legende des Baalschem,* first appeared in 1907, later in expanded and modified form in *Die chassidischen Bücher* (Hellerau: Hegner, 1928). It exists as *Legende des Baalschem,* rev. ed. (Zurich: Menesse, 1955) in the Stockholm library.

26. A copy of the typescript exists in the Nelly Sachs Collection, Stockholm. The notes are dated; the quotation can be found on p. 12, under the date 12 May 1973.

27. Buber, *Die chassidischen Bücher,* 6ff. The quotation comes from the original introduction to *Die Geschichte des Rabbi Nachman,* first published 1906.

28. Buber, *Die chassidischen Bücher,* xiff. The quotation comes from the *Geleitwort zur Gesamtausgabe* (dated 1927). Here Martin Buber uses the word "Zwiegespräch" [literally: conversation of two], xii. As Buber developed his philosophy of language, this word was replaced by "Zwiesprache," used as the book's title in 1930.

29. First edition in German published by Forsells Boktryckeri, Malmö, February 1951.

30. Letter to Emilia Fogelklou, 11 November 1945, *Briefe,* 43–44.

31. Buber, *Die chassidischen Bücher.*

32. Letter to Walter A. Berendsohn, 26 October 1950. Walter A. Berendsohn, *Nelly Sachs: Einführung in das Werk der Dichterin jüdischen Schicksals* (Darmstadt: Agora Verlag, 1974), 156. "In the Mos. Library yesterday I read anxiously in the Kabalah and profited from some of the things that are written about it in books. I was again happy to sense the secret connections that seem through the chaos to be opening their buds everywhere."

33. Ernst Müller, *Der Sohar und seine Lehre* (Vienna, Berlin: R. Löwit, 1920).

34. Gershom Scholem, trans., *Die Geheimnisse der Schöpfung* (Berlin: Schocken, 1935).

35. A handwritten note at the bottom of p. 29 relates to this thematic focus: "Attempt to make materiality transparent through inner languages."

36. Cf. the poems "Ein schwarzer Jochanaan" (A black Jochanaan), "Nicht nur Land ist Israel" (Israel is not only a country), "Daniel mit der Sternenzeichnung" (Daniel with the drawings of the stars), "Landschaft aus Schreien" (Landscape of screams). *Texte und Zeichen 11* 3, no. 1 (1957): 9–13.

37. First mentioned spring 1958; published at Easter, 1959, by the Deutsche Verlags-Anstalt, Stuttgart.

38. Poetry prize of the Swedish Authors' Union, January 1, 1958; Literature prize of the Kulturkreis im Bundesverband der Deutschen Industrie, 7 July 1959; Meersburger Droste Prize for Women Poets, 29 May 1960; Nelly Sachs Prize of the City of Dortmund, 1961; Peace Prize of the German Book Industry, 17 October 1965; Nobel Prize (together with Josef S. Agnon), 1966; named honorary citizen of the City of Berlin, 1967.

39. Letter to David Ben Gurion, 27 March 1962 (*Biographie,* 338).

40. Cf. "Im Eingefrorenen Zeitalter der Anden" (I, 355), from the cycle *Noch feiert Tod das Leben,* written between November 1960 and May 1961.

41. Cf. "Fortgehen ohne Rückschau" (II, 74); from the cycle *Glühende Rätsel III,* first published 1965.

42. Cf. "Diese Nacht" (II, 9); from the cycle *Glühende Rätsel I,* written 1962, first published 1963.

43. Unpublished letter of 25 February 1968; letter of 20 March 1968 (*Biographie,* 349–50). Both letters are privately owned; references here are to photocopies located in the Nelly Sachs Archive, Swedish Royal Library, Stockholm.

44. Written November 1960.

Chapter 3

"My Metaphors Are My Wounds": Nelly Sachs and the Limits of Poetic Metaphor

Ehrhard Bahr

Neither borrowing nor metaphor
[Weder Entlehnung noch Metapher].

—Paul Celan

Dealing with the limits of representation by poetic metaphor, I will con-
centrate on the major corpus of Nelly Sachs's poetry between 1947 and
1961. This focus will detract from her late poetry between 1961 and
1970, which still awaits discovery by a larger audience, yet it highlights
an issue that is at the center of Nelly Sachs's poetry. I have raised this
issue before in my *Nelly Sachs* of 1980 (79–86), and I will try to answer
this question here with new evidence. It is a dilemma that has plagued not
only literature, but also Western historiography from the mid-1970s on:
the issue of the limits of artistic and historical representation of the Nazi
genocide against the Jews.[1] This focus is justified in the case of Nelly
Sachs's poetry, because it was this event that elicited the response of her
poetry after 1943. Sachs had written poetry before, but she dated her
career as a legitimate poet from this date. She claimed she would not have
survived if she had not been able to write. "Death was my teacher. How
could I have written about anything else? My metaphors are my wounds.
This is the only way to understand my work," she later said.[2] The Nobel
Prize for literature was awarded to her as the voice of the suffering of
Israel, by which she meant not the state but the Jewish people. Her poetry
was characterized as the representation of the "world-wide tragedy of the
Jewish people."[3]

The genocide of the Jewish people is not only the central trauma of

German and Jewish history, but of twentieth-century history in general. During this century the concept of man as a human being was abolished, as André Malraux once said. It happened in Auschwitz, which is representative of all the other German extermination camps in Poland and which is no longer a place name but has become a metaphor for the inhumanity of this century. Since Auschwitz, our world has been defined as *l'univers concentrationnaire,* as David Rousset has labeled it.[4]

Historical scholarship has assembled and analyzed the available facts and dates; courts of justice have tried to sentence the persecutors; psychology and sociology have provided explanations; and philosophy and theology have tried to find an answer. George Steiner has declared that "the world of Auschwitz lies outside speech as it lies outside reason."[5] Martin Walser has said that we cannot project ourselves into the situation of the "inmates" because their degree of suffering is beyond comprehension.[6] What all these attempts to find an adequate answer to the problem of Auschwitz have in common is the fact that they ultimately arrive, as Saul Friedländer has put it, at "some non-defined, but clearly felt *limits of representation.*"[7] Literature is no exception to these limits, yet passive observance of these limits is unacceptable. Such an acceptance would be a surrender to the very same inhumanity that was put into practice in the extermination camps. Whoever surrenders human imagination to the limits of representation renounces the claim to historical existence. But total denial of limits is equally unacceptable. Even literature has no magic to overcome the limits of representation. Understanding evolves out of the dialectics of the failure of total comprehension. The very perception of limits of representation and their possible/impossible transcendence indicates that we are facing an exceptional situation that calls for a fusion of ethical and critical categories. It is not accidental that we have had a recent reaction against the ahistoricity of deconstructionism, as for example in J. Hillis Miller's *The Ethics of Reading* of 1987.[8]

Literature has been challenged by the Nazi genocide against the Jews in a very special way, because that murder called not only historical, but especially poetic, imagination into question. To what degree is literature able to represent the Nazi genocide using its traditional means of expression? What are the advantages of artistic representation, as compared to scholarly or philosophical representations? The recent *Historikerstreit* (historians' debate, 1986) in West Germany dealt with the exceptionality, the uniqueness of the Nazi genocide. The debate was decided in favor of that genocide's incomparability. The genocide confronts human beings with a kind of crime that was unequalled because, as the West German historian Eberhard Jäckel said,

> [N]ever before had a state decided, with the authority of its leader . . . totally to exterminate a certain group of people, including the old, the women, the children, the infants—and turned this decision into fact with the use of all possible instruments of power available to the state.[9]

Kafka's short story "In the Penal Colony" (In der Strafkolonie) can be cited only as an imaginative anticipation, but never as a direct confrontation with this crime, and therefore the novella leaves an impression of the fantastically absurd or bizarre. There was no tradition readily available in literature for the representation of the Nazi genocide against the Jews. This tradition had to be formed, and its means of expression had to be established. In the meantime, we have a corpus of texts of so-called Holocaust literature, to which Nelly Sachs made one of the most important contributions.

At the center of Holocaust literature is the problem of the representation of an incomparable crime via fictive literature's means of expression. Lawrence L. Langer was one of the first to identify this problem in his book *The Holocaust and the Literary Imagination* of 1975. He lists a number of recurrent themes and motifs, such as "the displacement of the consciousness of life by the imminence and pervasiveness of death; the violation of the coherence of childhood; the assault on physical reality; the disintegration of rational intelligence; and the disruption of chronological time."[10]

In Nelly Sachs's poetry after 1944, we can find a great number of these themes and motifs. Her first collection of poetry after World War II, *In den Wohnungen des Todes* (In the habitations of death), and her mystery play *Eli,* written after the first breakthrough in winter 1943–44, show Sachs breaking new ground by either totally avoiding metaphors or being very selective in choosing them. The title of the collection identifies existence within the realm of death. The theme of death is at the center of all poems of this cycle. In order to avoid any misunderstanding about the kind of death referred to, Sachs does not use metaphors for the first line of the title poem, but names the smoke stacks of the extermination camps' crematoria:

O the chimneys
On the ingeniously devised habitations of death

(*Chimneys*, 3)

[O die Schornsteine
Auf den sinnreich erdachten Wohnungen des Todes,

(I, 8)]

The buildings are deceptively constructed as houses, but they are not designed as houses for the living, but rather as "habitations of death." The human craft of house construction is totally alienated from its original function. The separation of this truly human activity from its original exposes the perversion of the design of these particular houses.

The third stanza addresses the bodily extremities used by the SS officers at the selection ramp to direct the victims to extermination or forced labor:

O you fingers
Laying the threshold
Like a knife between life and death—

(*Chimneys*, 3)

[O ihr Finger,
Die Eingangsschwelle legend
Wie ein Messer zwischen Leben und Tod—

(I, 8)]

The human gesture of pointing one's finger in a particular direction is meant to help people find their way, not to decide about their life or death. In the dehumanized system of the extermination camps, this gesture of assistance to the wayworn travelers is perverted into the gesture of the assassin or murderer.

During the 1950s, there was a discussion in West Germany about Holocaust literature, although the term had not yet been coined. This discussion revolved around Theodor W. Adorno's dictum that "to write poetry after Auschwitz is barbaric."[11] For Adorno, Auschwitz represents a complete rupture in human culture; it makes society and culture before and after the Nazi genocide against the Jews appear totally irreconcilable.[12] Although it has become almost a cliché, Adorno's statement needs to be included in our discussion of the limits of artistic representation of the Nazi genocide. It does not suffice to reconfirm that Nelly Sachs has written poems not only *after* Auschwitz, but *about* Auschwitz. Achievement and failure are close in this realm. Past criticism has been affirmative rather than analytical in reading her poetry from this point of view.

The problem raised by Adorno is the question of whether the writing of poetry can be justified after the Nazi genocide. The total collapse of Western culture has not prevented its restoration. This restoration carries the potential for repetition. Any participation in culture after Auschwitz will help to reproduce it.[13]

If literature could continue as it did before Auschwitz, then Adorno's verdict would be justified. German nature poetry after 1945 falls under this verdict. But literature also offers the opportunity to withdraw from "the assembly line of killers," as Kafka wrote in his diary on 27 January 1922.[14] In response to Adorno's verdict, one could raise the question of whether one should abandon poetry only because the restoration of culture could perhaps reproduce Auschwitz. Does not *l'univers concentrationnaire* require the counterbalance of art, literature, and music? Do not the victims have a "right to expression," a right to memory in artistic form? Adorno did indeed agree with this particular argument.[15]

But the problem of the artistic presentation of the Nazi genocide does not concern the "right of expression" of the victims, but rather the translation of the inhuman reality into the language of literature without that reality's diminishment, deletion, sentimentalization, or aestheticization. Adorno raised this argument against Arnold Schoenberg's oratorio *A Survivor of Warsaw,* saying that

> The so-called artistic representation of pure, bodily pain of the victims maltreated by rifle butts contains, even though remotely, a potential of aesthetic pleasure. The morality that commands art constantly to remember this slides into the abyss of the opposite. Aesthetic stylization . . . makes the inconceivable fate appear as if it had some meaning; there is transfiguration; some of the horrible is softened.[16]

This same idea is expressed in an essay of 1965 titled "To Describe Inhumanity" (Unmenschlichkeit beschreiben), by the West German critic Reinhard Baumgart. He explains that any aesthetic method betrays the representation of the Nazi genocide insofar as it constitutes aesthetic organization: "Even and especially the artistically successful poem or novella becomes suspect if it has succeeded in the artistic mastery of inhumanity."[17] The imminent risk of the work of art consists in the elimination of reality and the substitution of another reality that is a falsification or sentimentalization of that eliminated. Baumgart illustrates this danger of sentimentalization with a comment by a woman who had just seen a performance of the *Anne Frank* drama: she remarked that the Nazi should have saved at least this girl.[18] This psychological slip reveals a mentality that implicitly agrees with the genocide under the condition of saving one congenial victim. As much as the production of the play was able to enlighten the audience about a single victim, it failed in its main objective: to represent the Nazi genocide. The result was a sentimental audience-identification with the victim, which implied a concurrence with the genocide. As an example of the danger of falsification, Baumgart cites Rolf Hochhuth's play *The Deputy* (Der Stellvertreter), because it attempts to present the reality of the Nazi genocide by means of eighteenth-century historical drama. The conflict in Hochhuth's play is represented in terms of an individual's desire for truth; this individual proudly defies the threat of death, as was credible in the age of enlightened despotism, but not in an age of extermination camps that made it their first order of business to deny any individuality.[19]

It is therefore significant that Sachs, in the title poem "O the chimneys," calls the various objects of the extermination camp reality by their names. The synecdochal meanings of "chimney" and "finger" do not constitute an elimination of reality, but rather a concentration on the components of an inhuman system: the smoke stacks stand as *pars pro toto* for the gas chambers and crematoria, the fingers for the selection at the ramp.

The West German reading public showed no interest in Nelly Sachs's poetry during the first ten years of reconstruction between 1945 and 1955. Successful postwar poetry in West Germany was—with the exception of Günter Eich—limited to the idyllic topics of nature poetry. The economic miracle and the climate of restoration during the Adenauer period produced the Gottfried Benn renaissance of the 1950s. The situation was different in East Germany, where other poets were read. Nelly Sachs had her first postwar poems published by Peter Huchel in *Sinn und Form,* the journal of the Academy of Arts in East Berlin, which he was able to edit for more than ten years without censorship before he was forced to resign by the GDR's ruling party. Nelly Sachs's first volume of poetry was also published in East Germany, by the Aufbau publishing house in East Berlin and Weimar. Her second volume, *Sternverdunkelung,* published by Querido (Amsterdam) in 1949, was pulped due to lack of sales. The beginnings of the history of German postwar poetry will have to be rewritten, taking into consideration not only what was printed and well received, but also what was written and published, but not read for ideological reasons. German postwar poetry was not as escapist and idyllic as has often been claimed.

After West Germany's establishment of relations with Israel, and after the Eichmann trial in Jerusalem in 1961, public opinion in West Germany expressed the need for alibi figures. Nelly Sachs's image was manipulated to serve this need. During the 1960s, she received many awards and literary prizes in West Germany and was elected as a corresponding member to a number of academies of art. She was manipulated as representative of German-Jewish reconciliation, although she had never spoken of reconciliation—or of its opposite. What West German public opinion needed was a public gesture of reconciliation. After her numerous West German awards, Nelly Sachs received the Peace Prize of the German Book Trade in 1965. The award of the Nobel Prize for Literature, which she shared with Samuel Joseph Agnon, was perceived as a confirmation of West German efforts.

Since then, Nelly Sachs might have been forgotten if it had not been for the efforts of Bengt and Margarete Holmqvist and Ruth Dinesen. The historiography of German literature has neglected her during the last fifteen years, although "her poetry belongs to the best produced in the German language during this century," as Hilde Domin has said.[20] The reason for this disinterest or stagnation is the politicization of literature during the late 1960s. The "new subjectivity" in literature after 1975 did not result in a renewed receptivity for her poetry. With the deaths of Paul Celan and Nelly Sachs in 1970, a specific kind of poetry came to an end in Germany. While neglect has not affected Celan scholarship—there is a regularly published Celan yearbook—Nelly Sachs has suffered such neglect partially because of her closeness to Celan.

One of the misunderstandings regarding the poetry of Nelly Sachs is the fact that she was classified, celebrated, and forgotten as the "poet of the Jewish tragedy," although the Nazi genocide constitutes the dominant theme only during the first phase of her poetry and drama from 1943 to 1949. The second phase (1950–60) is dominated by Jewish mysticism, which is transcended by a universal mysticism during the last phase (1960–70). Her late poetry and her lyric dramas are largely undiscovered. The label of "poet of the Jewish tragedy" has blocked the approach to her late poetry and drama. Even reviews of her late works return to the label that applies most adequately only to her early production.

The poem I want to discuss in detail here belongs to her early work and may serve as a paradigm for the limits of artistic representation. The poem was written in 1947, when Sachs began to assemble the cycle for *Sternverdunkelung*, published in 1949. It was not selected for publication then but was finally published upon the express wish and recommendation of Hans Magnus Enzensberger, the West German editor of her *Gesammelte Gedichte* (Collected poems) of 1961. Sachs was evidently not satisfied with the poem. She thought that the topic had not been adequately treated.[21] It is important for the following discussion of the poem to keep in mind the poet's reservations about her own poem, and the popularity of a single stanza that was isolated from its context and repeatedly quoted in West Germany during the early sixties. This stanza has founded the fame—in this particular case we may almost refer to the dubious fame—of Nelly Sachs in West Germany. Her own reservations concerning the poem should be understood as an important contribution to the comprehension of the limits of representation or, more precisely, the limits of poetic metaphor.

Judging by the first stanza, it appears to be a nature poem, beginning, as it does, with references to "summer," "moon," "lilies," and "crickets":

When in early summer the moon sends out secret signs,
the chalices of lilies scent of heaven,
some ear opens to listen
beneath the chirp of the cricket
to earth turning and the language of spirits set free.

But in dreams the fish fly in the air
and a forest takes firm root in the floor of the room.

(*Seeker,* 147)

[Wenn im Vorsommer der Mond geheime Zeichen aussendet,
die Kelche der Lilien Dufthimmel verströmen,
öffnet sich manches Ohr unter Grillengezirp

dem Kreisen der Erde und der Sprache
der entschränkten Geister zu lauschen.

In den Träumen aber fliegen die Fische in der Luft
und ein Wald wurzelt sich im Zimmerfußboden fest.

(I, 153)]

But in the second stanza, nature is confronted with historical reality, and
her neutrality becomes intolerable in the face of Nazi genocide:

But in the midst of enchantment a voice speaks clearly and amazed:
World, how can you go on playing your games
and cheating time—
World, the little children were thrown like butterflies,
wings beating into the flames—

and your earth has not been thrown like a rotten apple
into the terror-roused abyss—

And sun and moon have gone on walking—
two cross-eyed witnesses who have seen nothing.

[Aber mitten in der Verzauberung spricht eine Stimme klar und
verwundert:
Welt, wie kannst du deine Spiele weiter spielen
und die Zeit betrügen—
Welt, man hat die kleinen Kinder wie Schmetterlinge,
flügelschlagend in die Flamme geworfen—

und deine Erde ist nicht wie ein fauler Apfel
in den schreckaufgejagten Abgrund geworfen worden—

Und Sonne und Mond sind weiter spazierengegangen—
zwei schieläugige Zeugen, die nichts gesehen haben.]

Shock is voiced at the fact that this terrestrial globe was not destroyed,
and that the sun and the moon, having seen the crime of genocide,
continued on their course like two witnesses who pretend to have seen
nothing. Sachs employs pathetic fallacy here, endowing nature with
human emotions. Even Goethe, with his almost pagan confidence in

nature, does not commit such a fallacy. In his poem "Das Göttliche" (The divine), he insists, rather, on the difference between man and nature:

> For unfeeling
> Is nature,
> The sun shines
> Upon evil men and good,
> And to the criminal
> As to the best
> The moon and the stars spend their light.

> [Denn unfühlend
> Ist die Natur:
> Es leuchtet die Sonne
> über Bös' und Gute,
> Und dem Verbrecher
> Glänzen wie dem Besten
> Der Mond und die Sterne.][22]

And Bertolt Brecht, Sachs's contemporary, asked in his poem "To Posterity" (An die Nachgeborenen): "What kinds of times are these / when a conversation about trees is almost a crime" [Was sind das für Zeiten, wo / Ein Gespräch über Bäume fast ein Verbrechen ist].[23] The voice of the poet who is preoccupied with nature will not be available to protest the crimes against humanity. Sachs, to be sure, does speak of trees, flowers, and butterflies in her poem, but she is not silent about the crimes committed. The expression of horror about the neutrality of nature appears not to be justifiable, because for the German tradition, with which she was familiar, nature is not a moral authority. The horror expressed can perhaps be explained in terms of a mystic belief confronted by God's withdrawal from his creation. Yet the system of such a belief is not provided by the context of this poem.

Without doubt, the following four lines belong to the best known of Sachs's poetry. Yet they are also perhaps the most problematic:

> World, the little children were thrown like butterflies,
> wings beating into the flames—

> and your earth has not been thrown like a rotten apple
> into the terror-roused abyss—

Out of context, these four lines make an anonymous "world" responsible for the crime of infanticide and reveal a dangerous tendency toward sentimentality. The poetic simile of the butterflies beating their wings diminishes the reality of the Nazi genocide because it asserts a similarity between human souls and butterflies while it downplays or hides the aspect of mass murder.[24] The conventional metaphor of butterfly and candle thus serves to protect the reader from a stronger representation of the reality of the extermination camps.

A quotation from Johann Gottfried Herder's *Letters for the Advancement of Humanity,* which take a stand on the same issue, may explain the problem. Herder writes:

> In novels, we weep for the butterfly whose wings are touched by rain; in conversations we overflow with noble sentiments; but for the moral decline of our human people, from which all evil comes, we have no eyes to see.

> [In Romanen beweinen wir den Schmetterling, dem der Regen die Flügel netzt; in Gesprächen kochen wir vor großen Gesinnungen über; und für jene moralische Verfallenheit unsres Geschlechts, aus der alles Übel entspringt, haben wir kein Auge.][25]

To return to Nelly Sachs's poem: there is the danger that the four lines and their central metaphor make the reader forget the difference between a human being and a butterfly. Shedding tears for the butterflies, the reader is allowed to forget the reality of six million victims, including children. Without doubt, this motivation has contributed to the popularity of these lines and their main image. The conventional metaphor enables the reader to put a distance between the historical event and its representation.

To be sure, the image of the butterfly as a representation of the human soul is one of the traditional symbols in Western literature from Greek mythology to Goethe. The butterfly is also one of the central symbols of Sachs's poetry; it can also be found as metaphor of the soul in Jewish mysticism as well as in the drawings of children from the Theresienstadt concentration camp and from the Warsaw ghetto. But even such associations cannot fully justify the use of the butterfly metaphor in this context. The comparison of small children with butterflies is not only sentimental, it also fails to provide an understanding of the process of destruction.

The similarities among the various ranges of experience provided by the butterfly metaphor do not cohere when it comes to the topic of genocide. The conventional metaphor blocks; it does not give structure to the historical experience.[26]

A comparison with André Schwarz-Bart's novel *The Last of the Just* (Le Dernier des justes) of 1959 and with a poem by Pablo Neruda may further explain the critical issue of the limits of representation. In a scene of the novel, the Jewish protagonist, young Ernie Levy, crushes a butterfly in his hands. In spite of his deep understanding of the mystic interpretation of the butterfly, Ernie enacts his revenge on the insect.[27] This action is a misplaced transference of his revenge for an attack by a gang of Hitler youths. Ernie's revenge makes him realize the transference of evil from the perpetrator to the victim: violence generates new violence. This experience makes Ernie understand the process of dehumanization. The image of the butterfly is legitimate in this context because the destruction of the butterfly is not employed as a simile to feel sorry for the victim, but rather as an example to expose the misguided revenge of a human being who aspires to be a just man. The experience teaches Ernie Levy to realize that he was not a just man, that it reduced him to nothing, as he has to admit.[28]

The lines from a poem by Neruda may help us further to understand the limits of the poetic simile employed by Sachs. The two lines are from a poem on the Spanish Civil War and read as follows:

and through the streets the blood of the children
just flowed like blood of children.[29]

[y por las calles la sangre de los niños
corría simplimente, como sangre de niños.][30]

In a desperately ironic tautology—the blood of children flows like blood of children—the poetic simile is deconstructed with the result that the horror of the event is represented without aesthetic distance. The rhetoric of lyric poetry fails when confronted with this event of the Spanish Civil War. Any simile would be a violation. The blood of children can only be compared to the blood of children. Any other analogy or metaphor proves to be unacceptable and a violation of the limits of representation.[31]

Nelly Sachs was evidently aware of the inadequacy of the simile employed. Her reservations regarding her own poem are an indication of her sensibility as a poet dealing with the Nazi genocide and the limits of its representation in poetry. A later poem, titled "My Place" (Mein Ort) and published in 1965, appears to be intertextually related to the poem of 1947:

Cut apart by the meridian of sighs
of tears
by the smile of the child
who was thrown into the flames
this foundation of suffering
where the globe gets beside itself
the architect with his flames
builds only haloes
further and further
away from death
who a nameless vision
decays backwards—

[Durchschnitten vom Meridian der Seufzer
der Tränen
dem Lächeln des Kindes
das in die Flammen geworfen wurde
diese Gründung des Leidens
wo der Erdball außer sich gerät
nur Glorien baut
der Baumeister mit Flammen
ferner und ferner
fort vom Tod
der eine namenlose Vision
rückwärts verfällt—[32]

(*Atlas*, 307)]

Avoiding the simile of the butterflies of the earlier poem, this text, referring to the smile of a child thrown into the flames, appears as a revision of the stanza of 1947. The new wording appears to constitute a realization of the limits of poetic metaphor in the representation of the Nazi genocide. The positive reception of the stanza of 1947 in West Germany during the 1960s—and I include myself among those who were moved by these four lines—was probably motivated by an ideological need for aesthetic distancing from the Nazi genocide.

Nelly Sachs's intertextual revision of 1965 is a prime example for critical study. Although she had said that her metaphors were her wounds, she deleted this particular metaphor of 1947, a poetic simile comparing children thrown into the flames of the crematoria to butterflies flapping their wings. The later poem of 1965 shows that Sachs was able to remove this metaphor, but none of her wounds. Her "place" to live is still "this foundation of suffering" [diese Gründung des Leidens]. Any serious future criticism will have to focus on examples like this to generate an awareness of the limits of representation of the Nazi genocide and the failures and achievements of poetic metaphor. In his penetrating remarks about the tension between poetic form and historical reference in poetry about the Nazi genocide, Berel Lang implies that successful poets like Celan make "the effort to give up one of these [impulses] in order to realize the other," while less successful poets, who "attempt to sustain both impulses, disclose a resultant dissonance in their work—not because of their use of *poetic* figure, but because of the effort to move in two conflicting directions at once."[33] But this dissonance is the very essence of poetry about the Nazi genocide, charged with the impossibility of its project: at once to incorporate and not to poeticize history.[34] As Paul Celan said when he had to remind one of the critics who persisted in questioning him about his literary allusions: in this kind of poetry—in this particular instance his own "Death Fugue" (Todesfuge)—the choice of words is, "God knows, neither borrowing nor metaphor" [weiß Gott, weder Entlehnung noch Metapher].[35]

NOTES

This essay is dedicated to Ruth (Angress) Klüger. Without her generously shared insights, I would not have been able to write it.

1. For the usage of the term *Nazi genocide,* as compared to *Holocaust* and/or *Shoah,* see Berel Lang, *Act and Idea in the Nazi Genocide* (Chicago: University of Chicago Press, 1990), xx–xxi.

2. See Olof Lagercrantz, *Versuch über die Lyrik der Nelly Sachs* (Frankfurt am Main: Suhrkamp, 1967), 43, 53; Bengt Holmqvist, ed., *Das Buch der Nelly Sachs,* 2d ed. (Frankfurt am Main: Suhrkamp, 1977), 28.

3. Horst Frenz, ed., *Literature 1901–1967: Nobel Lectures, Including Presentation Speeches and Laureates' Biographies* (Amsterdam: Elsevier, 1969), 612.

4. Lawrence L. Langer, *The Holocaust and the Literary Imagination* (New Haven: Yale University Press, 1975), 15–16.

5. Langer, *Holocaust and Literary Imagination,* 15.

6. Martin Walser, "Unser Auschwitz," in *Heimatkunde: Aufsätze und Reden* (Frankfurt am Main: Suhrkamp, 1968), 11.

7. I am indebted to Saul Friedlander, who coined this phrase in his opening remarks at the conference "Nazism and the 'Final Solution': Probing the Limits of Representation" at the University of California, Los Angeles, 27 April 1990. The papers from this conference have been edited by Friedlander and published as *Probing the Limits of Representation: Nazism and the "Final Solution"* (Cambridge: Harvard University Press, 1992).

8. Cf. Lang, *Act and Idea,* 122.

9. Eberhard Jäckel, "Die elende Praxis der Untersteller," in *"Historikerstreit,"* ed. Piper Verlag (Munich: Piper, 1987), 118.

10. Langer, *Holocaust and Literary Imagination,* xii.

11. Theodor W. Adorno, *Gesammelte Schriften,* (Frankfurt am Main: Suhrkamp, 1973–84), 10, pt. 1:30; 11:422.

12. Theodor W. Adorno, *Minima Moralia: Reflexionen aus dem beschädigten Leben* (Frankfurt am Main: Suhrkamp, 1976), 65.

13. Adorno, *Minima Moralia,* 65, 315–16.

14. Franz Kafka, *Tagebücher 1910–1923,* ed. Max Brod (Frankfurt am Main: Fischer, 1967), 406.

15. Adorno, *Gesammelte Schriften,* 6:355–56.

16. Adorno, *Gesammelte Schriften,* 11:423.

17. Reinhart Baumgart, "Unmenschlichkeit beschreiben," in *Literatur für Zeitgenossen: Essays* (Frankfurt am Main: Suhrkamp, 1966), 12–36.

18. See also Adorno, *Gesammelte Schriften,* 10, pt. 2:570.

19. Baumgart, "Unmenschlichkeit beschreiben," 28–35.

20. Hilde Domin, afterword to *Gedichte,* by Nelly Sachs (Frankfurt am Main: Suhrkamp, 1977), 110.

21. See Lagercrantz, *Versuch,* 18–20.

22. Johann Wolfgang von Goethe, "Das Göttliche," in *Werke,* ed. Erich Trunz, Hamburger Ausgabe (Hamburg: Wegner, 1949), 1:147–49.

23. Bertolt Brecht, "An die Nachgeborenen," in *Gedichte und Lieder* (Frankfurt am Main: Suhrkamp, 1979), 158.

24. I am indebted to George Lakoff and Mark Johnson and their discussion of the creation of similarity in *Metaphors We Live By* (Chicago: University of Chicago Press, 1980), 147–55. For a discussion of the legitimacy of Holocaust metaphors, see James E. Young, *Writing and Rewriting the Holocaust: Narrative and the Consequences of Intepretation* (Bloomington: Indiana University Press, 1988), 83–98; and Alvin H. Rosenfeld, *A Double Dying: Reflections on Holocaust Literature* (Bloomington: Indiana University Press, 1980), 180.

25. Johann Gottfried Herder, "Briefe zur Beförderung der Humanität, 1793–97," in *Sämtliche Werke,* ed. Bernhard Suphan (1883; rpt. Hildesheim: Olms, 1967), 18:235.

26. See Lakoff and Johnson, *Metaphors We Live By,* 47–55.

27. André Schwarz-Bart, *The Last of the Just,* trans. Stephen Becker (New York: Atheneum, 1960), 267–83.

28. Schwarz-Bart, *Last of the Just,* 272.

29. My translation.

30. Pablo Neruda, *Tercera Residencia (1935–1945),* 3d ed. (Buenos Aires: Editorial Losada, 1977), 50.

31. Michael Wood, "The Poetry of Pablo Neruda," *New York Review of Books,* 3 October 1974, 8–12.

32. *Atlas: Zusammengestell von deutschen Autoren* (Berlin: Wagenbach, 1965), 307.

33. Lang, *Act and Idea,* 140.

34. See Lang, *Act and Idea,* 140.

35. Letter of 19 May 1961 to Walter Jens, qtd. in Barbara Wiedemann-Wolf, *Antschel Paul—Paul Celan: Studien zum Frühwerk,* Studien zur deutschen Literatur 86 (Tübingen: Niemeyer, 1985), 85.

Chapter 4

Nelly Sachs: The Poem and Transformation

Johannes Anderegg

The complaint that Nelly Sachs is too little read and that the amount of critical attention paid to her work is disgracefully sparse can be heard from almost all literary critics who have concerned themselves with her work. One would hope for less reserve on the part of readers and critics vis-à-vis a body of work that deals so uncompromisingly with persecution and death in the Third Reich. Such restraint is nevertheless not surprising. The poetry of Nelly Sachs, which circles almost exclusively around the theme of death, stands in strong opposition to our "culture," in which dying is tabooed and trivialized. And those aspects of history that have entered Nelly Sachs's poetic oeuvre are hardly likely to promote her popularity.

As far as literary criticism is concerned, there is very little of importance left to do in the historical-biographical arena, given the state of the research materials; we can hardly count on controversies that might promote renewed attention; and Sachs's imagistic universe is not such a riddle that we could hope for surprising new insights.

Most noticeable in an encounter with Nelly Sachs's poetry, however, is the gap between interpretation or commentary, on the one hand, and poetry on the other: every word of a literary-critical commentary sounds too loud in the silence that is produced by her language.[1] Even when literary criticism goes about its work circumspectly and carefully, there remains an uneven relationship between that which can be experienced in a reading of a poem and that which literary criticism is capable of explaining. This is not to suggest that we would want to do without the illuminating commentaries and interpretive approaches such as those published by Holmqvist, Allemann, and others.[2] But even these interpreters will not deny that the attempt to demonstrate structures and meanings lags far behind that which the poem, the cycle, or even the collected works can make the reader experience.

In her letter of 7 January 1958 to Elisabeth Borchers and Peter Hamm, Nelly Sachs herself takes issue with a perspective that determines many an interpretation: "Occasionally I receive requests concerning the meaning of incomprehensible metaphors. But I never 'meant,'—I was torn open" (*Briefe*, 183).

The following does not entail an attempt to determine what Nelly Sachs "actually means." Instead, I want to try to show where I am taken by the reading of one of her poems, to indicate the direction in which it leads me. I hope in the process to be able to show that such a discourse—not so much *about* the poem as *from* or *of* the poem (that is, proceeding from the poem)—has its justification.

Sand and Light

The Dancer (D.H.)

Your feet barely knew the earth,
In a saraband they strayed
To the edge of it—
for longing was your bearing.

Where you slept, a butterfly slept
Transformation's most visible sign,
How soon you were to attain it—
Caterpillar and pupa and already a thing

In God's hand.
Light out of sand.[3]

[Die Tänzerin (D.H.)

Deine Füsse wußten wenig von der Erde,
Sie wanderten auf einer Sarabande
Bis zum Rande—
Denn Sehnsucht war deine Gebärde.

Wo du schliefst, da schlief ein Schmetterling

Der Verwandlung sichtbarstes Zeichen,
Wie bald solltest du ihn erreichen—
Raupe und Puppe und schon ein Ding

In Gottes Hand.
Licht wird aus Sand.

(I, 37)]

The poem "The Dancer" belongs to the early poem-cycle, "Grabschriften in die Luft geschrieben" (Epitaphs written into the air). We know from Sachs's letter to Emilia Fogelklou-Norlind of 18 July 1943 that it is written in memory of Sachs's friend Dora Horwitz, who died during the transport to Theresienstadt in 1942.[4]

The poem ends with a line whose startling terseness is almost insurpassable: "Light out of sand." *Light* and *sand* belong to the most central ciphers of Nelly Sachs's imagistic universe, and their opposition is fundamental for this universe. Many commentaries have been written on *light* and *sand* and their significance,[5] and their resonances are known to the reader of Sachs's poems. I shall therefore touch on just a few of these here.

Sand, dust, and *earth* are most closely related in their semantic field. Partially supplementing one another, partially overlapping, they constitute at their centers the fundamental image for the secular, terrestrial realm. The sign *sand* partakes especially of such biblical invocations of earth and dust as the following:

you are dust, / and to dust you shall return (Genesis 3:19)
[denn Du bist Erde und sollst zu Erde werden (1. Mose 3, 19)]

he remembers that we are dust (Psalm 103:14)
[er gedenkt daran, daß wir Staub sind]

they die / and return to their dust. (Psalm 104:29)
[so vergehen sie und werden wieder zu Staub]

all are from the dust, and all turn to dust again (Ecclesiastes 3:20)
[es ist alles von Staub gemacht und wird wieder zu Staub (Prediger 3, 20)]

Sand and dust lack water and fertility; the field cursed by God becomes sand. They are, therefore, the essence of the transitory and often also of that which has died, as in the line: "Sand that once was flesh" [Sand der einmal Fleisch war (I, 42)]. They stand as well for the secular corporeality of the human being—indeed, for that being's earthly constitution:

Oh you who still greet the dust as a friend
Who as speaking sand say to the sand:
I love you.

[O ihr, die ihr noch den Staub grüßt als einen Freund
Die ihr, redender Sand zum Sande sprecht:
Ich liebe dich.

(I, 56)]

Sand directs us moreover toward the sand desert, and precisely in this connection sand becomes humankind's designated element: the passage through the sand desert is an image for the life of the individual, for the Israelites' story of suffering, and for human history as a whole. Whenever sand is mentioned, therefore, there resonates always a moment of remembrance: the way of sorrow has inscribed itself in the sand; the wanderer leaves behind signs in the sand.

When she speaks of light, Nelly Sachs allows herself to be guided by a densely religious and especially a densely mystical tradition. What is captured by the word *light* is especially underscored by its opposition to the semantic field comprising darkness, blackness, gloom, and night, which refers to the secular realm with its threat, its anxieties, its dying—one need only think of titles like "Sternverdunkelung" (Eclipse of the stars) (I, 69), or words and phrases like "Erdennacht" [night of the earth] (I, 331), "schwarze Sonne" [black sun] (I, 381), "schwarze Sonne der Angst" [black sun of fear] (I, 56). As the place of suffering, of grief, of melancholy, the terrestrial is darkened;[6] but "the soul fled out of midnight" [Deren Seele . . . floh aus der Mitternacht (I, 51)], and whoever has "broken out of human nights" [aus Menschennächten losgebrochen] speaks "the language of the lights" [die Lichtersprache (I, 44)]. From the perspective of human oppression, *light* is thus a sign for the altogether other:

For from form to form
the angel in man weeps itself
deeper into the light!

(Seeker, 97)

[Denn von Gestalt zu Gestalt
weint sich der Engel im Menschen
tiefer in das Licht!

(I, 105)]

The last line of our poem not only juxtaposes the two realms of sand and light, it also postulates their relatedness by thematizing the *transformation* of *sand* into *light*. To be sure, this final line is closely connected to what precedes it, and it is also joined to the opening line by way of the semantic field *sand-earth*. But the closing line is also unmistakably separated from the preceding: it comprises a complete sentence consisting of only four words, moves into the present tense, and abandons the direct address to a "you." A new level of discourse seems to have been reached here: the preceding is not only continued, not only commented upon, but above all generalized. We now understand it as part of an apparently extensive, miracle-like process of transformation from *sand* into *light,* a process whose fundamental character finds expression in a kind of gnomic present tense—and this with a certainty beyond all doubt, which one would like to call a certainty of faith. Two things are spoken of here: that *sand* can become *light,* but also that light requires *sand,* because it arises from *sand* by way of transformation. Neither here nor elsewhere does Nelly Sachs stage a simple two-world image; she is, rather, concerned with that which connects the worlds, which plays itself out between them, in the transition from sand to light, in a transition that is more than the crossing of a threshold, that is a process of transformation whose goal is as yet totally unforeseeable.[7] This is also clear in "Chorus of the Dead" (Chor der Toten), for example, where the dead are associated neither with a clearly delineated "world beyond," nor with a realm of light that could be attained once and for all, but who seem, rather, to continue their earthly wandering:

We are moving past one more star
Into our hidden God.

(Seeker, 51)

[Wir reichen schon einen Stern weiter
in unseren verborgenen Gott hinein.

(I, 56)]

Signs of Transformation

In the imagistic network of caterpillar, pupa, and butterfly—with which we can also associate the sign *wing*[8]—*transformation* is also the theme of the second or middle stanza. Here Nelly Sachs appropriates a long-standing historical tradition, but she gives the conventional image an individual coinage. It is true that she, too, occasionally establishes a fairly direct connection between butterfly and soul, when we read, for instance, that "the butterfly-word *soul* burst from the cocoon" [sich das Schmetterlingswort *Seele* entpuppte (I, 89)] and the Christian idea of resurrection resonates when she juxtaposes an existence as caterpillar and pupa with the weightlessness of the butterfly, which appears to defy earth's gravity and, assigned to the realm of light, to lift itself above sand and earth. But the butterfly is not only an allegory of the soul that has been freed from corporeality and thus redeemed. To the butterfly are connected expectancy and hope; it anticipates the beyond in the here and now:

What lovely aftermath
is painted in your dust.
. . . .
What royal sign
in the secret of the air.

(*Chimneys,* 91)

[Welch schönes Jenseits
ist in deinen Staub gemalt.
. . . .
Welch Königszeichen
im Geheimnis der Luft.

(I, 148)]

The butterfly is thus above all a *sign,* a harbinger of transformation—a transformation that may include the process of physical dying:

Time of pupation
time of remission

ruined ones with their face in the dust
already sense the shoulder ache of wings

(*Chimneys,* 219)

[Zeit der Verpuppung
Zeit der Vergebung
Verfallene mit dem Gesicht im Staub
verspüren schon den Schulternschmerz der Flügel

(I, 364)]

The image of caterpillar, pupa, and butterfly in the second stanza does not, to be sure, speak of transformation or death in general; rather, the image serves to characterize a particular and individual fate; it is related to the dancer who is addressed by the poem with its "you." Here we must take the poem at its word: the dancer is not directly compared to the butterfly, nor is line 6 merely an apposition to *butterfly.* Line 5 lacks a comma at its end, and the verb *schlafen* thus becomes transitive: the butterfly *sleeps the most visible sign* of the transformation. The poem speaks not only of the process of transformation, it also tells us of the *production of a visible sign* that points to transformation—in the sleeping of the dancer as in the sleeping of the butterfly.

The Bearing of Longing

In the context of the first stanza it perhaps becomes clearer just how important it is that the second stanza contains references not only to a similarity with butterflies, but also to the *becoming visible of a sign of transformation.*

The poem begins by referring to feet: "Your feet barely knew the earth." This opening phrase is motivated not only by the theme of dance and dancer, as one might expect; it also belongs to an imagistic context of feet-wandering-earth-sand—which, centered around the traditional image of life as a journey, is fundamental to the structure of Nelly Sachs's entire work. The path of life, which is also always a path of suffering, is comprehended as a *Wanderung* or journey, especially as a journey through sand and the sand desert. The footprint (*Fußspur,* I, 27), the print in the sand (*Sandspur;* see I, 130, 191), is a print of life. The consciousness of the conditions of human suffering is thus connected to the feet. This is evident, for instance, in the poem "Der Hausierer," which precedes "The Dancer" by a few pages in volume 1 of her works:

But your feet, long accustomed to wandering
now knew the way, the other one

[Doch deine Füße, längst gewohnt das Wandern
Wußten nun den Weg, den andern

(I, 34)]

And it is for this reason that the loving remembrance in a poem addressing the dead beloved focuses on the feet:

Your feet!
The thoughts sped before them.
They came so quickly to God
That your feet grew weary,
Grew sore in trying to catch up with your heart.

(*Seeker,* 27)

[Deine Füße!
Die Gedanken eilten ihnen voraus.
Die so schnell bei Gott waren,
So wurden deine Füße müde,
Wurden wund um Dein Herz einzuholen.

(I, 26)]

In the poem "The Dancer," the imagistic network feet-journey-sand undergoes, to be sure, a significant modification. That the feet of the dancer barely knew the earth not only reminds one of the lightness, of the weightlessness, sought in dancing; it also characterizes—especially in contrast to the counterimages of journeys of suffering—the dancer herself as a person little imprisoned in the terrestrial. The expression of lightness is also served by the modification of the journey, which does not lead through a desert here, but is instead—dance and wandering converge—brought into connection with music: "In a saraband they strayed."

In the original, the rhyme forces a German pronunciation of "Sarabande." Perhaps there is here a resonance of the word *Band,* or ribbon, if the reader's imagination conjures the image of graceful movement along a prescribed line that might have been traced by a ribbon. One might also register an instance of ties that bind. Here, again, the reference is not only to a single dance, but also to the life of the female artist *as* artist, a life that leads, like the dance, to the edge. And again this image of going to the edge, which is spatial despite all its abstraction, stands for both: for an inner distantiation from earth and for an art that gives expression to such distantiation, which in fact aims in its very essence at the attainment and visible representation of such distantiation—the dance. The dash that ends the line "To the edge of it" imitates the pause at the boundary; at the same time it points, like the movement of the dance, beyond the edge to something else, to an other that does not, to be sure, find its way into language. For, in the aftermath of the silence, the poem's language turns back, as it were, to justify what has been said: "for longing was your bearing."

Holmqvist has correctly noted that the word *longing (Sehnsucht)* has degenerated these days into an everyday household word, but that, in the context of Nelly Sachs's poetry, it becomes "loaded" and must be seen as weighty and seminal.[9] Care must be taken, however, not to reduce longing to the longing for death that is an unavoidable undertone in many poems. In the poetry and world of Nelly Sachs, longing is inscribed into all wandering, all life; it is the expression of being-under-way; it belongs to a path that leads to death—and longing is therefore surely also the hope, indeed perhaps the certainty, that this path is a path to God—but which is not thought of as concluding with death. Longing has no object; it does not aim at a possession or a state of being that would be describable in the language of our world, for it means precisely the transcendence of this world—it is longing for the other, longing for *transformation*. Thus, in another passage, we read that "*longing* is seed for a new world" [Samen für eine neue Welt (I, 113)]; and in "Chor der Sterne" (Chorus of the stars), the earth is "richest in longing / Who began her task—to form angels—in dust" (*Chimneys*, 39) [die Sehnsuchtsvollste / Die im Staube begann ihr Werk: Engel zu bilden" (I, 60)]. In this same poem, longing is connected with a movement that overcomes gravity and rises away from the earth:

Has no one's longing ripened
So it will rise like the angelically flying seed
Of the dandelion blossom?

(*Chimneys*, 39)

[Ist niemandes Sehnsucht reif geworden
Daß sie sich erhebt wie der engelhaft fliegende Samen
Der Löwenzahnblüte?

(I, 60)]

Similarly, in "The Dancer," the distantiation from the terrestrial, the movement to the edge, is understood as an expression of longing.

Longing defines the movement of the dancer, but not only in the sense of an inner motivation: indeed, it becomes *visible as bearing* or *gesture*. In other poems as well, Nelly Sachs connects the motif of longing with the image of an externally visible bodily gesture that is determined by longing:

contorted
in the vise of longing.

[verrenkt
im Schraubstock der Sehnsucht

(I, 267)]

And the princess in the ice coffin is also contorted by longing.[10] But the bearing of the dancer is not a contortion she has suffered, and the longing is not compared to the influence of an external power. Longing is, rather, the *visible basic figure* of the dance; it is that of which its signifying potential gives evidence. The feet of the dancer barely know the earth to the extent that their wandering is one transformed out of longing, namely dance. And as a movement or wandering transformed out of longing, dance is, in its essence, the *bearing or gesture of longing*.

Signs of Transformation

The second stanza joins the theme of signifying potential with the motif of sleep. In so doing, it not only alludes to other literary contexts, but also to our everyday experience of sleep as a state of neither-nor, of in between. Sleep is not life and not death but is related to both. It belongs to life but is already removed from it as a kind of anticipated death. While sleeping, we are in a border area, we are *at the edge*. Characterized by "no longer" and "not yet," sleep is a condition of *transformation*. The "Chor der verlassenen Dinge" (Chorus of abandoned things) also makes reference to this: "Ash sleeps itself new into a constellation" [Asche schläft sich neu zur Sterngestalt (I, 49)].

Butterflies do not sleep; the sleep of the butterfly is its pupation. Thus the sleeping butterfly is no longer caterpillar but not yet butterfly, and as this no-longer and not-yet it is—it *sleeps*—the *sign of transformation*.

The sleep of the dancer is compared to the sleep of the butterfly: Like the butterfly, she, sleeping, is a sign of transformation. It is not, or at least not only, a matter here of the physiological process of sleeping, but rather of the dancer's own "no longer" and "not yet," of *her* pupation, which is to say: of her dancing, her being-dancer. As dancer, dancing, she no longer belongs entirely to the earth, but she has also not overstepped the *edge* of the terrestrial—or perhaps only to the extent that her gesture and bearing of longing, hence her art, points beyond that edge.

A kind of breach occurs in the middle of the second stanza; here the poem no longer speaks of the dancer's way of life or of dance, but rather of a crossing of the boundary, of reaching a new state of being, and this implies—although the word is not mentioned—also of death. The imagistic realm caterpillar-pupa-butterfly joins the two parts of the stanza. Moreover, line 6 does not end with a full stop, as one might expect; the language does not pause; it arrives unexpectedly at the theme of death, whose prematurity is expressed not only in "soon" and "already," but also in the progress of the sentence that leaves us no room to take a breath.

Already (schon) is frequent and important in Nelly Sachs's poetry:[11] "We are moving [already] past one more star" (*Seeker,* 51) [Wir reichen schon einen Stern weiter (I, 56)]; "a bud of death already on the eyelids" (*Seeker,* 379) [schon eine Knospe Tod auf den Lidern (I, 386)]. *Soon* and *already* articulate not only the unexpected prematurity of transformation and a moment of surprise and astonishment; that which, longed for, seemed to lie at a great distance has *already* moved surprisingly close, or may even be completed.

The second stanza also closes surprisingly with the totally unexpected word "thing" [Ding], which points back with its rhyme to "Schmetterling," but which seems entirely inadequate to the butterfly existence: we use *thing* to refer to that which is worthless, formless, indefinite—also to that which is dead. But then we notice that the sentence does not end here but carries over into the last stanza, and we understand that only one perspective—the terrestrial one—is expressed in the word "thing," while the decisive transformation—the casting off of "thingness"—occurs in the transition from the second to the third stanza: the thing in God's hand is not a thing—it is a butterfly. The literal emptiness after the second stanza is juxtaposed in the ninth line with the image of being sheltered.

The Epitaph

There is no explicit mention of death in the poem; but the title of the poem cycle "Epitaphs Written into the Air" reverberates for us as an indispensible context here. We remember, moreover, that the poem refers to the life and the dying of an identifiable individual, and that it cannot be separated from the writer Nelly Sachs. And we recall the concrete historical context: the persecution of the Jews and their murder in the concentration camps of the Third Reich.

We may read the poem cycle's title as suggesting that the smoke of the cremating ovens was the only "epitaph" of those murdered in the camps. But "written into the air" means also, and primarily, *not* engraved in stone, not legible in the customary way, not intended to be read in the here and now. The epitaph written into the air resists categorization according to traditional genre norms to which it nonetheless alludes in the process of distancing itself: it is more than and different from a remembrance of the dead, can be equated neither with the lamentation for the dead nor with a memento mori, not to mention the latter's inversion into a carpe diem. As the discourse of the dead person or the address to that person, it aims at a "speaking across." Its *you* is more than rhetorical apostrophe or a fictional staging.

To the extent that the epitaph intends to "speak across," it contains inherently a "no" and a "nevertheless" *(dennoch):* it wants to grasp what cannot be grasped by our everyday language; it wants to move beyond that which cannot be transcended. In the gesture of this nevertheless it wants to approach the unapproachable, and it distances itself in the process from the everyday disposition *(Verfaßtheit)* of our speech. In undertaking to perform that which cannot be performed with our language, it makes of this language a language at the *edge*, a language that points beyond the edge.

Longing is the bearing, the basic figure of the epitaph written into the air, whereby longing should not be identified with the death wish any more than it is in the case of the dance. Longing is directed toward the nearness of the deceased and toward the overcoming of the boundary that separates the deceased from the living, and, more generally, toward the overcoming of the limitations of common speech. It is for this reason that the epitaph lets us experience, with particular acuity, the insufficiency of our everyday language. The only kind of speech that can make sense here, at the boundary, is that which is not imprisoned by the narrowness of the everyday, not indebted to our quotidian reality, but rather aims at its opening up.

To be sure, the language of the epitaph remains human. But as the language of longing it is no longer everyday language, no longer an instrument for the description of the familiar world that is already understood. Suspended between this "no longer" and "not yet," it is *language in transformation*. As such, it does not keep its boundary at its back—if I may be allowed the image—rather it moves toward its limitations. In moving toward the *edge,* and in pointing beyond, it enables the experience of limitation.

The dancing of the dancer leads, as transformed lightfooted wandering, to the *edge;* the epitaph, too, leads to the edge as transformed language. And in this respect epitaph and dance are the same: they are signs of transformation. In speaking of the dance of the dancer, Nelly Sachs deals simultaneously with her own speech: just as the dance is something other than wandering, although it belongs to its category, so, too, is the epitaph written into the air not communicative speech—from which, however, it emerges—but rather bearing, that is a sign of transformation.

This also means, to be sure, that epitaph and poem are equated for Nelly Sachs. In a poem from the cycle *Prayers for a Dead Bridegroom* we read:

You remember the mindless words
That a bride spoke into the air to her dead bridegroom.

(Seeker, 29)

[Du gedenkst der geistesverlorenen Worte,
Die eine Braut in die Luft hineinredete zu ihrem toten Bräutigam.

(I, 27)]

If one may connect these verses to the immediately preceding poem (cf. I, 26), in which the dead bridegroom is addressed, the words spoken *into the air* may be understood as an explicit reference to Sachs's own writing: that speech at the edge which constitutes her poetic enterprise.

The Epitaph as Paradigm for the Poem

The necessity of language's transformation reveals itself nowhere more clearly than in the border region of the epitaph. But as language in transformation, the epitaph is no longer part of our everyday communication; it obstructs our quotidian mode of understanding. In this position of obstruction, leaving everyday speech behind it, the epitaph—with reference to the work of Nelly Sachs—can be considered the essence (embodiment) of poetry; beyond Sachs's work, it can be understood as a paradigm for the poem. To comprehend the poem by way of the epitaph—and it is a fact that the epitaph belongs, historically, to the early poetic forms[12]—means to comprehend it as a language of the "no longer" and the "not yet"; its language is no longer language of the quotidian and not yet an entirely different, new language; it is, however, language in transformation, language in pupation and thus also, in its essence, *bearing, sign of transformation.*

As *language in transformation* and *as sign of transformation* the poem withdraws itself from use—just as this is paradigmatically demonstrated by the epitaph. It abandons the temporally conditioned character of our discourse—as does the epitaph in its untimeliness—points beyond the situation that gave rise to it or which it thematizes, and thus explodes the common "property relations," the customary classifications of our speech. It is more and other than the expression of a speaker or a writer, and, like the epitaph, it resists, as transformed speech, being assigned to a specific addressee. On the contrary, it waits for us to make it our own, to become aware of its properties as sign. As language in transformation, the poem is released for "appropriation"; as language of transformation it awaits transformation into something of our own.

To understand the poem by way of the epitaph therefore also means to understand that it cannot be back-translated into our speech, as though it spoke of that which we can talk about in our language. All commentary and interpretation remain secondary to that which the poem can be: a sign of transformation.

To understand the poem by way of the epitaph—does this also mean that our encounters with poetry contain the instance of an encounter with death as well? This is not to say that every poem would have to focus thematically on death; this is immediately refuted by everyone's experience. But that which in its radicality can probably be experienced only in the vision of death's boundary determines not only the epitaph, but also the *bearing* of the poem: as speech at the edge, it lets us experience the limitations and questionableness of our reality.

Concluding Remark

Many critics have pointed out that dance and poetry are also closely related in the biographical-factual realm of Nelly Sachs's life. In her letter to Walter A. Berendsohn of 25 January 1959 (*Briefe,* 201), she writes of her enthusiasm for dance, about her habit of dancing to her father's piano playing, and about her early desire to become a dancer. And she establishes a direct connection between that which she can accomplish as a poet and that which she sought to attain as a dancer.

> Dance was my means of expression, even before words. My innermost element. It is only because of the hard fate I had to suffer that I moved from this manner of expression to another. To words![13]

It becomes clear in the same letter that dance and poetry are equated for her to the extent that both are defined by the bearing of longing and point beyond the edge:

> My interest in mime and in that musical kind of poetic writing that occasionally, as though soundless, arches over all boundaries, is grounded in this innermost disposition of mine.[14]

But even without all this biographical underpinning, Nelly Sachs's poems give us cause to see dance and poetry as interrelated. Thus, for instance, she relates the concept of transformation, central to the poem "The Dancer," in another context to her own poetic enterprise:

> I hold instead of a homeland
> The metamorphoses of the world—
>
> (Chimneys, 145)

> [An Stelle von Heimat
> halte ich die Verwandlungen der Welt—
>
> (I, 262)]

And in a kind of personal confession, Sachs addresses herself as "you" to summarize that which connects the dancer with the poet, which determines the symbolic quality of her art at the boundary:

You
in the night
busy unlearning the world

(Chimneys, 193)

[Du
in der Nacht
mit dem Verlernen der Welt Beschäftigte

(I, 333)]

Translated by Marilyn Sibley Fries

NOTES

1. This applies especially to the methodological self-assurance in the interpretations of Ulrich Klingmann; see his *Religion und Religiosität in der Lyrik von Nelly Sachs* (Frankfurt am Main: Lang, 1980).

2. See, for instance, Bengt Holmqvist, "Die Sprache der Sehnsucht," and Beda Allemann, "Hinweis auf einen Gedichtraum," in *Das Buch der Nelly Sachs,* ed. Bengt Holmqvist (Frankfurt am Main: Suhrkamp, 1968), 7–70 and 291–308, respectively; here especially 7ff. and 291ff.

3. I am grateful for this translation to Geoffrey Hartman, who composed it at my request a few years ago—not with a view toward publication, but rather for discussion in a small group.

4. On Dora Horwitz, see also the letters of 20 March 1947, 7 January 1958, and 26 April 1960 (*Briefe,* 74, 184, 24).

5. See especially Paul Kersten, *Die Metaphorik der Nelly Sachs: Mit einer Wort-Konkordanz und einer Nelly Sachs-Bibliographie* (Hamburg: Lüdke, 1970), 73–76; see also Allemann, 297ff.

6. See Matthias Krieg, *Schmetterlingsweisheit: Die Todesbilder der Nelly Sachs* (Berlin: Institut Kirche und Judentum, 1983), 108ff.

7. Compare Matthias Krieg and his critical discussion of Luzia Hardegger, *Nelly Sachs und die Verwandlungen der Welt* (Bern: Lang, 1975).

8. See, for instance, I, 331: "aufgeflügelt sind seine Gebete" [his prayers have winged up *(Chimneys,* 189)].

9. Cf. Holmqvist, "Die Sprache der Sehnsucht," 9ff.

10. Cf. Holmqvist, "Die Sprache der Sehnsucht," 16.

11. Surprisingly, the words *bald* and *schon* are missing from Kersten's concordance.

12. Cf. for instance Jan Assmann, *Stein und Zeit: Mensch und Gesellschaft im alten Ägypten* (Munich: Fink, 1991), 169ff.

13. "Der Tanz war meine Art des Ausdrucks noch vor dem Wort. Mein innerstes Element. Nur durch die Schwere des Schicksals, das mich betraf, bin ich von dieser Ausdrucksweise zu einer anderen gekommen: dem Wort!" (*Briefe,* 201).

14. "Mein Interesse für den Mimus und jene musikalische Art des Dichtens, die sich zuweilen wie lautlos über alle Grenzen beugt, beruht auf dieser meiner innersten Veranlagung" (*Briefe,* 201).

Chapter 5

The Poetics of Inadequacy:
Nelly Sachs and the Resurrection
of the Dead

William West

But all that binds us together now is leave-taking,
The leave-taking in the dust
Binds us together with you.

("Chorus of the Rescued," *Chimneys*, 27)

[Aber zusammen hält uns nur noch der Abschied,
Der Abschied im Staub
Hält uns mit euch zusammen.

("Chor der Geretteten," I, 51)]

There is a story that Simonides of Ceos at a banquet one night sang a
poem in honor of his host that also praised the heroes Castor and Pollux.
His host told him that since only half the poem had been about him, he
would pay only half the usual fee; the rest, he said, Simonides could col-
lect from the divine twins. A little later a servant came in to say that there
were two young men outside asking to see Simonides. Simonides got up
and went out, but there was nobody waiting for him out in the street. He
turned to go back in, and at that moment the roof of the house suddenly
collapsed, killing everyone inside the building. The bodies of the ban-
queters were so badly mangled that their families could not tell them
apart to bury them. Simonides, though, was able to identify the bodies by
remembering where each man had been reclining during the meal. Cicero
tells this story in *De oratore* to illustrate the origin of the art of memory,[1]
but it serves equally well to emblematize the structure of epitaphs. The
epitaph lies at the coincidence of death and memory; it is no accident that

the same Simonides who first takes this call and later remembers the dead was also the most famous Greek writer of epitaphs.

Even before de Man's reading of Wordsworth's *Essays on Epitaphs,*[2] the epitaph was seen as a genre of presence through memory—it allows the dead to speak in memory and so become recoverable to the living. It provides a last chance for closure and ensures the preservation of memory and meaning. The *peripeteia* of death is also the removal from the danger of further *peripeteiai,* and the epitaph can therefore be seen as a still point from which the life of the dead person can be appraised and so also made whole. All these aspects intersect in de Man's recognition of the master trope of the epitaph as prosopopoeia, the giving of a voice to what lacks one, and so an attempt to represent the speechless dead.[3] The nature of this recovery and preservation varies from text to text. For Wordsworth, the memorial is a kind of mirror between life and death that enables each to be known to the other and so to recognize their relation as one of symmetry rather than mere opposition; de Man describes this relationship as a move "from life *or* death to life *and* death."[4] Wordsworth chooses to see in epitaphs, or at least in successful ones, a kind of naive sincerity; he does not mention the long and sophisticated tradition of this naïveté, which is a generic convention going back at least to book 7 of the Greek Anthology, a Hellenistic collection of literary epitaphs. The early Greek concept of the relation of the living and the dead is more disproportionate but tends to produce a similar result. Dead souls twitter impotently like bats, and in the underworld of the *Odyssey* they are mute and strengthless until they have been given blood to drink. Death is life infinitely attenuated, although the oblivion of the soul is never quite reachable and the dead persist in memory in the wasted likeness of the living.[5] In both cases, though, the dead soul stands in a determinate relation, whether of inversion or of diminution, to the living one, and this likeness of the dead to the living is what allows the dead individual to be recovered by the epitaph. The epitaph can make the departed soul, whether or not it is conceived of as existing outside the memory of it, speak, and the epitaph provides a memorial that can represent the dead person for memory and so bring him by a *via negativa* into a determinate state of absence that functions like a representation of him. In this view of the epitaph, it is the representation of the dead man that creates pathos.[6]

When Nelly Sachs writes a section entitled "Grabschriften in die Luft geschrieben" (Epitaphs written into the air) in her first volume of poetry after the Holocaust, *In the Habitations of Death* (In den Wohnungen des Todes), she sets her work both within the ancient genre of the poetic epitaph and also against it. In her work, the epitaph has a different task and a different way of functioning than it does in the tradition that she follows temporally and structurally. It works, in fact, as a kind of inversion of the tradition as understood by Wordsworth and others. This difference is immediately visible in the reversal of the usual positions of epitaphic speaker and addressee in the passage above from "Chorus of the Rescued." Here the saved address the dead, whereas the usual trope in epitaphs is for the dead to speak to the living. The near interchangeability of the dead and the living is also shown in the shared verb *zusammenhalten* (binds) that both holds the living together and two lines later holds them together with the dead. Most striking is that "Abschied" [leave taking] is what performs both bindings. This is also an inversion of the usual epitaphic gesture that brings the dead back for the memory of the living; here it is paradoxically the departure of the dead that preserves them.

It is too facile to declare that the scope of the death that Sachs memorializes makes her project entirely different from that of similar collections like book 7 of the Greek Anthology or Edgar Lee Masters's post–World War I volume, *Spoon River Anthology*.[7] Sachs's epitaphic *In the Habitations of Death* differs in part from similar works not through a kind of direct ratio, but as a kind of inversion. What Sachs records is not the loss of an individual recorded by a community of survivors; a community itself has been lost, and Sachs in exile is a different kind of survivor, whom the possibility of remembering, I will argue, leaves almost dead. Sachs begins with a problem that reverses the one usually proposed by epitaphic writings—as the quotation from "Chorus of the Rescued" suggests, the dead are not absent in her work, but too present, so that even leave taking, whether it is theirs or that of the saved, binds them together with the living. In fact, though, not only in Sachs but in much of the tradition that precedes her, the operation of the epitaph seems to be more complex than a simple inversion of the dead that reproduces their life and that still allows for a kind of presence. I will return to this passage and to Sachs's inversion of the genre in which she is working, but before this is possible some groundwork for the structure of the genre must be laid. To suggest a different way of understanding the epitaph, I will first look at some traditional examples before returning to Wordsworth and suggesting how his model, too, knows better than it seems to admit about the resurrection of the dead. At that point I will reexamine Sachs's reformulation of the tradition of the epitaph separated from its usual psychologizing or pathetic explanations to determine both the problem it responds to and the solution it offers.

The *Siste, viator* is one of the oldest and most common types of epitaph; it is perhaps most familiar from its frequent appearance on early American gravestones:

> Behold and see as you pass by,
> As you are now so once was I,
> As I am now so you must be;
> Prepare for death and follow me.[8]

The epitaph, speaking for the dead man, addresses a passerby, commanding the addressee to stop and read. The contrast between the traveler who is addressed and the motionless corpse who is given a voice in the epitaph is developed in the next two lines by the pairing of simple oppositions: I-you; now-once; an implied now-future. A closer reading reveals that these binary oppositions only seem balanced. Despite the balanced chiastic structures that the poem hints at, the second line is not simply inverted in the third into the expected "As I am now so you will be," but into "As I am now so you *must* be." The sentences shift from an indicative mood to one of necessity, a near imperative that not only predicts but demands: "must be" instead of "will be." The last line is a command like the first, but rather than undoing the command of the first line and releasing the traveler to go on, the now stationary traveler is urged to "follow" the dead man, metaphorically set in motion during the course of this poem, into death, not later, but now. De Man has suggested that the epitaph in Wordsworth presents death as an inversion of life through a dangerously unstable trope of binary opposition that threatens to tip either way, and so can as easily kill the living as animate the dead.[9] In this poem, though, what has happened in the change from stillness to motion in the first and last lines and the shift of the intervening couplet is not a mere reversal, but an irreversible transfer of motive power from reader to speaker that is brought about by the passage of time and the presentation of a demand. Life and death are not brought into mutual presence, as in Wordsworth's mirroring metaphor. Instead, they are shown to occupy different moments in time, although ones that are linked by a one-way street. With this recognition, the future death of the reader slides back into the present moment of life, and the reader steps away from the stone with life no longer in a balanced opposition to death, but as its prelude. This epitaph does not make any attempt to represent the dead person, except to the extent that it ventriloquizes him, or to reaffirm a memory among the living. We are much closer to the trench that Odysseus fills with blood to feed the strengthless ghosts. Here, though, what is required in exchange for the voice of the dead is not the blood of sheep, but of the reader. The poem threatens, or at least warns of, the reader's death through a reversal of the moving and the static that can be turned once but not back.[10]

Some of this malignancy is attributable to the memento mori character of this epitaph, but even epitaphs that do not draw on that particular element of the tradition offer a kind of threatening pathos to their readers. A seemingly dissimilar Greek epitaph runs as follows:

asbeston kleos hoide philêi peri patridi thentes
    kuaneon thanatou amphebalonto nephos
oude tethnasi thanontes, epei sph' aretê kathuperthen
    kudainous' anagei dômatos ex Haideô.

[Setting unquenchable fame *(kleos)* on their dear fatherland, these men wrapped themselves in the dark cloud of death. They have not died, dying, since excellence *(aretê)* down from above, glorifying them, leads them up from the house of Hades.][11]

The form of this epitaph differs most noticeably from the earlier one in that it involves no direct address to the reader and no appeal. We recognize again, though, binary oppositions like those that set up the possibility of reversal in the previous epitaph: "kleos" is unquenchable and so metaphorically a fire, while the cloud of death is "kuaneon," a color that is often used of the sea and so is associated with moisture; also, there is a contrast between the excellence that comes down from above and the ascent of the dead up from below in the underworld. In addition, there is a moment of near sublimation of the difference between death and life in the paradox of "they have not died, dying." Those commemorated occupy a kind of middle ground. Here, though, the element of pathos is generated, not, as in the first epitaph, by the relation of inversion between speaking dead and reader and by its grim resolution that draws the reader toward death, but by the failure of the poem to realize what it narrates. The phrase "excellence down from above, glorifying them, leads them up" describes what is clearly meant to be an instance of prosopopoeia and *enargeia* that restores the dead to memory, but it fails to enact the event. In spite of the poem's assurance of unquenchable fame, we have no idea who these men are or anything else about them except that they are dead. A reader might ask what kind of "asbeston kleos" burns with so fine a flame that it can illuminate only its own existence and not the actions that earned it or the men it is attributed to. The cloud proves to be an apt image for death in this poem, for the dead are obscured by their deaths, in fact all but obliterated. This epitaph is no more a memorial than the memento mori was.

The Greek notion of a good death, James Redfield has suggested, required the complete acculturation of the dead man by the dissolution of his natural body into the entirely cultural constructions of *sêma* and *kleos*.[12] A *sêma* is in particular the mound or any other grave marker set up over a corpse, but in a broader sense any sign at all. *Kleos* means fame or glory; it is the reputation of a man as it circulates through one or more communities, a man's remembered existence after death. Etymologically it is "being heard of"; it is related to *kluô* (I hear), used especially in prayers, and perhaps also to *kaleomai* (I call). Redfield's observation allows us to conceive of the monument to the dead as split rather than simple—that is to say, constructed like a sign—and to contrast the *sêma,* or sign, and what is in the usual model of epitaphs its signified, the *kleos* of the dead man. If the words carved on the marker are part of the *sêma,* they do not include the *kleos,* literally the thing that is heard, that is needed to complete them and is assumed to be in circulation apart from any physical monument.[13]

The epitaph is what Hartman describes as a "dependent" genre; it is "conscious of the place on which it was written" and so requires a determinate context to give it meaning.[14] What Redfield and Hartman observe independently is that certain poems require particular elements that are missing from the text in order to be fully read, and so produce gaps in understanding at the very points that they present as thematically most important. This inadequacy is not, of course, confined to the genre of epitaph, but while other genres try to mask it, the epitaph emphasizes it. This lack is most obvious when the reader is detached from the context of the epitaph and so does not fill in what is missing easily; gaps like this associated with, for instance, Kennedy's grave, might be less visible to us, since we supply the missing elements so easily, or, more exactly, fail to recognize them as gaps. In the epitaph, the missing elements correspond to Redfield's *kleos* and act as a kind of summons or a demand to be filled. What is called to fill these gaps is, in this case, history. Only when we know that the men for whom this epitaph was written were Spartans and that they were killed at Plataea driving the last of the Persians out of Greece in the Persian Wars is the epitaph complete. It can of course be understood without knowing this, but not without the reader being aware that he lacks something. Unlike other signs, the epitaph gestures explicitly at its own incompleteness and turns to the reader to fill it. Sachs's poems are recognizably epitaphic in part because the Holocaust serves us as a ready instance of unthinkability; since it is in a sense acknowledged as somehow ungraspable, it offers itself as a gap already established, as a chasm of unrepresentability that is also a sign of that unrepresentability.

This is more obvious in the most famous epitaph by Simonides, that of Leonidas and the Spartans at Thermopylae:

ô xein', angellein Lakedaimoniois hoti têide
    keimetha tois keinôn rhêmasi peithomenoi.

[O stranger, tell the Spartans that here we lie, obeying their words.][15]

This seems almost prosaic, or perhaps, appropriately, laconic. The unexceptional present tense of "keimetha" [we lie] is followed by the startling use of the same tense in "peithomenoi" [obeying], rather than the expected aorist or perfect "having obeyed"; this changes the value of "keimetha" from the lifeless lying down of a corpse to the vigilant lying in wait of soldiers on guard, as if the Spartan contingent were still at their posts even in death. Like the last one, this epitaph calls history, and it is the richness of the history that lies outside the text that explains the poem's well-established appeal as a source of wartime propaganda.[16] History is so much a part of it that it is impossible to read without it— not that the poem would be incomprehensible without the history, but that the absent knowledge of the heroism of the Spartans is so firmly attached to this poem that a reader cannot think it away. But that the reader be able to produce the history of the epitaph as memory, or more accurately, that he or she be able to recognize the gap into which such memory must be inserted, is not the poem's only demand. The poem also charges the reader to make it known to the Spartans what has happened; that is, the call of the poem for what it lacks, now not only its history but the ability to communicate (and in fact the missing history is filled in for this reason, too—to make the poem communicate with the reader), is laid at the reader's feet as a demand for fulfillment.

This makes the connection between these three epitaphs clearer. In each case an inadequacy is revealed in the poem that the reader is charged to make good, whether by following the fictive speaker into death or merely by recalling history or relaying a message. The epitaph does not simply gesture toward a particular being whose loss the reader mourns, as we might assume; the epitaph signals its own inadequacy to gesture to this absence and then demands that the reader make good its failure. The epitaph cannot produce memory or preserve it, only demand or charge it. But the demand of the epitaph also is impossible to fulfill, because, regardless of the reader's response, the epitaph will always repeat its message. The obedient reader returning from Sparta to Thermopylae will be greeted with the same words that sent him away in the first place. Like the stupid writing that Socrates criticizes in *Phaedrus,* the epitaph seems to speak like a person but always says the same thing. With repetition, loss becomes accusation or demand, as when Sachs's "Chorus of the Orphans" (Chor der Waisen) changes its refrain from "We lament to the world" [Wir klagen der Welt] to "O world / We accuse you!" [O Welt / Wir klagen dich an!] (*Chimneys,* 29–31; I, 54–55). In his analysis of mourning, Rickels suggests that mourning is not for a lost object, but for a lost relation with that object, and in effect the imitation of the object's grief at its own loss of the subject—an interesting psychoanalytical solution to a problem that is also, and perhaps first, textual.[17] The lack within the epitaph—the epitaph's loss—is transferred to the epitaph's reader in the same way that Rickels sees the mourner assuming the grief that belongs to the object. It is the double failure of both the poem and the reader to delineate this absence adequately that generates pathos, rather than simply the knowledge of a determinate absence that can be easily inverted into presence. It is not the memory of a lost object or person that causes grief, nor complete forgetfulness of it; it is the memory of forgetfulness, the consciousness that memory has failed, that produces the experience of mourning in epitaphs like these.

Following such a reading of epitaphs before Wordsworth, Wordsworth's own discussion of epitaphs reveals an accord with the idea of double failure and in fact clarifies the exteriority of the truth of the dead soul to the epitaph. Wordsworth regarded as vitally important the generalization of the contents of the epitaph. Its purpose is not to anatomize or scrutinize the dead person, but to present this figure "through a tender haze or a luminous mist."[18] Stripped of its positive valorizations, this corresponds to the figure of death as a dark enveloping cloud in the Plataea epitaph. That which seeks to preserve the individual can do so only by blurring his individuality. This verbal haze requires

> that it shall contain thoughts and feelings which are in their substance common-place, and even trite. . . . But it is required that these truths should be instinctively ejaculated or should rise irresistibly from circumstances . . . not adopted, not spoken by rote, but perceived in their whole compass with the freshness and clearness of an original intuition.[19]

But this transformation from triteness to truth can never take place except through an act of memory or interpretation that lies outside the text of the epitaph. The reader must recognize behind the "common-place" some instinctive or natural response; the good epitaph, until it is read by some suitably sensitive soul, is indistinguishable from its trite, unspontaneous double. Of an epitaph that fails through its insincerity to memorialize the deceased, Wordsworth observes that "the composition is in the style of those labored portraits in words which we sometimes see placed at the bottom of a print to fill up lines of expression which the bumbling artist had left imperfect."[20] But not only failed epitaphs but all epitaphs need to have this kind of supplement attached to them in the form of memory or of a judgment of sincerity in order to seem complete. The epitaph, as it seeks to balance the demands of the particular and the general, succeeds only in pointing out that somebody is dead without being able to say who. What can individuate the dead is not what is in the epitaph itself, but what is not in it: what the epitaph calls. This inability of the epitaph to present adequately the absence of a particular individual is then passed on as a demand to the reader. The result of this absence of genuine dialectic and counterbalance produces the sense of the "hollowness" that Wordsworth feared in life if there were no conviction of immortality for each individual and death were not conceived as life's mirror image.[21] The living reader cannot peer through the veil of death to see a corresponding image on the other side; the reader sees only what he or she puts there, and the epitaph tells the reader so. Whether hidden by the cloud or death or by the hazy clichés of the epitaph, the dead individual disappears and is replaced by a gap that must be filled in by the reader.

We cannot assume that this appeal to the reader may not at times approach success and bring life out of death. Because in its declared inadequacy the epitaph calls on the reader to supply what it lacks, though, the failure of the epitaph to recover the dead is often masked by its success as a machine for generating emotion, since it is the first failure that produces this success. The call itself may even appear to be a representation of the dead person through its mimicry of his or her voice or its display of knowledge or affect proper to the dead person. In this case the structure that produces pathos is inverted completely, and the epitaph appears as a site of plenitude of meaning set against the reader's impoverishment. It is at this point that a Wordsworthian reading of the epitaph as harmonious coexistence of life and death can appear. But the call, like the epitaph itself, at this moment exceeds the individuality of the dead person as it previously fell short of it and so again fails to recover the dead. Herman Altman's epitaph from Edgar Lee Masters's collection of literary epitaphs, *Spoon River Anthology,* shows the impossibility of relying on memory or something exterior to the epitaph to answer the call and bring the dead back:

> Therefore, build no monument to me,
> And carve no bust for me,
> Lest, though I become not a demi-god,
> The reality of my soul be lost,
> . . . .
> My lovers and their children must not be dispossessed of me;
> I would be the untarnished possession forever
> Of those for whom I lived.[22]

The concern for the loss of the reality of the soul through the construction of a monument is an explicit statement of the constitutive inadequacy within the epitaph, but this explicitness is only possible because the monumental epitaph is subordinated to another, supposedly truer one in the memory of the "lovers and their children." Such a simulated interiority is possible because the device of the literary epitaph allows for a split between a written epitaph and a dead individual speaking in his or her own, and thus authentic, voice; this is clearly not possible in the absence of such a split. The memory of Altman's lovers will be his real epitaph, and so Altman's death will be recovered as a simple absence rather than a double, irreversible one. This would seem to be a recovery of death as absence by an exclusive reliance on *kleos,* to use Redfield's terms, rather than *sêma.* But Altman's living memory, figured as an "untarnished possession," is curiously ossified and monumental. The distinction between proper memorialization in human memory and its perverted opposite in a monument proves moot, since before the end of the poem Altman's soul hardens into a possession that seems already monumentalized. The vague impersonal grandeur of the epitaph's language does nothing to discourage this reading. The recuperation of memory as a better kind of epitaph finally falls short because memory of the dead cannot be separated with certainty from the epitaph itself; memory too assumes the form of an epitaph, inaugurating an endless regression of epitaphs that all fail to do what they must. As a mark of lost plenitude, the epitaph may compel the production of more epitaphs, as the gap opened by each new epitaph requires another moment of plenitude to fill it, which will itself immediately become hollow and epitaphic.[23] The dead have only what the living give them, and the epitaph is the endless demand for the gift. An epitaph is not, then, a death mask, the rim over the cavity left by the loss of a soul that records its absence in negative outline. It is a death mask that has been lost and so does not indicate anything except its own failure to do what it should; it indicates, not like a finger pointing at an empty space, but like a string tied around a finger to jog the memory. Epitaphs thus practice what we may term a poetics of inadequacy, a poetics that relies on falling short of what it seems to attempt in order to generate pathos from its own failure and that of its reader.

Sachs's "Talking to air in words of flame" (Die Kerze) is an almost emblematic dramatization of this reading of the epitaph as an indication of its own inadequacy and a charge to the reader to fill it. It is not an epitaph itself so much as the representation of the reading of one.

Talking to air in words of flame that leap and wave
The candle I have lit for you burns tall,
Water drips from my eye; out of the grave
Your dust calls clearly to the life eternal.

O high encounter in the room of need.
If I but knew what the elements intend;

They define you, for everything indeed
Always defines you; my tears never end.

(Seeker, 21)

[Die Kerze, die ich für dich entzündet habe,
Spricht mit der Luft der Flammensprache Beben,
Und Wasser tropft vom Auge; aus dem Grabe
Dein Staub vernehmlich ruft zum ewgen Leben.

O hoher Treffpunkt in der Armut Zimmer.
Wenn ich nur wüßte, was die Elemente meinen;
Sie deuten dich, denn alles deutet immer
Auf dich; ich kann nichts tun als weinen.

(I, 23)]

Lighting the memorial candle, the narrator brings together three of the
four elements of ancient physics, the air, the candle's flame, and the water
of her tears; the lack of the fourth element conjures the response of the
earth of the addressee, which calls audibly to eternal life. This call is
simply the fantasy of the epitaph's successful resurrection of the dead
individual, which is here not confused with an actual representation of
the dead addressee. The poem shows that the dead addressee does not
call through its own power, but only as the result of the conjunction of
the other elements that results from the narrator's actions. When the call
fails and the addressee is not restored, the narrator ascribes the failure to
her own lack of understanding of "what the elements intend"; she sees
them pointing to the addressee, like an epitaph does, but she assumes that
there is a level of meaning that she fails to read. The quasi-mystical union
of elements is perceived as a demand for interpretation. The space for this
missing level opens up between the hermeneutic *deuten* and the deictic
deuten auf, between explanation and indication. The poem must in fact
be read backward to reveal the development of this division of ignorance
and knowledge, narrator and nature. The elements are credited with the
possession of *meaning* ("meinen . . . deuten") only because ("denn") the
narrator sees them *point to* ("deutet . . . / Auf") the missing addressee.
But gesture is not explication or representation, and this gap between her
lack of knowledge and their presumed knowledge causes her to weep.

   This demand, whether for understanding, attention, or anything else,
is what is performed also by the *Siste, viator* that is a founding moment

of the epitaph. The experience of the demand to the traveler is drama-
tized in an epitaph from Masters's *The New Spoon River*:

U. S. Stopp

Walking in town, a little drunk,
I saw from the road the humble stone
Of Isaac Waite, which said "I. Waite"
And I read the words, "Thy will be done,"
As "You will be done."
And then and there I laughed and chose
That epitaph, "You will be done,"
Which, passer-by, you see![24]

The remarkably named Stopp reads the epitaph of the equally
remarkably named I. Waite correctly as an address to him, although this
reading is linked to the abnormal mental state of being "a little drunk."
Instead of trying to recover Isaac Waite from the epitaph, though, as the
narrator of "Talking to air . . ." does with the call of the dust, Stopp reads
the name as an allegory. By dismissing the possibility of recalling the dead
by means of an epitaph and instead recognizing at once their
unrecoverability and the demand that is being placed on him, Stopp is
able to read without grieving. His laughter signals his acceptance of the
epitaph's charge for him, and he passes on the charge to the reader of his
own epitaph. The charge forms a chain from I. Waite through U. S.
Stopp, constituting the same one-way link that appears in the New
Preston memento mori, and like the obedient reader of that verse, Stopp
prepares for death by deciding on his own epitaph "then and there," the
same one that is for the present reader here and now. What the reader
reads, though, is not only Stopp's epitaph, but also Waite's demand as it
passes through Stopp's. The reader receives the double charge of both
epitaphs that Stopp had avoided by echoing Waite. The reader can be
unburdened of the weight of the charge only by accepting it and death
together, as Stopp does, and not treating it as an obligation that he or she
fails to uphold. The epitaph as Stopp reads it demands not a
representation of the dead but an acceptance of their unrepresentability
and the passing on of the charge. With this acceptance, the epitaph's need
becomes the same as the reader's; the void the epitaph exhibits can only

be matched by the acceptance of a similar void in the reader rather than by any attempts to fill or complete the epitaph by making the dead even negatively present. The response to loss is acceptance of loss and thus, paradoxically, its deferral onto another. What endures in this poem is neither the living nor the dead as negative presence, but the demand itself as a kind of subjectless immortality. Stopp and Waite appear not as individual subjects, but as allegories of the call of the epitaph to its reader. While this epitaph defuses one danger, though, it suggests another. In reading the shift from the first epitaph's mildly exhortative indicative *I. Waite / I wait* to the imperative *U. S. Stopp / you stop* of the second, the possibility appears that just as more epitaphs generate more pathos, a longer chain of epitaphs produces more insistent charges. With Altman's epitaph, this would suggest that the regression from epitaph to epitaph, whether such epitaphs are written in stone or in memory, defers the demands on the reader, but at the price of making it unbearable if it is ever accepted.

This is the problem that haunts Sachs's first volume of poetry after the war, *In the Habitations of Death*. Sachs's poems do not seek, in general, to recover the dead; the dead in her work are already too present and bring too much mourning with them. There is thus relatively little need for prosopopoeia. Like Masters's Stopp, *In the Habitations of Death* explores the possibilities of resisting the demand that the epitaph makes and so avoiding the call to mourning and the production of pathos that, in the post-Holocaust world, are ultimately deadly to their receiver.

O the chimneys
On the ingeniously devised habitations of death
When Israel's body drifted as smoke
Through the air—
Was welcomed by a star, a chimney sweep,
A star that turned black
Or was it a ray of sun?

O the chimneys!
Freedomway for Jeremiah and Job's dust—
Who devised you and laid stone upon stone
The road for refugees of smoke?

O the habitations of death,
Invitingly appointed

For the host who used to be a guest—
O you fingers
Laying a threshold
Like a knife between life and death—

O you chimneys,
O you fingers
And Israel's body as smoke through the air!

(*Chimneys, 3*)

[O die Schornsteine
Auf den sinnreich erdachten Wohnungen des Todes,
Als Israels Leib zog aufgelöst in Rauch
Durch die Luft—
Als Essenkehrer ihn ein Stern empfing
Der schwarz wurde
Oder war es ein Sonnenstrahl?

O die Schornsteine!
Freiheitswege für Jeremias und Hiobs Staub—
Wer erdachte euch und baute Stein auf Stein
Den Weg für Flüchtlinge aus Rauch?

O die Wohnungen des Todes,
Einladend hergerichtet
Für den Wirt des Hauses, der sonst Gast war—
O ihr Finger,
Die Eingangsschwelle legend
Wie ein Messer zwischen Leben und Tod—

O ihr Schornsteine,
O ihr Finger,
Und Israels Leib im Rauch durch die Luft!

(I, 8)]

In contrast to many other epitaphs, this poem, the first in the volume, takes the unrecoverability of the dead as a starting point; already they are "drifting," "dust," "smoke through the air." The chimneys act as a passage between the individual bodies of the victims and the amorphous smoke they become. They similarly connect the literal things of the poem—the guards' pointing fingers, the threshold of the building—and their metaphorical referent, which is the chimneys themselves. The concrete things named by the poem fade into one single thing, thresholds becoming metaphors for fingers that in turn are metaphors for chimneys, dissolving like the dead into undifferentiation. The chimneys also have a doubled status as both object and symbol. The smokestacks of the death camps are an ironic grave marker because they not only remain in the absence of the dead like any other grave marker, but are also the vehicle by which the dead are made to disappear, at once the threshold that marks a limit and the knife that cuts it off. They are thus a metaphor for epitaphs generally, and this impression is reinforced by the association of the smokestacks with the pointing fingers that, like epitaphs, gesture toward the indeterminate space of the threshold without being able to define it or point beyond it.

From this point on, the possibility of re-collecting the scattered dead in an epitaph is given little consideration. Even poems that seem to offer some form of redemption of the dead are cast in terms that suggest dispersal; the "Chorus of the Dead" (Chor der Toten), for instance, is able to speak only from a position from a further star within a hidden God (*Seeker,* 51; I, 56). The problem the volume offers is that this dissolution and dispersal of the dead carried out by the chimneys is also a broadcasting or dissemination of them in the indeterminate form of dust or smoke through the air. The "road for refugees of smoke" is, ironically, itself *smoke,* and so the escape of the dead relies on their being infused into the very air that the living still breathe. With the dead so present in the world even in their death, the blackening of the star or the sunbeam by the smoke takes on an additional symbolic weight, as does the title "Grabschriften in die Luft geschrieben" (Epitaphs written into the air). This is the old image for the vainest of inscriptions, which makes up John Keats's epitaph: "Here lies one whose name was writ in water." Writing in a shifting medium like water or air is usually a mark of impermanence, but in Sachs's work it is an indefinition that is painfully indissoluble. In the next poem, "To you that build the new house" (An euch, die das neue Haus bauen), even the walls and furniture of the house prove to be tainted with *Staub,* the dust that is literally and figuratively the dead. The result is that the world becomes one vast epitaph or tomb and, as in "Talking to air . . . ," every object demands a recognition of the failure of the onlooker to represent the dead. While the dead themselves are never present anywhere, their demands are everywhere. They appear in the forms of hollows or absences that charge their observer to fill them—literal hollows like the empty shoes that appear throughout the work, the footprints that fill themselves with death (I, 27), the Spinoza researcher's shell (I, 36), the forgotten pitcher in the rubble (I, 48), or the mother's hands curved into bowls (I, 16), and also more figural emptinesses like those of the forgotten things (I, 48), the survivors (I, 50) or the orphans (I, 54), each of which has its status through the loss of something else. These hollows outline an adjacent realm of absence without being able to represent the object that could fill the space. Shoes, if they are filled at all, are filled not with feet but with sand, the undifferentiated remains of the dead in common rather than those of any identifiable individual. The dead are everywhere present en masse, but individually they are lost; thus mourning and remembrance remain always under way and always incomplete. Every object that has come into contact with the dead is transformed into an epitaph for them, sometimes literally gaining a voice like the "Chorus of Stones":

When someone lifts us
He lifts in his hand millions of memories
Which do not dissolve in blood
Like evening.
For we are memorial stones
Embracing all dying.

(*Chimneys*, 35)

[Wenn einer uns hebt
Hebt er Billionen Erinnerungen in seiner Hand
Die sich nicht auflösen im Blute
Wie der Abend.
Denn Gedenksteine sind wir
Alles Sterben umfassend.

(I, 58)]

If this dispersal of memorials is allowed to take place, life becomes unlivable, and each expression of mourning produces further pain instead of relief, because it so clearly falls short of bringing the dead back:

Do not sigh when you bed your sheets,
Else your dreams will mingle

With the sweat of the dead.

(*Chimneys*, 5)

[Seufze nicht, wenn du dein Laken bettest,
Es mischen sich sonst deine Träume
Mit dem Schweiß der Toten.

(I, 9)]

The dead Patroclus visits Achilles in a dream in *Iliad* XXIII, a soul and image without a core, but the dead here do not return even insubstantially in dreams. Only their sweat returns, another reminder that, like the candle or the hollowed things, their remembrance will not bring them back but only provoke further grief and further mourning in a cycle that shows no sign of having an end.

The endless regression of epitaphs that Altman's epitaph threatened is here revealed to be not merely pathetic, but deadly. When the "Chorus of the Rescued" announces that "Our constellation is buried in dust. / . . . / It could be, it could be / That we will dissolve into dust" (*Chimneys*, 25) [Unser Gestirn ist vergraben im Staub. / . . . / Es könnte sein, es könnte sein / Daß wir zu Staub zerfallen (I, 50–51)], the image is the same as that of the star masked by smoke in "O the chimneys." Here, though, the threat of the dust's contagion appears. The dust that buries the stars figures the dead and threatens to choke out the survivors until they too collapse into its formless mass and lose their identity. To recognize the call of this epitaphic dust is to become dust oneself. If the recurring hollows reveal a world that is truncated by absences, the series of choruses shows, literally, the world becoming reproach. Mourning becomes fatal; a poem that begins with a mother "Already embraced by the arm of heavenly solace" (*Chimneys*, 15) [Schon vom Arm des himmlischen Trostes umfangen (I, 16)] ends, inevitably, with her death as the embrace of grief becomes no less lethal than the more usual metaphor of the embrace of death. As her failure suggests, mourning is also insufficient; near the end of the volume, the "Chorus of Comforters" (Chor der Tröster) confesses that "The blossoms of comfort are too small / Not enough for the torment of a child's tear" (*Seeker*, 59) [Die Blüten des Trostes sind zu kurz entsprossen / Reichen nicht für die Qual einer Kinderträne (I, 65)]. Grief has no power to lessen the demand placed on the living by the dead but only hooks the living into a cycle of further mourning that leaves them as dead as those they have lost. Representing and recollecting the dead is no longer the main problem, and in fact seems impossible, as the logic of inadequacy suggests. In *In the Habitations of Death,* the main difficulty is resisting the potentially lethal call of the dead to the living that is known as survivor's guilt.

A possible alternative to perpetual mourning or collapse into dust appears in "Der Steinsammler" (The stone collector):

> In the stones, you have collected
> The stillness of earth's ages.
> How many early dawns gleam in the beryl
> How much distance in the crystal
>
> With the bee that brewed
> The honey of millenia on a vetch plant,
> But the opal, with its seer's look
> Long since made you familiar with your death.
>
> You, broken away from human nights
> Speak the language of light out of the cracks—
> Which one speaks when the shell has been penetrated
> And of which we know only the flashes.
>
> [Du hast der Erdenzeiten Stille
> Gesammelt in den Steinen.
> Wieviel Morgenröten im Berylle
> Wieviel Fernen im Kristalle scheinen
>
> Mit der Biene, die auf einer Wicke
> Abertausendjährgen Honig braute,
> Doch Opal mit seinem Seherblicke
> Längst dein Sterben dir schon anvertraute.
>
> Du, aus Menschennächten losgebrochen
> Sprichst die Lichtersprache aus den Rissen—
> Die man spricht, wenn das Gehäus durchstochen
> Und von der wir nur die Funken wissen.

(I, 44)][25]

Like many of the poems in the volume, this one is both an epitaph and the representation of a reaction to the epitaphs around it. In contrast to the *Malerin* (woman painter) of another epitaph, who provides an exemplar for inadequacy and the possibility of generating grief through her inability to represent even her most well loved as anything other than "Sand—Sand—Sand—" (I, 42), the stone collector is like the bee who gathers sweet honey from vetch in his ability to gather history statically in his stones. Read tendentiously, the *Steinsammler* is a *Grabstein-sammler*, a collector of tombstones, as his collection of silence *(Stille)* also suggests. But in Sachs, *Stille* is what is needed; the dead do not need to be brought back to life, but laid permanently to rest. The representational art of the *Malerin* fails to produce anything but that eerily haunted substance *Sand*, while the unmimetic, inhuman art of the *Steinsammler* entrusts him with his own death in advance ("dein Sterben dir schon anvertraute"). Although his voice is as lost to the living as the voice of the dead—we know only its flashes, just as the dead speaking in epitaphs are known only in their absence—he falls not into dust but into light.

The narrator of *In the Habitations of Death* shows herself, like the *Steinsammler*, collecting what she needs from the dead in order to resist the demands left behind in their epitaphs. The epitaph is not a call from the dead, as we have seen, but from the living to themselves that takes the form of such a call or demand. By acknowledging the source and effectiveness of the demand to be her own failure of memory, the narrator is able to resist the call of death by finding a void in herself—her failure—corresponding to death's void. In this, also like the *Steinsammler*, whose stones are almost animate and who himself leaves the realm of the human for a more enduring one, the narrator becomes epitaphic. Mourning and the memory of loss that epitaphs produce must be put behind the reader of epitaphs:

> When you come to put up your walls anew—
> Your stove, your bedstead, table and chair—
> Do not hang your tears for those who departed,
> Who will not live with you then.
>
> *(Chimneys, 5)*

> [Wenn du dir deine Wände neu aufrichtest—
> Deinen Herd, Schlafstatt, Tisch und Stuhl—
> Hänge nicht deine Tränen um sie, die dahingegangen,
> Die nicht mehr mit dir wohnen werden.
>
> (I, 9)]

This realization that the grief cannot be carried into the future without the risk of its becoming overwhelming comes in "To you that build the new house" (An euch, die das neue Haus bauen), just after "O the chimneys" (O die Schornsteine), in which the unrecoverability of the dead was recognized. But the acceptance of this as practice is not as easy as the intellectual formulation of it. To acknowledge the need to forget is not the same thing as forgetting, and there is the additional problem that absolute oblivion does not seem to be desirable either. The rest of *In the Habitations of Death* can be read as the tension between the need to forget in order to survive and not be crushed by grief, and the need not to give in to a deathlike state of forgetfulness.

There are two moments when a solution seems to be grasped. The first is the poem that breaks off the cycle of "Grabschriften in die Luft geschrieben," the epitaph of "The Woman Who Forgot Everything"— "Die alles Vergessende." The series of epitaphs becomes almost self-perpetuating, each epitaph signaling its failure to recover the dead and so requiring another, when one appears that seems to lay the others to rest:

> But in old age all drifts in blurred immensities.
> The little things fly off and up like bees.
>
> You forgot all the words and forgot the object too;
> And reached your enemy a hand where roses and nettles grew.
>
> *(Seeker,* 47)

> [Aber im Alter ist alles ein großes Verschwimmen.
> Die kleinen Dinge fliegen fort wie die Immen.
>
> Alle Worte vergaßt du und auch den Gegenstand;
> Und reichtest deinem Feind über Rosen und Nesseln die Hand.
>
> (I, 46)]

The old woman's solution is not that of the beelike *Steinsammler,* but an inversion of it; it is like bees that the things of the world elude her rather than her being like a bee to gather them. Her relation to the world is one of loss rather than collection. In forgetting everything, the old woman achieves a kind of peace and, having lost her ability to interpret, reaches indifferently across both roses and nettles to an enemy that might as well be her friend. It is impossible to tell if the last line is horrible or wonderful, perfect incomprehension or perfect forgiveness. In fact it is neither; like death, it is an indeterminate absence that cannot be represented completely, not the negation of any particular quality like understanding or hatred. This oblivion is a kind of death before death. What distinguishes the old woman from the truly dead is her gesture of reaching out, apart from any meaning we seek to find in it. Like the *Steinsammler,* the old woman leaves a world of words and things for another one, but not without leaving behind a trace that calls for interpretation; unlike the *Steinsammler,* though, she herself is the uninterpretable trace she leaves. If the *Steinsammler* is really a *Grabsteinsammler,* the old woman is really a *Grabstein* (gravestone). The old woman's gesture is the empty gesture that the epitaph makes to its reader, the display of inadequacy that the reader understands as a demand to be filled. But she is not the only epitaph. Like Stopp accepting Waite's message, the narrator relays the gesture of the old woman without trying to fill it and without responding to its call for pathos. What puts an end to the series of epitaphs is the miming of the old woman's inscrutable gesture by the narrator, and so the turning-epitaph of two readers, the old woman and the narrator. The acceptance and passing on of the epitaphic demand for death renders each neither wholly alive nor wholly dead but sets them both between memory and forgetfulness. This is to take up the place of the epitaph oneself. Like the refugees *(Flüchtlinge)* whose way out of smoke is to become smoke themselves, the reader's way out of epitaphs is to become like an epitaph.

The "Chöre nach der Mitternacht" section also threatens to get out of control and unleash an endless sequence of mourning. The poem that puts this section to rest is called, unlike the other poems that are choruses, a *Stimme,* "voice," although perhaps a collective one; as the last, it occupies the place of the epitaph of the volume.

The voice of the Holy Land

O my children,
Death has run through your hearts
As through a vineyard—
Painted *Israel* red on all the walls of the world.

What shall be the end of the little holiness
Which still dwells in my sand?
The voices of the dead
Speak through reed pipes of seclusion.

Lay the weapons of revenge in the field
That they grow gentle—
For even iron and grain are akin
In the womb of earth—

But what shall be the end of the little holiness
Which still dwells in my sand?

The child murdered in sleep
Arises; bends down the tree of ages
And pins the white breathing star
That was once called Israel
To its topmost bough.
Spring upright again, says the child,
To where tears mean eternity.

(*Chimneys*, 45)

[Stimme des heiligen Landes

O meine Kinder,
Der Tod ist durch eure Herzen gefahren
Wie durch einen Weinberg—
Malte *Israel* rot an alle Wände der Erde.

Wo soll die kleine Heiligkeit hin
Die noch in meinem Sande wohnt?
Durch die Röhren der Abgeschiedenheit
Sprechen die Stimmen der Toten:

Leget auf den Acker die Waffen der Rache
Damit sie leise werden—
Denn auch Eisen und Korn sind Geschwister
Im Schoße der Erde—

Wo soll denn die kleine Heiligkeit hin
Die noch in meinem Sande wohnt?

Das Kind im Schlafe gemordet
Steht auf; biegt den Baum der Jahrtausende hinab
Und heftet den weißen, atmenden Stern
Der einmal Israel hieß
An seine Krone.

Schnelle zurück, spricht es
Dorthin, wo Tränen Ewigkeit bedeuten.

(I, 68)]

Despite the title, we hear at least two voices, not one. First, what is presumably the voice of the title speaks in indignant rage at the gory dissemination of the word *Israel*. Its angry question in the second stanza seems a rhetorical expression of continuing outrage, which is to say, not a question at all. Surprisingly, the dead reply. Their voice is explicitly epitaphic, speaking in its absence "through reed pipes of seclusion," and the demand it makes in response to the question of the Holy Land is a form of the familiar memento mori; the first speaker is asked to set vengeance aside and be like the dead earth, which produces iron and grain indifferently. As in "The Woman Who Forgot Everything," it is hard here to say how literally lethal this moment of forgiveness is meant to be. It also seems to be a rebuttal of the first voice; the addition of "but" [denn] when the first voice repeats its question suggests that the answer that it wanted was precisely the act of vengeance that the answer of the dead has forestalled.

The repetition raises the possibility that the dialogue to this point will simply repeat itself with ever increasing intensity and no opportunity for discharge. But this threat of an endless stasis of a reader confronting an epitaph is broken by a narrative voice not clearly identifiable as belonging either to the dead or to the Holy Land. Like the chimneys of "O the chimneys," the children in the first line are between figurative and literal language, at once the dead metaphor of the inhabitants of a place as its children and the literal dead and absent children killed during the war. The children are seemingly resurrected in the last stanza as a single child, but this is again not simply the fulfillment of the fantasy of the epitaph to bring the dead back. The initial metaphor gives way to a figure that abandons any attempt to realize what it refers to. Its schematization marks it as allegorical. Unlike the first reply of the *Stimmen der Toten,* this answer has no voice of its own; the direct response of the dead is replaced by a strange, sourceless description of an action. The poem shifts, then, from a fantasy in which the dead can speak clearly—even if they give an undesirable answer—to a version in which the response demonstrates their inability to be absent in a reversible way. We cannot finally distinguish exact meanings of the allegorical figures of child, tree, crown, and star without an indissoluble vagueness. At the same time, the figures are monumental in vagueness, demanding an act of interpretation through the same doubtfulness that makes a decisive interpretation impossible. The figures are thus like tombstones or epitaphs themselves and so offer an alternative to a life haunted by grief or a deathlike oblivion. The alternative is between the children *(Kinder),* living or dead but individuated and bound together by the bloody writing, and the allegorical child *(Kind)* who stands somewhere outside the binary opposition of living and dead.

At the moment that some kind of sublimation seems to have been achieved and peace found outside of oblivion, though, prosopopoeia reappears as "it" ("es") speaks. "It" could be the child, as in the English translation, but it is also an indeterminate epitaphic voice placing a demand on an indeterminate addressee. The speech is not addressed to the reader, though, like the familiar epitaphic command. Because of the line break, the punctuation of the sentence remains uncertain, as does the word modified by "Dorthin." Speech and leap are turned inseparably together, "To where tears mean eternity" [Dorthin, wo Tränen Ewigkeit bedeuten]. As it comes in the position of the last epitaphic word and promises freedom from the destructive cycle of grief, this leap back ("Schnelle zurück") can only be a return into the body of the text behind it. Are tears an assurance of eternity—that is, does grief guarantee the persistence of the memory of the dead? Or are tears just the signs that mourning, once begun, never ends, so that tears and mourning create a cycle in which epitaphs must multiply both themselves and pathos, and that this cycle is eternal and eternally unchanging—in a word, dead? Whatever their relation, the point at which "Tränen Ewigkeit bedeuten" is *dorthin,* back in the poem, and with this line the poem, and indeed the whole volume, folds in on itself. This reflexiveness would ordinarily suggest a kind of fulfillment or wholeness, but here the turn inward appears not as a result of plenitude, but of lack and so of demand. But by turning in on itself instead of leveling its demand at the reader, the final poem dramatizes a freeing of the reader from the burden of reading and from the cycle of epitaph and pathos. How far this is an actual escape and how far it is only another version of the memento mori, a calling to a forgetfulness and oblivion, we cannot read.

The words of the "Chorus of the Rescued" cited in the beginning of this essay can thus finally be read themselves as a reading of the reader's relation to the epitaph. In the face of a world full of epitaphs, it is only *Abschied,* leave taking, that can preserve those who have been saved from death. The task is not to bring the dead back, but to let them go or to take leave of them oneself. But this leave taking, while it preserves the lives of the saved, also turns them into epitaphic representations of the dead. Their leave taking is like the leave taking of the dead, and so their *Abschied* not only holds the living together, but holds them together with the dead. To live *in the habitations of death* and in *In the Habitations of Death* is to become oneself an epitaph. In a sense, then, to be alive is to become dead to the dead, to mark their lost place but not to answer their call.

NOTES

My thanks to Tim Bahti, who first suggested that I work on this topic, and to Frauke Lenckos, Patricia Simpson, and Marilyn Fries, each of whom gave me valuable help in bringing this essay to a conclusion. It is dedicated to the memory of my grandparents, without whom it could not have been written.

1. Cicero, [Marcus Tullius], *De oratore,* trans. Edward W. Sutton and Horace Rackham, 2 vols., Loeb Classical Library (Cambridge: Harvard University Press, 1988), II.lxxxvi.350–54.

2. Wordsworth wrote three short pieces on epitaphs, two of which were published and the third of which remained in manuscript, as well as many poems that have since been discussed in epitaphic or inscriptional terms. Paul de Man's "Autobiography as De-facement," *Modern Language Notes* 94 (1979): 919–30; and Geoffrey Hartman's *Beyond Formalism: Literary Essays 1958–1970* (New Haven: Yale University Press, 1970), 206–30 and *Wordsworth's Poetry 1797–1814* (New Haven: Yale University Press, 1964), 3–30 are groundbreaking studies on the epitaphic especially in Wordsworth that address the issues of authority and closure more skeptically; Karen Mills-Courts's recent *Poetry as Epitaph: Representation and Poetic Language* (Baton Rouge: Louisiana State University Press, 1990) is a book-length study of the epitaphic as typical of poetry generally, but all four works set themselves against, and so to some extent within, the Wordsworthian tradition.

3. For de Man, "Autobiography as De-facement," 926, and following him, Werner Hamacher, "The Second of Inversion: Movements of a Figure through Celan's Poetry," *Yale French Studies* 69 (1985): 278–79, the trope of prosopopoeia is the founding trope of the epitaph. According to Hamacher, when it is unsuccessful what speaks is not the conceivable "something dead," but the ungraspability of death itself. Benjamin discusses death as the moment that a life takes on "tradierbare Form" and meaning, and as a source of authority in "Der Erzähler" (II, 449–50 and 456–57); see Ute Ecker's conclusion to her *Grabmal*

und Epigramm: Studien zur Frühgriechischen Sepulkraldichtung, Palingenesia Band 29 (Stuttgart: Franz Steiner, 1990), 233–35, for a brief recapitulation of the importance of both these themes in Greek epitaphic practice.

4. De Man, "Autobiography as De-facement," 925.

5. In his *Themes in Greek and Latin Epitaphs,* Illinois Studies in Language and Literature 28, nos. 1–2 (Urbana: University of Illinois Press, 1942), 21–22, Richmond Lattimore suggests that these are attempts in early Greek thought to represent dead souls as a kind of real absence or genuine nonbeing.

6. In Laurence A. Rickels's wide-ranging meditation on mourning and epitaphs, *Aberrations of Mourning: Writing on German Crypts* (Detroit: Wayne State University Press, 1988), 7–16, it is the presence of the deceased within the mourner that creates melancholic grief, while normal mourning is expressed in outward representations. In either case, representation functions as a cause.

7. Edgar Lee Masters, *Spoon River Anthology* (New York: Macmillan, 1919).

8. John R. Kippax, *Churchyard Literature: A Choice Collection of American Epitaphs* (1876; rpt. Williamstown: Corner House, 1978), 69; from a stone in New Preston, Connecticut, dated 1794. Lattimore, *Themes,* 256–58, finds numerous examples of the same sentiment in ancient Greek and Latin epitaphs and traces some descendants up to Tudor England.

9. De Man, "Autobiography as De-facement," 928; Hartman, *Wordsworth's Poetry,* 17–22, both on this phenomenon in Wordsworth.

10. Cf. de Man, "Autobiography as De-facement," 927–28.

11. Simonides 121D. Greek poems are all taken from David A. Campbell, *Greek Lyric Poetry* (London: Macmillan, 1967); the translations from the Greek are mine.

12. "Herodotus the Tourist," *Classical Philology* 80 (1985): 105.

13. Mills-Courts, *Poetry as Epitaph,* 183–84, notes that Wordsworth's "tender fiction" of the presence of the dead requires a similar supplement. Imagination must occupy the epitaph in order to produce the semblance of the dead person speaking from it.

14. Hartman, *Beyond Formalism,* 207.

15. Simonides 92D.

16. Roderick H. Watt, in his "'Wanderer, kommst du nach Sparta?' History through Propaganda into Literary Commonplace," *Modern Language Review* 80, no. 3 (1985): 871–83, discusses the use of this epitaph as German propaganda following the loss of Stalingrad in 1943 (passim), the British use of the story of Thermopylae during the evacuation of Greece in 1941 (875 n. 12), and French Resistance code words using "Thermopylae" around D-Day (883). See also his later essay, "'Wanderer, kommst du nach Sparta?'—a Postscript," *Forum for Modern Language Studies* 23, no. 3 (1987): 278–79, for a revised version of the epitaph placed at the base of the Vietnam War Memorial.

17. Rickels, *Aberrations of Mourning*, 16.

18. William Wordsworth, *The Prose Works*, ed. Alexander B. Grosart, 3 vols. (London: Edward Moxon, Son, and Co., 1876), 36.

19. Wordsworth, *Prose Works*, 58.

20. Wordsworth, *Prose Works*, 53.

21. Wordsworth, *Prose Works*, 29.

22. Masters, *Spoon River Anthology*, 232.

23. Mills-Courts, *Poetry as Epitaph*, 189, proposes that the "lacunae" in Wordsworth's *Prelude* "force the poet to keep writing." The obsessive accumulation of epitaphs in the Greek Anthology, in Masters's *Spoon River Anthology* and *New Spoon River* (New York: Macmillan, 1968), and Sachs's "Grabschriften in die Luft geschrieben" suggests a similar operation at work in each of these.

24. Masters, *The New Spoon River*, 249.

25. Editors' translation.

Chapter 6

Nelly Sachs and the
Dance of Language

Elisabeth Strenger

The Hasidic tales collected by Martin Buber constituted part of Nelly Sachs's initial significant intellectual and poetic contact with Jewish culture. The following anecdote, titled "Silence and Speech," evokes the historical reasons Sachs had for maintaining the struggle for her poetic voice, at first as the memorializer, then as the singer, of her people:

A man had taken upon himself the discipline of silence and for three years had spoken no words save those of the Torah and of prayer. Finally the Yehudi sent for him. "Young man," he said, "how is it that I do not see a single word of yours in the world of truth?"

"Rabbi," said the other to justify himself, "why should I indulge in the vanity of speech? Is it not better just to learn and to pray?"

"If you do that," said the Yehudi, "not a word of your own reaches the world of truth. He who only learns and prays is murdering the word of his own soul."[1]

In her own poetry, Nelly Sachs synecdochically locates the poetic voice in the throat *(die Kehle)*, at times, more specifically, the nightingale's throat. In the nightingale, we recognize the Romantic icon of Brentano's and Eichendorff's poetry and also the baroque emblem of the German metaphysical poets. One is reminded especially of Friedrich von Spee's devotional "Trutz Nachtigall." The conscious use of the nightingale reveals Sachs's continuing interest in the baroque and Romantic poetic traditions. In addition to these intertextual possibilities, the throat, as a physiognomic feature, signifies the frailty of the voice and of the physical aspect of life. This constellation of associations, juxtaposed with the bio-

105

graphical incidence of Nelly Sachs's loss of voice occasioned by a Gestapo interrogation ("I lived for five days without language during a witch trial"),[2] underscores her dual vulnerability as a Jewish woman and her realization of that vulnerability.

The fact of exile and exodus determined the poles of Nelly Sachs's experience of culture and history as a German Jew. She serves as an example of an intensification of the question of identification faced by all Jews writing in the German cultural context. The equation was solved differently by each individual: either the Jewish or German side is weighted with varying degrees of assimilation or commitment to Judaic tradition in response to historical, political, or personal pressures. The Nuremberg laws forced a realignment, a reevaluation of points of orientation. The content of German culture, now radically shifted to a position of "otherness," was called into question. In Nelly Sachs's case, critical attention has been focused on her rejection of the literary norms of German romanticism and her subsequent exploration of Hasidic mysticism and the adaptation of its ontological and semiotic systems.

Sachs's metamorphosis into a Jewish poet acknowledges her continuous development of Jewish issues and motifs that exist in a symbiotic relationship with the German language, for, as a modernist poet, she posits language and its ability to bear meaning as her poetry's formative theme. The German language was discredited as a system encouraging meaning because it had been the language of the disruptive oppressors. She developed a strategy for salvaging her means of expression and communication—her system of metaphors, which is, in effect, a reinvention of language. Her system affirms the existence of bonds between words and their meanings, while opening up a new range of meanings, and it challenges words to describe what has been termed the indescribable.

To reject completely the German language would imply the loss of her poetic voice and the structuring element of her personal and cultural experience. For Sachs, inspired by the theological and linguistic precepts of Kabalistic and Hasidic mysticism, the agent that initiates and sustains the creation and the creative process is language. Her poetic and semiotic experiments are conducted in German, on German, and through these she attempts to transform the language of the oppressors ("die Jäger") and reclaim it on behalf of the oppressed ("die Gejagten"). Two pieces that illustrate the process by which she appropriates and reshapes German as a medium to express the Jewish experience are "Chassidische Schriften" (Hasidic Scriptures, 1949) from the collection *Sternver-*

dunkelung (I, 72–154; *Eclipse of the Stars, Chimneys,* 47–95; *Seeker,* 61–147) and the scenic poem "Der magische Tänzer" (The magic dancer, 1955; III, 239–52). "Chassidische Schriften" represents the initial stage of this process where she begins to develop a metaphoric system based primarily on the Book of the Zohar, one of the central Kabalistic texts from thirteenth-century Spain. The dramatic poem *Der magische Tänzer,* with its evocation of Kleist's "Über das Marionettentheater" (On marionettes), reveals the deeply problematic relationship between the German and Jewish cultural spheres. It questions the possibility of reconstituting the language and posits two extensions to the traditional poetic medium: silence and dance.

Within the Jewish mystical tradition we find a perception of human language that emphasizes the ambivalence of language itself as a possible system of access to divine understanding. Human language is opposed to the immanent Creative, Divine Word. Medieval German Hasidism delivers perhaps the most unequivocal faith in the power of language. In this movement, with its belief in mystic ascent, as Gershom Scholem describes, "[T]he emphasis is no longer on the approach of the mystic himself to God's throne, but on that of his prayer. It is the word, not the soul, which triumphs over fate and evil."[3] But when commenting on Jewish mysticism's relationship to language, Scholem asks, "[H]ow can words express an experience for which there is no adequate simile in this finite world of man?" There is a strong sense that we can only know by analogy or association. The Kabalistic tradition also operated within metaphors—these being the only means by which to "name" the *deus absconditus,* "that which is infinite, that which is not conceivable by thinking. At best these are words with close approximations."[4] Sachs stretches the limitations of language so it can form a bridge between experiential *Bezogenheit* and the place in which language has its source—the place before language.[5]

Fashioning one's own language is in keeping with the great Jewish mystic traditions: from the secret passwords for protection on ecstatic journeys to the Zohar's artificially reproduced Aramaic. So, too, Nelly Sachs seeks to transform her language into one that expresses the inexpressible. Her transformed language includes nonverbal communication strategies. Her highly visual metaphors become emblems in the reader's eye. The human body itself is pressed into service: gestures and dance are summoned to convey meaning both to the reader, and, in prayer, to God.

A consideration of the physical, sensual aspect of her imagery and communicative strategy, as represented by description and inclusion of gesture, leads to the observation of how verbal and nonverbal communication merge in the image of having the word, or sign, inscribed upon the body. Even in transcendent poems describing mystic projections, the reader finds Sachs's attention on the intersection between the material and the spiritual. In *Der magische Tänzer,* the body becomes the word: first in dance, and then, finally, when the heart is torn from the body. Unmediated communication via the body takes place as the Hasidic mystic completes his journey to the place before language.

If we continue to interpret Sachs's poetry as attempts at transcending the strictures of the material world, we will only focus on the abstract qualities of her metaphorical system, which, as Ruth Dinesen pointed out in 1985, is one of the obstacles to her critical reception.[6] At the core of her transcendent impulses lies an acute awareness and understanding of the materiality that constitutes the human experience of one's surroundings, of history, and of self. In the reading and the speech of bodies are found occasions not only for vertically channeled contact between the divine and human spheres, but her poems also record the touching between bodies as a means of establishing lateral bonds, or community. Sometimes the simple human or animal gestures echo contact between man and God. A mother stroking her child's hip in "A dead child speaks" (Ein totes Kind spricht) parallels Jacob's encounter with the angel:

> So that it should not strike me,
> My mother loosed her hand from mine.
> But she lightly touched my hip once more—
> And her hand was bleeding—
>
> (*Chimneys,* 13)[7]

> Die Mutter löste ihre Hand aus der meinen,
> Damit es mich nicht träfe.
> Sie aber berührte noch einmal leise meine Hüfte—
> Und da blutete ihre Hand—
>
> (I, 13)

Although feminist questions on the identification of a woman through her body and with her body arise in relation to certain aspects of Sachs's poetry, I am not basing my analysis on the theories of critics such as Hélène Cixous and Julia Kristeva. But the fact remains that Sachs does concretize the body in her poetry; although this body is not always a feminine body, hers, the poet's, is, and feminist implications, especially in evaluating the link between biography and poetry, should not be overlooked. Throughout her oeuvre we find the cosmos, that same starry realm that represents the patriarchal promise to Abraham, associated with feminine terms: the Milky Way, if we wish, becomes the mother's milk way. We find umbilical cords binding us to the divine in the form of crystalline wombs. And pervasive is the blood, not always the blood of victims or death, but the blood of exuberant, painful, beginning life. Sachs gives birth to language renewed, and this metaphorical feminine presence is far more pervasive than is warranted by traditional Jewish mysticism and the limited role it ascribes to the Shechinah, that feminine manifestation of God.

Johanna Bossinade, in her article "Fürstinnen der Trauer" (1984), began the feminist exploration of Sachs's work. She discusses the importance of the feminine identity for Sachs's poetics in terms of Freud's theory of the female wound, the wounded female. She, too, has noted that many of Sachs's images of separation or loss are opposed to metaphors of maternal security, or *Geborgenheit*.[8]

Sachs lets her body, the body, be heard, but not in a manner easily accounted for by a single theoretical model. And for Sachs, it is not just a question of what the body says, but what the body hears. What experiences does the body react to, testify to? Mystics transcend the body, but the locus of their experience remains the body, and their bodies are said to bear signs of light or blood in response to that experience. It is significant that the strongest statement we have about Sachs and the production of her poems is that she felt them burning within her. One can read these either as the signs of a changing woman's body, or as the searing ecstacy of a mystic. Her epoch has seen the fragility of the body; she writes against this thoughtless, horrific waste. Her epitaphs for the Holocaust's nameless victims, collected in the cycle *In the Habitations of Death*, contain detailed descriptions of their bodies or gestures, of their physical existence as well as testimonies to their spiritual presence.

The poem "Chassidische Schriften" (I, 141; "Hasidic Scriptures," *Seeker,* 131–33) serves as a significant marker in Nelly Sachs's quest to transform language. Blomster, Klingman, and Weissenberger have viewed this poem as a poetic-mystic manifesto and have discussed it in terms of how systematic her analysis and integration of Kabalism and Hasidism have been.[9] Sachs's mysticism is not a system of abstractions. She poeti-

cally transforms personal memory of experienced reality into an evoca-
tion of the cosmos and fate of a people. In this poem, she seeks to pro-
duce her own Hasidic text: a mystical contemplation on the opening pas-
sages of the Kabalistic Book of the Zohar. But whereas the Zohar's
author was inspired to seek the layers of illumination contained within
each word of the Creation narrative, Sachs's meditation telescopes the
entire Torah as it moves from Creation through Exodus.

The poem's epigraph reads: "It is said: the commandments of the
Torah equal the number of a man's bones, its prohibitions the number of
the veins. Thus the whole law covers the whole human body" (*Seeker,*
131) [Es heißt: die Gebote der Thora entsprechen der Zahl der Knochen
des Menschen, ihre Verbote der Zahl der Adern. So deckt das ganze
Gesetz den ganzen Menschenleib (I, 141)]. It invites us to contemplate
the convergence of word and body, although the dynamics of this con-
vergence remain a mystery—a mystery that the poem goes on to invoke
as the space in which all is whole and intact, and for which all creatures
long.

The epigraph is echoed within the poem: "and the bones live the magic
number of the commandments / and the veins bleed to the end" [und die
Knochen leben die magische Zahl der Gebote / und die Adern bluten sich
zu Ende]. The poet's eye transgresses the boundaries of the body, passes
through the permeable barrier of skin. The skeletal and bleeding body,
the bones and open veins, transcend their conventional association with
death to connote life as well, a life encompassed by—or, more accurately,
circumscribed by—the Laws of the Torah. The body, an object of death
and genocide in *Wohnungen des Todes,* functions here primarily as the
living symbol of a god's covenant with his people. The gender-specific
sign of circumcision is replaced by the whole inscribed body. In a fashion
reminiscent of Christianity's saints, who bore stigmata as signs of a mys-
tical union, the body becomes the sign of God's Covenant with his peo-
ple. It can be "read" according to Kabalistic numerology, and one per-
ceives the possibility of an unmediated experience of divinity.

The poem places the reader at the beginning of creation as light is born
of darkness in the protective, nurturing matrix of the universe. The entire
process is distilled into the elemental images of night, stars, water, and
sand that we find recurring in Sachs's poetry. The agent that initiates and
sustains the creation is language: "and the word went forth / . . . Names
formed / like pools in the sand" (*Seeker,* 131) [und das Wort lief aus /
. . . Namen bildeten sich / wie Teiche im Sand" (I, 141)]. Inasmuch as

human beings participate in the naming of activity, they participate in creation, as Blomster has elaborated in his essay on Sachs's theosophy of the creative word.

In this poem, darkness and light have universal significance, but Sachs expresses her hopeful belief in transformation when she imagines the night giving birth to the stars. Dark and light are not in perpetual conflict; rather, one can engender the other. Similarly, she transforms the image of the stone (hard, lifeless matter and symbolic of exile in the barren desert) into a petrified darkness that still contains the promise of divine movement and light. Even threatening quicksand becomes a metaphor for the potential for change on the most elemental level.

In conjunction with the final images of fertile seeds and stars, sand assumes yet another dimension inspired by the Bible (Genesis 22:17). God promises Abraham: "I will shower blessings on you, I will make your descendants as many as the stars in heaven and the grains of sand on the seashore." The poem closes with the image of another stigmatized figure—Jacob, whose injured hip bore the trace of his encounter with his deity. No longer the Jew victimized by history, Jacob is the emblem for an Israel that continues to sleep with the stars that betoken the promise to engender a people. If we can "read" God's presence in or on our bodies, then the possibility exists that we might reverse the direction of communication in accordance with the mystics' belief that the path *to* God is the reversal of the path *from* God. For the psalmist David, for the Hasidic pious, and for Nelly Sachs, the body could then speak back to God, in dance. Hellmut Geißner has attempted to describe the nature of dance as it is understood and applied by Nelly Sachs according to anthropological categories of ritualistic dance.[10] He defines it as "enthusiasmic" dance, which is at once inward and outward turning, seeking both to conjure God and to join with him. Such an ethnographical definition ignores both the communal and the personal/psychological aspects of dance. These other forces operating on dance are represented in Sachs's work by Hasidic dance and by the expressive/interpretative dance of her childhood. Only when one considers dance within this triad of contexts can one understand the complex dynamics of dance as an act of communication.

This volume, and the conference that preceded it, are testimony to the weight of biography/autobiography in her works, including her symbolic biography, à la Bahr: "Nelly Sachs wanted to disappear behind her work, to remain anonymous."[11] Her individuality may have been suppressed, but not her humanity. Of the few facts that can be gleaned from her self-representations, from her autobiographical sketches or references in letters, the most consistently mentioned by biographers and critics is her fascination with dance. She expresses her feelings especially pointedly in a letter to Walter Berendsohn (25 January 1959):

> First of all, there was my father's music, his fantasizing piano improvisations that often went on for hours in the evening after his work, and to which—from childhood on—I danced with total dance abandonment and surrender. . . . For they [her poems of dance and music] grew entirely in this common atmosphere that bound my father and me so deeply together, even though it was almost without words. . . . [Dance] was my innermost element. It is only because of the hard fate I had to suffer that I moved from this manner of expression to another. To words! My interest in mime and in that musical kind of poetic writing that occasionally, as though soundless, arches over all boundaries, is grounded in this innermost disposition of mine.[12]

Note the change to the present tense and the discussion of her later scenic poetry: as a mature poet, she still feels that dance, not the word, is her natural element. In the scenic poem *Der magische Tänzer* dance is the return to cosmic harmony, harmony with the breath that animates the universe. Again in her correspondence, Sachs writes:

> But in this respect, too, my father was my best teacher, because he discovered the connection of rhythmic beat of the [dance] movements with the beat of our breathing long before its time; he had ideas that were quite revolutionary for the times, and which enabled every human being to regain a natural rhythm that had seemed lost.[13]

Beside the desire to recover a lost harmony, a desire strongly associated with nostalgic attachment to her father, Sachs's autobiographical reflections on dance contain another mystical aspect that illuminates her relationship to language. Of her dancing as her father played, she writes: "I followed him for a long way in order to reach the distant places; I leaned over the boundary into a speechless realm."[14] (One more piece of biographical evidence suggests that dance had not lost its attraction as a means of personal expression for the mature poet. Lili Simon reports Ingeborg Drewitz's anecdote that tells of Sachs dancing with abandon when she saw the Berlin Tiergarten again for the first time after twenty-five years. She had returned to Germany to receive the Peace Prize of the German Book Industry in Frankfurt, 1965.)[15] In light of the constant experimentation with mime and movement that accompanied her poetic endeavors, we cannot easily dismiss this interest's origins in childhood.

Theorists of dance and of its essential component, movement, emphasize the developmental aspects of kinesthetic awareness. Kinesthetics has been defined as

> the sensual discrimination of the position and movement of body parts based on information other than visual, auditory, verbal. . . . sensors in the muscles, tendons, and joints, as well as the vestibular apparatus of the inner ear . . . provide a constant, though subliminal, knowledge of the arrangement of body parts. This awareness is enhanced by the sense of touch . . . [the] contact and pressure sensors provide additional information about body position.[16]

In infancy, kinesthesis and physical contact with the external environment are instrumental in helping the individual "begin to conceptualize the world as an orderly and understandable place."[17]

Conceptualization then is grounded in movement. Isadora Duncan and the proponents of dance education/dance therapy insisted that the relationship between movement and the conceptualization of the self and the world extends throughout one's life. Isadora Duncan writes in her essay "Dancing in Relation to Religion and Love": "[A] child can understand many things through the movement of its body which would be impossible for it to comprehend by the medium of the written or spoken word."[18]

Beyond the tactile exploration of one's own body, movement is incorporated early into a pattern of communication strategies. For infants there are the touches, gestures, and facial expressions of caregivers. This stage of kinesthesis is found in many moments in Nelly Sachs's poetry: the cow licking her calf, the mother stroking her child's hip, the old women combing their hair. These gestures, seen as either direct expression of emotion or as symbolic, establish the communal matrix onto which language (verbal communication) is grafted.

The power of Hasidic dance is best observed in its communal implications. For the Hasid, dance is much more than the expression of a single individual's encounter with God; the message the dancer conveys to his pious observers is an equally important function. Through dance, the Hasid teaches and inspires. The Hasidic tales contain many reports of the infectiousness of dance; strangers, passersby, skeptics are drawn into a communal ecstacy. Their oral tradition also tells of rabbis who communicated their enlightenment through dance: The Ba'al Shem Tov, founder of eastern European Hasidism, danced with the Torah, and when he set it down in the midst of the dance, one of his disciples proclaimed, "Now our master has laid aside the visible, dimensional teachings, and has taken the spiritual teachings unto himself."[19] And of a nameless, pious grandfather it is remarked, "You may believe me: he has made all his limbs so pure and so holy, that with every step he takes, his feet accomplish holy unifications."[20]

Nelly Sachs emblematizes the Hasidic dancer in her scenic poem *Der magische Tänzer.* The stage directions for the first scene describe impoverished surroundings hung with laundry. Marina, who has devoted her life to David, the former stage-dancer turned mystic, struggles to support him by taking in washing. The scene's opening dialogue between Marina and her neighbor is about a head of cauliflower. This portrayal of quotidian life reminds one of the lack of disjuncture between daily and mystical/religious experience advocated by the eastern European Hasids.

The figure of David gives the impression of being a large wounded bird ("den Eindruck eines großen angeschossenen Vogels"), and in this posture are suggested his vulnerability as a hunted object, his ungainliness, and his interrupted flight. His metaphoric association with the bird indicates that he is not completely earthbound; he occupies a space between the material and celestial realms. David sits with his head dropping down until it hangs between his knees in the contemplative position of the early Merkabah or throne mystics. After fasting, this position was required for the soul's mystic journey through the gates to the throne of God. It is a position many religions have in common: it influences the blood's progress to the brain—induces physical and psychological "symptoms." The rushing heard in the ears, the play of light against the eyelids, the changing body temperature are all translated into different aspects of the ecstatic experience.

In the first scene of *Der magische Tänzer,* the entire onus of David's functioning (as a subject, as an object of our gazes, as someone who interprets or configures reality as well as someone who invites interpretation) is placed on his postures, gestures, and movements. He is speechless, and the only way he communicates his mystical experience is through dance. His utterances during the second scene mark the stages of his spiritual journey through history and the cosmos. His seeking for the doorway into the night parallels experiences of the Merkabah mystics who confronted gatekeepers at each stage of their ascendancy to God's throne.

An ironic juxtaposition to this silent yet expressive figure is created by the figure of the neighbor, who is represented by a marionette with a built-in tape for a voice. Through this figure, Sachs dehumanizes the subject. This dehumanization is appropriate for the neighbor who, completely focused on material reality, is lacking in sympathy for David's ecstatic reenactment among the clotheslines of King David's dance before the Ark. This David's Ark is Marina's keepsake chest. Of course, the saint appears as crazed to the neighbor, to someone representing society's norm, just as King David's dance was derided by his wife, Michal.

For the second scene, the stage is transformed by lighting techniques into a crystalline globe in which the figures of David and Marina are encased. The crystalline globe creates the effect of a cosmic womb and indicates the return to a precreation state. The visualization of the womb pierced by light parallels the Book of the Zohar's Creation myth in which the male ray enters the female womb. David's somnambulistic dance continues, and a cosmic wind, the breath of the universe, sets the clotheslines into movement. The magic dancer, portrayed by a marionette, appears and the stage retains an enormous amount of kinetic energy until the piece concludes. David's somnambulism indicates the movements of one who has no self-consciousness.

The marionette's presence on stage and David's unself-conscious movements stand in an interesting intertextuality with Heinrich von Kleist's critical musings "Über das Marionettentheater" (On marionettes), published in 1810 in his *Berliner Abendblätter*. This echo may serve as yet more evidence of Sachs's continuing connection to the German Romantic literary heritage. The most striking parallel with Sachs's understanding of dance is the reason given for preferring marionettes over the self-conscious, hence distorted, movements of dancers, because they have the advantage of being antigravitational, or defying some of the rules of materiality. Kinetic energy overcomes considerations of mass and gravity:

Furthermore . . . these puppets have the advantage that they are anti-gravitational. They know nothing of the inertia of materiality, of all properties that which is most counteractive (antithetical) to dance: because the force that lifts them into the air is greater than that which binds them to the earth.[21]

Dance, pure movement, for Kleist and Sachs presents the possibility of transcending materiality. Sachs's dancer takes on some of the characteristics of Kleist's marionettes in order to problematize the paradox of achieving transcendence of the body, through the body.

The magic dancer serves as a guide along the mystical journey; he assists in preparing David for his ecstatic encounter. In a stark counterpoint to the scene of cultic, ritual preparations in Euripides' *Bacchae,* where Dionysius suggests transformative actions to Pentheus, who dons the costume of a Baccante, the magic dancer shapes David's perception of the process in which he is engaged by means of naming. Urged to burst from his skin, David flings off his coat; a belt is perceived as a tonguing snake. While the magic dancer's kinetic energy dismantles the world projected on the hanging linens and unravels the meridians, hence negating the distinctions, divisions, and confinements imposed by humanity upon the *geos,* David continues stripping until, in his shredded undergarments, he bares his chest.

The mention of the snake, its mouth open, winding about David's waist, introduces the theme of Eden and the Fall of Man, which figures in Kleist's deliberations on the causes of humanity's loss of physical grace, of *Anmut und Grazie* (charm and grace). This loss is associated with Adam's and Eve's shame upon becoming conscious of their nakedness. If we superimpose a mystic's reading of this scriptural passage, the awareness of nakedness represents a distinct separation from God. Kleist couches the idea of retracing our steps to God in satirical wit: "Consequently, I said somewhat distractedly, we would have to eat again from the tree of knowledge in order to return to the state of innocence? To be sure, answered Herr C.; that is the last chapter of the history of the world."[22]

David continues his dance, unwinding the confining threads, unraveling the cocoon so that he can undergo his final metamorphosis. The butterfly, that royal sign, Sachs's metaphor of transformation, is here embodied in David's dance. The concluding gesture of his dance is to tear the heart from his bared chest. With this, the interior becomes the exterior, *ex*pression occurs through the body, since the living heart, not the work, becomes the bearer of the self and, ultimately, of meaning.

For Nelly Sachs, the human capacity to communicate, to express, to configure reality includes both verbal and nonverbal languages. The rhythmic movement of dance can overreach the body's boundaries of space, time, and gravity. Jewish mystical voices cry out over the uninitiated language of the German oppressors. Sachs's German dances in a new rhythmical ascendance to spiritual freedom. She explores and acknowledges the paradoxical nature of the mystic journey to God: the body is both the starting point of that journey and the vehicle through which the goal of transcendence is attained.

On every sabbath eve Rabbi Hayyim of Kosov, the son of Rabbi Mendel, danced before his assembled disciples. His face was aflame and they all knew that every step was informed with sublime meanings and effected sublime things. Once while he was in the midst of dancing, a heavy bench fell on his foot and he had to pause because of the pain. Later they asked him about it. "It seems to me," he said, "that the pain made itself felt because I had interrupted the dance."[23]

NOTES

1. Martin Buber, *Tales of the Hasidim,* trans. Olga Marx (New York: Schocken Books, 1947), 228.

2. "Fünf Tage lebte ich ohne Sprache unter einem Hexenprozeß." Ehrhard Bahr, *Nelly Sachs* (Munich: Beck, 1980), 39–40; editors' translation.

3. Gershom Scholem, *Major Trends in Jewish Mysticism,* trans. George Lichtheim (New York: Schocken Books, 1941), 101.

4. Scholem, *Major Trends,* 12–13.

5. Scholem, *Major Trends,* 4.

6. Ruth Dinesen, "Verehrung und Verwerfung: Nelly Sachs—Kontroverse um eine Dichterin," in *Kontroversen, alte und neue: Akten des VII. Internationalen Germanisten-Kongresses,* ed. Albrecht Schöne (Tübingen: Niemeyer, 1986), 10:130–37.

7. Translation modified by editors.

8. Johanna Bossinade, "Fürstinnen der Trauer: Die Gedichte von Nelly Sachs," *Jahrbuch für Internationale Germanistik* 16, no. 1 (1984): 133–57.

9. W. V. Blomster, "A Theosophy of the Creative Word: The *Zohar*-Cycle of Nelly Sachs," *Germanic Review* 44, no. 3 (1969): 211–27; Ulrich Klingman, *Religion und Religiosität in der Lyrik von Nelly Sachs* (Frankfurt am Main: Lang,

1980), 107; Klaus Weissenberger, *Zwischen Stein und Stern: Mystische Formgebung in der Dichtung von Else Lasker-Schüler, Nelly Sachs und Paul Celan* (Bern: Francke, 1976).

10. Hellmut Geißner, "Sprache und Tanz," *Das Buch der Nelly Sachs,* ed. Bengt Holmqvist (Frankfurt am Main: Suhrkamp, 1968), 363–80.

11. "Nelly Sachs wollte hinter ihrem Werk verschwinden, wollte anonym bleiben" (Bahr, *Nelly Sachs,* 30).

12. "Da ist in erster Linie die Musik meines Vaters, die er oft stundenlang des Abends nach seinem Beruf auf dem Klavier phantasierte und die ich mit Hingegebenheit und gänzlicher Fortgerissenheit von Kindheit auf im Tanz begleitete. . . . Denn sie [ihre Tanz- und Musikgedichte] sind ganz aus dieser gemeinsamen Atmosphäre erwachsen, die meinen Vater und mich so gut wie wortlos und doch im Innersten verband. . . . [Der Tanz war] mein innerstes Element. Nur durch die Schwere des Schicksals, das mich betraf, bin ich von dieser Ausdrucksweise zu einer anderen gekommen: dem Wort! Mein Interesse für den Mimus und jene musikalische Art des Dichtens, die sich zuweilen wie lautlos über alle Grenzen beugt, beruht auf dieser meiner innersten Veranlagung" (qtd. in Bahr, *Nelly Sachs,* 32; editors' translation).

13. "Aber in meinem Vater hatte ich auch in dieser Hinsicht den besten Lehrer, da er selber lange vor seiner Zeit jenen rhythmischen Takt der Bewegung mit dem des Atems in Verbindung brachte und für damalige Zeit ganz revolutionäre Ideen hatte, die es jedem Menschen gestatteten, einen natürlichen und verloren gegangenen Rhythmus wieder zu gewinnen" (qtd. in Bahr, *Nelly Sachs,* 33; editors' translation).

14. "Ich folgte ihm weit hinweg, um die Fernen zu erreichen, beugte mich hinaus in ein sprachloses Gebiet." These lines (cited by Bengt Holmqvist, "Die Sprache der Sehnsucht," in *Das Buch der Nelly Sachs,* ed. Bengt Holmqvist, 2d ed. [Frankfurt am Main: Suhrkamp, 1977], 26) reveal a striking parallel to an anthropological observation of dance's function. Through dance, primal peoples "touch unknown and unseen elements, which they sense in the world around them." Jamake Highwater, *Dance: Rituals of Experience* (New York: Alfred von der Marck, 1985), 27.

15. Lili Simon, "Nelly Sachs: Dichterin der großen Trauer," *Neue deutsche Hefte* 35, no. 4 (1988): 695.

16. Carol-Lynne Moore and Kaoru Yamamoto, *Beyond Words: Movement Observation and Analysis* (New York: Gordon and Breach, 1988), 60.

17. Moore and Yamamoto, *Beyond Words,* 70.

18. Isadora Duncan, "Dancing in Relation to Religion and Love," in *Theatre Arts Monthly,* 11, 8 (1927): 389.

19. Buber, *Tales of the Hasidim,* 53.

20. Buber, *Tales of the Hasidim,* 171.

21. Heinrich von Kleist, *Werke in einem Band* (Munich: Hanser, 1966), 805; editors' translation.

22. Kleist, *Werke in einem Band,* 807; editors' translation.

23. Buber, *Tales of the Hasidim,* 98.

Chapter 7

Approaches to a Theory of Language: Walter Benjamin's Early Essays and Nelly Sachs's Dramatic Scenes

Dorothee Ostmeier

The works of Walter Benjamin and Nelly Sachs resemble each other in their approach to drama as a drama of language. For Benjamin, talking about dramatic language calls language itself into question. This premise corresponds to Nelly Sachs's dramatization of language in her scenes, which reflect critically, perhaps destructively, on their own genre.

Nelly Sachs's poem "Vor den Wänden der Worte" (Before the walls of the words), written after she had stopped working on dramatic scenes, points to the intricacies of words functioning as theatrical elements. Addressing words metaphorically as stages, the poem isolates and alienates from each other all processes that take place onstage, offstage, and backstage. The spatial prepositions "before" [vor], "behind" [hinter], "through" [durch], "over" [über], and "in" set up these theatrical spaces through which different theatrical languages—words, silence, revelations, and bodily movements of the eyes, hands, dance—are estranged from each other. These languages try to reach out, beyond themselves, without ever being able to reach each other.

> Before the walls of words—silence—
> Behind the walls of words—silence—
> Revelations of melancholy grow through the skin
> Eyes wander over the glacial waters of suffering
> In the dark hands grope
> for the white pinnacles of nonbeing
> Outside
> dance breaks into God's spaces of love
> the star preserves the wound of life—[1]

[Vor den Wänden der Worte—Schweigen—
Hinter den Wänden der Worte—Schweigen—
Offenbarungen der Schwermut wachsen durch die Haut
Augen gehen über die Gletscherwasser des Leidens
Im Dunkeln tasten die Hände
nach den weißen Zinnen des Nichtseins
Außerhalb
bricht Tanz ein in den Gottesraum der Liebe
der Stern erhält die Wunde des Lebens—

(II, 112)]

Instead of setting up bridges between their walls, "words" open up endangering gaps of "silence," "melancholy," "suffering," and "darkness" between them. These dangers exist and threaten without ever having been isolated, and without the possibility of ever being isolated.

Walter Benjamin also confronts such gaps inscribed in the structure of language. In his theory of drama, he places the dramatic principles of dialogue ("Gesetzlichkeit der gesprochenen Rede zwischen Menschen" [II, 137]) in the context of his theory of language. He says at one point: "The word acting according to its meaning of pure bearing becomes tragic. As the pure bearer of its meaning it is the pure word,"[2] and, at another: "The counterplay between sound and meaning remains ghostly and horrible in the mourning play."[3] Benjamin ignores conventional etymology by isolating the first syllable *Trag* from the word *Trag-ödie* and relating it to the German verb *tragen* (to carry or bear). He examines the relation of the two words *Tragödie* and *Trauerspiel* to the literal meaning of their constituent elements: *Trag* in *Tragödie*, *Trauer* (mourning) and *Spiel* (play) in *Trauerspiel*. In one case, meaning is borne; in the other, it is disrupted by a counterplay. In the *Trag-ödie*, words bear meaning. That does not mean that borne and bearer merge into each other, rather that they operate according to a relation indicated by the German syllable *trag*. Considering that the semantic implications of this syllable in German are quite different from those of its roots in the Greek word *trágos* and its French and English modifications, it becomes obvious that the semantics suggested by the German word are obscured by its translation into other languages. Here the problem of naming in different languages comes into play, suggesting the stress on the material rather than the semantic aspect of the word: the focus lies more on the word as a physical carrier than on that which it carries. This is different in the *Trauer-*

spiel. Rejecting the translation of this term as "tragic drama," Samuel Weber insists on its literal translation as "mourning play."[4] In so doing, he correctly points out that these dramatic terms are not interchangeable. In the mourning play a "ghostly and horrible counterplay *(Widerspiel)*" intrudes between sound and meaning, between signifier and signified. The clash of these linguistic elements disrupts their conventional reciprocal relation. Their conflict underlies the human discourse represented on the stage. One cannot define the borders between signifier and signified, between the bearer and that which it bears. The loosening of the defined structure of words opens up the possibility of various dramatic forms realized only after Benjamin wrote his book on the German mourning play. Benjamin talks about the open future of this form as a "form of mystery."

> The *Trauerspiel* is affirmed as a form of saint's tragedy by means of the martyr-drama. And if one only learns to recognize its characteristics in many different styles of drama from Calderon to Strindberg it must become clear that this form, a form of mystery, still has an open future.[5]

Because the dramatic form of the *Trauerspiel* is doubly open—in its structure, and in its "future"—*form* becomes a fragile term. One can no longer distinguish between that which forms and that which is being formed, and so one must ask how form is generated at all. How does language generate dramatic form and how does drama generate its language?

Benjamin retains for the baroque mourning play the term *mystery play,* but he revises it: in the course of secularization, mystery is removed from any conventional religious connotation.

> But from the outset these efforts remained confined to a context of strict immanence, without any access to the beyond of the mystery plays and so, for all their technical ingenuity, limited to the representation of ghostly apparitions and the apotheoses of rulers. It was under such restrictions that the German baroque drama arose and matured. (*Origin,* 80)[6]

The language of the modern mystery play is no longer related semantically to any idealistic order and is reduced to its theatrical functions of presenting (*Dar-stellung,*[7] *Vor-stellung*) and staging. The spectacle of the stage replaces the idealistic order. The immanent structures of language now become the focus of the texts. In fact, Benjamin identifies the mourning play as "the scene of the actual conception of word and speech in art."[8] Only mourning plays offer words the possibilities to establish themselves as art forms. Benjamin focuses on the word, identifying the drama of its structure, the aforementioned counterplay, as the play's subject; he distinguishes his theory of drama from classical theories, which confine themselves to tragedy and describe it thematically as the representation of ethical problems or historical events. Benjamin's "ghostly and horrible counterplay" no longer occurs as a demonic fate intruding into tragedy. Instead of being mimetically represented, this counterplay is introduced as a given condition of language. Language no longer functions as a reliable medium of representation: the play takes place within it. Benjamin refers on one hand to the intriguer and, on the other, to Hamlet as examples of theatrical figures facing this split in language. The intriguer takes advantage of this structure by employing wit and gaiety to deceitful ends. In the case of Hamlet, Hamlet's silence unmasks the word of wisdom as deceitful.

> The rest is silence. For everything that has not been lived sinks beyond recall in this space where the word of wisdom leads but a deceptive, ghostly existence. (*Origin,* 158)[9]

Instead of regulating semantic relations, words of wisdom reveal their delusory function. Benjamin exploits the ambiguous connotations of the German word *Geist* by referring to its abstract as well as its literal and sensuous meanings as spirit, apparition, phantom, and ghost. If words start wandering and haunting like phantoms, they fulfill their performative function by shifting their written or tonal appearance into visual theatricality *(Geistererscheinungen, Herrscherapotheosen)*. With this transformation—that is, translation from one language to another—they open up an enigmatic realm between the visible and the invisible, the figurative and the nonfigurative. Benjamin observes that the dramatic events of baroque mourning plays usually take place around "the witching hour" of midnight (I, 1, 314). The visualization of words as phantoms, images, figures, or scenic events occurs only in the dark. The darkness obscures this process of visualization by intruding between the words that are already spoken, or visualized as image, dramatic figure, or scenic event.

Benjamin also refers to the darkness as "depth" and "abyss" in order to stress the threat of the unknown and the unknowable. In the mourning play, meaning or wisdom are present only as fraud or delusion.

In essays written before his *Habilitationsschrift* on the mourning play, Benjamin acknowledges a transcendental autonomy of language from its sounds. The essay "The Task of the Translator" (Die Aufgabe des Über-setzers [IV, 1]) calls this autonomous language "the pure language." But in the *Trauerspiel* book itself, he shifts this split between sound and meaning toward a split between different signs—between written and acoustic signs, for example—a split that no meaning can resolve. By focusing on the sensuous and material aspects of language, he can trace their allegorical relation to the visual language of theater.

The heroes both of the tragedy and of the mourning play confront these linguistic splits, but in different ways. Fighting physically on the agonistic battlefield, the tragic hero does not argue in words against given circumstances. Speechless and enclosed within himself (*Origin*, 115), he silently subjects himself to the conditions of physical laws and limits: "[T]he hero, as tragic hero, always remained the same, always the same self, defiantly buried in itself" (*Origin*, 112).[10]

According to a literal reading of this sentence—which quotes Franz Rosenzweig's conception of the antique hero—the self is exposed to death from the very beginning. Rosenzweig distinguishes the silent self of a figure from its personality because it is exactly the personality that con-stitutes itself by marking itself off from others through speech. The ago-nistic battle extinguishes the last barriers that inhibit the hero's identification with self and therefore with death, thus erasing the last traces of his personality. Rosenzweig calls the speechlessness and silence of the tragic hero a language—a language of the ineffable, a language that precedes all common language, and a language in which the hero can remain only as self.[11] Death therefore isolates the language of self from all other possible languages. No sign is closer to that which it signifies than the dead body. It undermines the basic structural characteristics of a sign because the dead body only points to itself as a relic of life. That means that the conventional definitions of language are not applicable to the language of death, self, and muteness. The audience of a tragedy con-fronts this impersonal cryptic language only indirectly by facing the hero's alienation from any communal language, and therefore it experi-ences it as the sublime of linguistic expressions. Whereas Rosenzweig focuses on this sublime muteness of the self,[12] Benjamin stresses its effect on the audience: "In the presence of the suffering hero the community learns reverence and gratitude for the word with which his death endowed it" (*Origin*, 109).[13] Whereas the deaths in tragedies draw the audience's attention toward the mute language hidden by the common language, the deaths in the mourning plays institute and proclaim a language that opposes death itself.

In confrontation with his death, Socrates removes the difference in the relations of audience and hero to language: his disdain of physical limitations serves Benjamin as a characteristic model for all protagonists in the mourning play. Even though they do not fight death, these figures withdraw from their dependence upon physical conditions. They postulate immortality and base further actions and the roles they play on this assumption. "Socrates looks death in the eye as a mortal . . . but he recognizes it as something alien, beyond which, in immortality, he expects to return to himself" (*Origin*, 114).[14] Exempting himself from physical laws, Socrates entrusts himself to the perceptions of language. Confronting his own tragedy just as the ancient Greek audience confronted the tragedies of their heroes, he usurps the place of tragedy and learns a language from which the tragic hero remains excluded. But is this still the same sublime language? "The agonal has disappeared from the drama of Socrates . . . and in one stroke the death of the hero has been transformed into that of a martyr" (*Origin*, 113–14).[15]

Wherein lies the difference between the death of the hero and the dying of the martyr? Benjamin perceives the essence *(Wesen)* of the mourning play, and especially the deaths it sketches, as "an appeal of the kind which martyrs utter" (*Origin*, 137).[16] In this comparison, mourning plays take over the role of their own figures: the setup and plot of the play and the main figure reflect one another. One theatrical figure figures the other and thereby reaches beyond its own present. For the martyr, death no longer indicates an absolute limit or border. Conventionally, he entrusts himself to a prestructured eschatological order, but such an order is abolished by the mourning play. The appeal of such theatrical figures as the martyr and the mourning play itself therefore evokes nothing less than their own continuation and supplementation. The endless "counterplay" between sound and image makes all imaginable conclusions impossible. As Benjamin says, "[T]he resumption is implied in the mourning play" (*Origin*, 137), that is, each end of a play merely masks its endlessness.

Socrates changes the relation to death: by defying mortality, he opens up prospects such as immortality, which are based exclusively on the performative power of language. His confrontation with death initiates a new way of speaking.

> Whereas the tragic hero, in his "immortality," does not save his life, but only his name, in death the characters of the *Trauerspiel* lose only the name-bearing individuality, and not the vitality of their role. This survives undiminished in the spirit-world. (*Origin*, 136)[17]

The wandering words in the mourning play also become independent of the characters, whose death does not eradicate them. Like spirits, ghosts, or phantoms, they appear and disappear, performing or withdrawing from performance—retaining the "vitality of their roles" and the possibility for new performance. In fact, by continuing their existence within "the vitality of their role," the characters of the mourning play distance themselves from the conditions of their visual and physical appearance. When John Osborne translates "Geisterwelt" as "spirit-world," he stresses the idealistic or transcendental and diminishes those connotations on which I am basing my reading.

The tragedy and the mourning play bear a contrasting relation to each other: whereas the muteness of the figures in tragedies and their alienation from all forms of expression restrict them to physical laws, the speaking of the figures in the mourning play allows them to go beyond these laws. This is crucial. Words become spirits, theatrical figures that populate the stage. Although the speakers will be transformed, their parts in the play, their "roles," remain. "In his own lifetime the hero not only discovers the word, but he acquires a band of disciples, his youthful spokesmen" (*Origin*, 117).[18] Because the disciples resume Socrates' way of speech after his death, his presence will be preserved in language. Only by participating in this language, in the "role" of speaking, can Socrates claim immortality. If there is any reference implied to a being beyond this special language, it is uncertain. What does it mean to expect to return to oneself after death as Socrates does? Since this self can be separated from the "name-bearing individuality," it can only be the self that inscribes itself into language, according to theatrical language into a "role" that turns into theatrical and performative presence. By doing this, the self distinguishes its existence in language from its actual physical presence on the stage, its linguistic from its theatrical presence. With his way of speaking, Socrates establishes these fragmented conditions of each presence and thereby institutes an alienation from all forms of expression.

Not entrusting himself at all to the common language, the ancient hero—a figuration of Rosenzweig's "self"—in his silence negates its power absolutely. Socrates, by contrast, offers the autonomy of his spoken words in defiance of death's silence. Only Hamlet unmasks the cunning play of this language in the silence of his mourning. Whereas the silence of the ancient hero marks his radical withdrawal from the spoken language altogether, Hamlet's silence confronts language in its inevitable "role," its delusive play, and its theatrical function. The modern hero experiences himself as always already drawn into this play of the word's spirits, through which language conceives itself by imaging itself.

The main figures in Nelly Sachs's dramatic scenes are always involved in searching for a language they cannot attain. Even when this language *appears* on the stage *visually* as letters or *acoustically* as voice, it presents itself as an agency that *resists being grasped*. The main figures confront the space between different languages, attempting to see what cannot be heard and to hear what cannot be seen. Because these different theatrical languages never coincide, Nelly Sachs's dramatic scenes introduce the search for a language as a search within theatrical limbo. In the scenes I discuss, this liminality is introduced by the figures of disappearing, death, and dying.

First, I examine the relation between the search for a language—which I refer to as a language of words, language of dance, or music—and the processes of disappearance and dying in three scenes written in 1944, 1955, and 1961, during the writer's Swedish exile—an exile from country and language. Second, I discuss another dimension of the scenes: although language is the subject of these plays, they also take place in language. Therefore the problems of its figurative and scenic-poetic presence have to be addressed.

The dramatic scenes I consider do not fit into the framework of the classical drama, in which words describe actions, reflect in monologues upon a dramatic context, or establish a dialogical relation and communication between the figures on the stage. Here words refer to themselves as intrinsically limited signs. Calling their own signifying power into question, they complicate the conditions of their own emergence, and constitute scenes—as we shall see—that stage the intricacies of relating to a language that is absent.

On the one hand, the figures name their attempts "longing," "searching," and "hunting" for this language, or "drowning" and "suffering" for the connection to it; on the other hand, they act out exactly these processes they name. In the sense of the German verbs *darstellen* and *vorstellen,* they concretize, show, present, and perform the very actions they are talking about. By this they distinguish themselves from the personae of realistic or naturalistic dramas. They might be described as abstract—not only absurd and not only symbolic. Because of their self-referentiality, the scenes containing these figures might also be called scenic or concrete poetry or lyrical dramas. This shift in terminology points to the questions at hand. What happens when words are enacted and theatrically visualized, when written or spoken words are transformed into bodily movements and gestures of actors and into images of stage settings, especially when we consider—in the case of Nelly Sachs's scenes—that these figurations take place in the context of death and dying? What dies? The written word itself, or the spoken word? No; what dies are the relations the words constitute, and therefore the figures. What does the theatrical process risk when it relates death to the processes of figurative language?

Two dramatic scenes among Nelly Sachs's very short lyrical dramas literally stage the search for a language. In both dramas, the main figures, Abram and Beryll, are so powerfully attracted by sounds and words from an unseen source that they risk sacrificing their physical lives in order to get into touch with this invisible voice. In one drama, this is called "the voice of night," in the other, "the voice out of night." In listening to this voice, which they hear but do not see, both these figures experience something that they have lost and that they try to find again by breaking through various kinds of boundaries, especially the boundary of their physical life.

In *Abram im Salz* (Abram in Salt [III, 93–122]), the protagonist escapes a death that is politically imposed by Nimrod.[19] Abram comes out of the grave, responding to the voice that calls his name. In running and searching for this name, he leaves the stage, disappearing into an indeterminate space and indefinite time, again leaving conventional life.

In the dramatic scene with three titles—*Beryll sieht in der Nacht oder Das verlorene und wiedergerettete Alphabet: Einige Szenen aus der Leidensgeschichte der Erde* (Beryll sees in the night, or The alphabet lost and rescued again: Some scenes from the history of earth's sufferings)—Beryll is the only figure alive after the Great Flood (II, 287–304). Here, Nelly

Sachs rewrites the biblical story and merges parts of the Babel myth with the myth of the Great Flood, presenting it as a myth of lost language. The text refers to language as having been killed, forgotten, and "drowned."

> You beat your alphabet to death—
> You forgot your letters—
> Your word is drowned in the Flood.[20]

Humanity has distanced itself from language: the gap of death separates humanity from the alphabet, the letters, and the word. The language that has disappeared is abstractly called "Vorbedeutung," meaning before the meaning, premeaning. Figuratively, the text refers to this premeaning, this lost language as "Gesicht des Wassers," which would, at first glance, be translated as "the face of the water." In German, however, *Gesicht* means not only face, but can also refer to prophetic vision. These connotations suggest the translation of "Gesicht des Wassers" as "the prophetic vision of the water." The water motif is associated with another image that calls the lost language "the language of the fish." This is a silent language. Its meaning is not split from its visions and images; it lies already in them. As "meaning before the meaning" it is more fundamental than any other meaning. This language can never be reduced to meaning, but neither is it the mere sensuous positivity of signifiers. The question arises: can we conceive of a language with no communicative function, a language in which signifier and signified are not split from each other, or a language from which either the signified or the signifier is withdrawn and removed?

This conceptualization of language is related to a tradition of earlier theories, especially Jacob Böhme's theory about the original language of Adam and Eve. It appears that Nelly Sachs quotes the figure of the tongue tree from Böhme.[21] But whereas Böhme distinguishes the tree of one kind of tongue from that of various tongues in order to distinguish paradisiacal from decadent languages, Nelly Sachs contracts these two figures into one, undermining Böhme's triadic concept of the history of language and shifting his diachronic view to a synchronic one. Instead of two different figures for two concepts of language, there is only one ambivalent figure in modernity. The one symbolic figure for the original language of Adam and Eve is lost. This is one example of the ambiguity of Nelly Sachs's figures that resist symbolic interpretation. There is no way to present "meaning before the meaning" as an unambiguous figure on the stage.

Nevertheless, Beryll attempts to search for his language, as though it were merely hidden. Beryll cannot be seen on the stage for most of the play: seeking this language—to rescue and enliven it—he sinks into the water. This sinking is called alternately "dying" and "reading": "Beryll reads in/while drowning" [Beryll liest im Ertrinken (III, 289)]. The process of reading is present as a tragic gesture of disappearance. Any spiritual relation to language is substituted by a physical relation to it—in this case a destructive relation.[22] The dying and drowning body is the reader. Drowning has to be read literally as a process of radical immersion into reading, an immersion that risks the loss of the autonomy of the figure Beryll.

Moreover, in this drama one suicidal scene merges with another. The voice of the night reports:

Someone has opened his veins
Blood fills the radiant chain of the alphabet—[23]

As a figure of radical martyrdom, Beryll gives up his life and bursts open his physical isolation, narrowness, and seclusion. After the Great Flood there is no home, his mere bodily existence has no purpose in itself, and he attempts to have language take over his corporal dimensions. The destruction of the body implies a singular exchange between corporeal life and language; language itself is supposed to become corporealized: "My veins [are] empty—space for the dwelling of the name."[24] The drowning, which the scene also calls "reading," empties the veins and creates a physical space in which the language of the name may settle. But this suicidal act does not have the intended effect: although the language of the silent and the mute appears magically in the form of gleaming and flying signs and letters, Beryll remains separated from it. The stage directions read: "Fish fly in the air, forming the glory of the alphabet over his head."[25] The emergence of the alphabet—a motif that quotes and synthesizes different images from Judaic and especially Hasidic traditions—is dependent on Beryll's sacrifice and longing for it. Beryll's radical disappearance causes the self-activation and appearance of the language. But he can only participate in this language by losing it again and again. A tragic exchange takes place: as soon as Beryll lives and becomes visible on the stage again, the visible language dies and disappears. The physical presence of language and of the human figure exclude each other. Here, death and dying cannot be functionalized in any way. There is no way of merging them. This is in contrast to concepts that see death as a transforming agent, as is typical in the conventional martyr plays described earlier.

Beryll as a figure for the search for language assumes a very ambiguous function. On the one hand, the figure itself remains separated from the language he is looking for; on the other hand, he activates it without controlling it. Even though the two activities are dependent on each other, they pass by and miss each other.

The dramatic scene *Der magische Tänzer* (The magic dancer) (III, 239–52) focuses on the human body as an absolute barrier and hindrance. It is true that the words of the magic dancer seem to promise otherwise: "the skin is no boundary" (III, 245), he says. But the scene raises the question: is there anything beyond corporeality? In this scene, words are spoken only in order to make themselves superfluous: the art of dancing replaces the art of speaking.

The magic dancer, a marionette, teaches the ecstasy of dance to the human figure David, who is named after King David, the biblical dancer. The marionette—who appears later as the young David—meets David at a moment in which David has completely withdrawn from his successful artistic career in dancing (modeled after Nijinsky's) and has submitted to the laws of gravity and passivity. The stage directions read:

> At right front David sitting on a chair, a black coat around his shoulders. The sleeves hang down. Impression of a large bird wounded by shooting. His head bends lower and lower until it hangs down between his knees.[26]

One cannot imagine a more striking figure of melancholy. In this depersonalization, the body is estranged from all natural and creative relations and becomes itself a mere thing. The stage directions explain this posture as the pose of deepest contemplation in Hasidic mysticism (III, 241). In becoming this body of contemplation, David passes over from one language to another, from motion to immobility. The rupture of his dance and his speechless and stiff apathy are the preconditions for the appearance of the magic dancer.

The magic dancer does not teach an artistic dance; he teaches a dance that tries to burst through the limits of the body. He urges:

> the skin is no boundary
> burst it open—burst it open![27]

Whereas Beryll opens his veins, David has to learn to break through his skin. In her letters, Nelly Sachs uses this very vocabulary of exploding and bursting existing structures to describe her own writing experience. She writes: "These dramatic experiments came about where the poem did not seem to suffice and the boundaries exploded themselves."[28] Nelly Sachs's unusual reflexive use of the verb *sprengen* as "explode"—in the sense of "bursting oneself open"—indicates a profound tension within poetic form. The form does not seem to be strong enough to hold itself together; instead, it suddenly breaks out, explodes, and destroys itself. It expands into something that is no longer a poem. It grows indeterminately. What does Nelly Sachs address when she speaks about dramatic scenes, especially when—as I have pointed out—human bodies in these scenes function like bodies of poems: they explode and burst? What advantage does this figuration of poetic texts have over poetic texts themselves?

In Sachs's scenes, anthropomorphized figures having no psychological or subjective characteristics are reduced to their physical shapes. These shapes can produce other shapes by remodeling, or by destroying, themselves. In *The Magic Dancer*, David finally gives up all his efforts to dance; he undresses himself and tears his heart out of his body: "[He] utters a heart-rending cry, tears off his shirt, tears out his heart, and sinks . . . down."[29] Here, the conventional metaphor of the broken heart is staged literally as David tears his heart out of his body. At the same time, he cuts off all metaphysical and psychological connotations of the metaphor. "Heart" cannot be read any longer as soul, mind, or spirit. David strips the metaphor of its own metaphoricity, so that the heart is restricted to physical laws of gravity. The last illusion of inwardness, hidden by metaphorical language, is lost.

Notice that, in comparison to the other two dramas, death is here radicalized. With the destruction of his body, David also interrupts and destroys his search for a language. He tears his body apart, but in doing so he does not reach out to a language that is not present on stage. What can be inferred from this? A poetic figure can exploit only its own figurative elements, it is stuck in its own structures and cannot reach out beyond them.[30]

To return to the text: when David comes to the end of his search for the absent language, he screams. This scream borders language. It is exactly the sound of losing all capacity for controlled expression (i.e., language).

The magic dancer, assuming the shape of the very young David, reminds David of the strength of sounds (III, 246). He teaches the dance as an endless pirouette, without the interruptions characteristic of traditional dances. One can dance oneself out of the physical laws of space and time. This ecstasy of dance opens up memory, especially the memory of a time when spoken or written words were not yet a part of the child's own language, when the child translated visual impressions into sound, visual expression into musical expression. Roman Jakobson calls this period, during which a child can produce all imaginable sounds but no recognizable words, the "babbling period."[31] The child loses this variety of the natural and arbitrary play with sounds as soon as it tries to relate to language as a medium for communication. Saussure's linguistic system as well as all the succeeding ones and their means of distinguishing the linguistic sign are based and anchored in this arbitrary play. In Nelly Sachs's scene, the magic dancer calls up the memory of this play as music itself when he briefly turns his speaking into singing and then into the humming of a child. He says:

When Rachel woke up
your mother
from her bed of stone
singing:
and each stone had already become music
and you took the stone—the stone—the eye stone
and played like this . . .

Now the stage directions call for "humming music."[32]

Everything that memory brings back—mother, music, the motherhood of musical sound—lies beyond the competence of spoken or written language. In the mother-child relation, the firm, the fixated, and the dead become music.

After the magic dancer who is David's childhood departs, David can no longer remain in his prelingual musical and transcendentalizing approach to visuality. An inversion takes place: his screaming tears his body apart. The death scene is enacted as a dismembering of visual and bodily structures and a disavowal of any transcendence.

Abram is still running toward the voices he hears; Beryll experiences the language he seeks as removed from himself. For David, the language is lost. The quest for a language is relinquished in *The Magic Dancer,* where the enactment of death becomes purposeless. Death cannot be functionalized; its only consequence is to concretize the split that it marks—the split that separates all kinds of expressions from each other.

Whereas Socrates distinguishes his physical from his verbal existence in order to entrust himself to the latter, Nelly Sachs's figures subvert such trust. The speaking that releases them from physical laws confronts them again with such laws. This is shown on different levels of the plots:

1. It is demonstrated thematically in the failure of the search for language. The more the figures search, the more the language seems to withdraw from them. Each play moves between proposing and negating the existence of such a language and ends in an open ambiguity. Abram disappears from the stage, continuing his search in invisibility and silence, where no language exists any longer. Beryll listens to a death's head, a figure of the dying night and its singing. Beryll, the blind man who could only see in the night, now also loses this source of light. His encounter with the night leaves him doubly blinded and suffering. "Gesang ist Leiden" [Song is suffering] the night says at the end.

2. It is evident in the staging of this search. It takes place in an encompassing theatrical context in which gestural, scenic, imagistic-visual, and acoustical elements work off each other in such a way that they can never coincide. Dissonance separates them. Experimenting with different enactments of death, Nelly Sachs explores the limits in and of language.

This results in the undoing of rhetorical forms and therefore in the problematization of poetic aesthetics in general. Notice, for example, the inversions that occur in *Beryll sieht in der Nacht*: the night not only opens up the sight for the blind (the view into the Ark) but also the possibility to hear its, night's, voice. The acoustic scene seems to set up the visual in order to demonstrate the impossibility of this synaesthetic relation: the rhetoric of synaesthesia extends to a scenic event of merging acoustic and visual scenes that, while splitting again, tear this synaesthetic relation apart. Poetic expression is here theatrically represented as a tension between two scenic elements; in fact, the possibility for this poetic expression is called into question. On this level of the scenario, the search for language is taking place in theatrical languages that seem to destroy the conventions of rhetorical poetics.

I conclude with a summary that brings together some of my points. The figures of Nelly Sachs's plays—Abram, Beryll, and David—can be regarded as martyr figures of the modern mourning play in Benjamin's sense, which is to say that the pre-Socratic concept of tragedy, in which the sign is restricted to its bearing function, is excluded. The figures strive to merge with a language by expanding and transforming their own figurative presence theatrically. In trying to overcome their limitations, they reveal themselves as limited. Different concepts of language seem to be struggling with each other: the Socratic concept realized in mourning plays, where the sign itself (the body of the philosopher) is a reduced and inefficient medium, and a Kabalistic concept according to which the sign itself is the absolute carrier of its effects. According to Kabalistic doctrine, the letters are divine forces of creation. Nelly Sachs had intensely studied Gershom Scholem's translation of a chapter from the Zohar called "Die Geheimnisse der Schöpfung" (The secrets of the creation). It is an interpretation of the first book of Genesis in which the unfolding of the alphabet—which composes God's name—creates the world.[33] Although Nelly Sachs's figures momentarily encounter unique signs of such an absolute other language, they experience themselves as being split from them. As figures of the splits, abysses, and darknesses that Benjamin detects in the language of the mourning play, they wander like the ghosts in baroque plays on their endless search.

NOTES

1. Editors' translation.

2. "Das Wort nach seiner reinen tragenden Bedeutung wirkend wird tragisch. Das Wort als reiner Träger seiner Bedeutung ist das reine Wort" (II, 138). Translations by Dorothee Ostmeier unless indicated otherwise.

3. "Das Widerspiel zwischen Laut und Bedeutung bleibt dem Trauerspiel ein Geisterhaftes, Fürchterliches" (II, 139).

4. Samuel Weber, "Genealogy of Modernity: History, Myth and Allegory in Benjamin's *Origin of the German Mourning Play*," *Modern Language Notes* 106, no. 3 (1991): 465–500.

5. "Das Trauerspiel ist als Form der Heiligentragödie durch das Märtyrerdrama beglaubigt. Und wofern nur der Blick deren Züge unter mannigfaltigen Arten des Dramas von Calderon bis Strindberg zu erkennen sich schult, wird die noch offene Zukunft dieser Form, einer Form des Mysteriums, ihm evident werden müssen" (I, 292). The translations in *Origin* have been frequently modified by the author or editors.

6. "Gebannt aber blieben diese Versuche von vornherein in eine strenge Immanenz und ohne Ausblick auf das Jenseits der Mysterien, in der Entfaltung ihres gewiß reichen Apparates auf die Darstellung von Geistererscheinungen und Herrscherapotheosen beschränkt. In dieser Beklemmung erwuchs das deutsche Barockdrama" (I, 258).

7. On *Darstellung,* see Rainer Nägele, *Theater, Theory, Speculation: Walter Benjamin and the Scenes of Modernity* (Baltimore: Johns Hopkins University Press, 1991), ix–xviii.

8. "Stätte der eigentlichen Empfängnis des Wortes und der Rede in der Kunst " (II, 140).

9. "Der Rest ist Schweigen. Denn alles nicht Gelebte verfällt unrettbar in diesem Raum, in dem das Wort der Weisheit nur trügerisch geistert" (I, 335). A better translation for the second sentence would be: "For everything that has not been lived is irretrievably lost, decaying beyond rescue in this space in which the word of wisdom wanders in mere deception."

10. "[D]er Held aber war als tragischer Held immer der gleiche, immer das gleiche trotzig in sich vergrabene Selbst" (I, 291).

11. Franz Rosenzweig, *Der Stern der Erlösung* (Frankfurt am Main: Suhrkamp, 1988), 87.

12. Rosenzweig, *Der Stern der Erösung,* 83.

13. "Im Angesicht des leidenden Helden lernt die Gemeinde den ehrfürchtigen Dank für das Wort, mit dem dessen Tod sie begabte" (I, 288).

14. "Sokrates sieht dem Tode ins Auge wie ein Sterblicher . . . aber er erkennt ihn als ein Fremdes, jenseits dessen, in der Unsterblichkeit, er sich wiederzufinden erwartet" (I, 293).

15. "Aus dem Sokratesdrama ist das Agonale herausgebrochen . . . und mit einem Schlage hat der Tod des Heros sich in das Sterben eines Märtyrers verwandelt" (I, 292–93). (A more precise translation of the first part would read: "The agonal has broken out of the drama of Socrates . . .")

16. "[E]in Apell, wie ihn denn Märtyrer auch formulieren" (I, 315).

17. "Wenn der tragische Held in seiner 'Unsterblichkeit' nicht das Leben sondern den Namen allein rettet, so büßen die Trauerspielpersonen mit dem Tode nur die benannte Individualität und nicht die Lebenskraft der Rolle ein. Ungemindert lebt sie in der Geisterwelt auf" (I, 314–15). "Geisterwelt" translates as world of spirits, ghosts, apparitions, or phantoms.

18. "Dem Helden selber wächst in seiner eignenen Lebenszeit nicht nur das Wort, sogar die Schar der Jünger, seiner jugendlichen Sprecher zu" (I, 296–97).

19. *Abram im Salz: Ein Spiel für Wort—Mimus—Musik* (II, 93–122).

20. "Ihr habt euer Alphabet erschlagen— / Eure Buchstaben vergessen— / Sintflutertrunken ist euer Wort" (III, 108–21).

21. Jacob Böhme, *Mysterium Magnum, oder Erklärung über Das Erste Buch Mosis* (1623), *Sämtliche Schriften,* vols. 7 and 8 (Stuttgart: Fr. Frommanns Verlag, 1958).

22. One might think of the death of the victim in Kafka's "In der Strafkolonie" (In the penal colony). But there the judgment is brutally carved into the body. This death by language has to be distinguished from that in Nelly Sachs's drama because different modes of language are involved.

23. "Einer hat seine Adern geöffnet / Blut füllt die Glorienkette des Alphabetes—" (III, 291).

24. "Meine Adern leer—Raum für die Wohnstatt des Namens" (III, 291).

25. "Fische fliegen in der Luft, bilden über seinem Haupt die Glorie des Alphabetes" (III, 291).

26. "Vorn rechts David auf einem Stuhl sitzend, einen schwarzen Mantel um die Schultern. Die Ärmel hängen herab. Eindruck eines großen angeschossenen Vogels. Sein Kopf beugt sich tiefer und tiefer bis er zwischen den Knien herunterhängt" (III, 241).

27. "[D]ie Haut ist keine Grenze / sprenge sie—sprenge sie!" (III, 245).

28. "Da wo das Gedicht nicht auszureichen schien und die Grenzen sich sprengten, kamen diese dramatischen Versuche zu Stande" (*Briefe,* 240).

29. "[Er] stößt einen herzzerreißenden Schrei aus, reißt den Trikot herunter, reißt sein Herz heraus und sinkt . . . hin" (III, 252).

30. Before David's final self-destruction, the text suggests an alternative ending: David is turned into a dancing cherub. In the logic of the play, I interpret this end as an analogy to the scene in *Beryll sieht in der Nacht* in which the radiant chain of the alphabet appears as a sign of the language that cannot be encompassed.

31. Roman Jakobson, *Kindersprache, Aphasie und allgemeine Lautgesetze* (Frankfurt am Main: Suhrkamp, 1969).

32. "Als Rahel aufwachte / deine Mutter / aus ihrem Bett aus Stein / *singend:* / und jeder Stein war schon Musik geworden / und du nahmst den Stein—den Stein—den Augenstein / und spieltest so: // *Summende Musik*" (III, 248).

33. Similarities of the images in Scholem's and Sachs's texts suggest the appropriateness of reading Nelly Sachs's drama as a rewriting of and—for this reason— a commentary on the Zohar. Gershom Scholem, *Die Geheimnisse der Schöpfung: Ein Kapitel aus dem Sohar* (Berlin: Schocken, 1935), 49ff.

Chapter 8

Benjamin's Metaphors of Origin: Names, Ideas, Stars

Stéphane Mosès

From very early on, Benjamin's thought is marked by a search for the origin, this being understood as at once a *beginning* and a *foundation*. For the young Benjamin—just as, later, for the Benjamin of the *Arcades Project*—the ultimate truth that all knowledge aims at is simultaneously a first truth: it designates at once that which grounds knowledge and that which constitutes its point of departure. But at the same time, the very fact that the foundation of truth is also its beginning implies that, in its very being, *truth has a history*. Benjamin affirms this in his earliest texts and maintains it as one of his central themes up to the *Arcades Project* and the "Theses on the Philosophy of History." What changes across the different stages of Benjamin's thought is the nature of this history, or rather, the nature of the code by means of which that history can be deciphered: the historicity of truth is read first as a theological history of language, then as a history of works (and above all of texts), to reveal itself finally—this is the project of the *Arcades Project*—as a history of social facts.

The principles of the theological vision of the origin are posed by Benjamin in his two essays "On Language as Such and on the Language of Man" (Über Sprache überhaupt und über die Sprache des Menschen, 1916 [II, 140–57]) and "The Task of the Translator" (Die Aufgabe des Übersetzers, 1921 [IV, 9–21]). In the history of Benjamin's thought, one may consider these two studies as foundational texts. In effect, Benjamin here develops the central intuition that will dominate his entire oeuvre, namely, *that the place of truth is language*. This idea, which will be taken up again and deepened two years later in the essay "On the Program of the Coming Philosophy" (Über das Programm der kommenden Philosophie [II, 157–71]), should be understood as an affirmation of the primacy of the signifier over the signified. In "The Task of the Translator," this signifier, across which the hidden truth of every literary text reveals itself, is called "the mode of signifying" [die Art des Meinens]. In the book on the baroque *Trauerspiel,* it is the analysis of a paradigmatic signifier—allegory—that permits the deciphering of the baroque's worldview. In the series of great literary essays—on Proust, Kafka, Leskov, Baudelaire—it is the study of narrative or poetic forms that leads to ideological interpretation. Finally, in the *Arcades Project,* the description of social facts ought not to be taken as an end in itself; in truth, they play the role of signs that point to the most hidden meaning of modernity.

It is only in appearance that the two early texts, "On Language as Such" and "The Task of the Translator," treat the origin of language; in truth, they speak of the language of the origin. If there is a question of genesis, of beginning, it does not concern a point of historical departure, but rather an ontological foundation that is projected, in the manner of a myth, into an immemorial past. Biblical narrative here plays the role of a founding text, at once because in the story of Creation a central place is accorded the birth of language, and because in the manner in which that story is recounted, the language shows itself to be closest to its original power. In "On Language as Such," the narrative of Creation appears at the same time as the story of humanity's loss of that original power and as the illustration of its survival. Of the three episodes of Genesis that Benjamin reinterprets, the first (Gen. 1:1–31) designates language in its purest essence, that is, in an ideal form to which human beings have never had access: that in which no difference exists between language and reality. Here, it is not a matter of saying that at this stage, language accords perfectly with reality, that the word recuperates the very being of the thing that it designates. No, at this primordial level the duality of word and thing does not yet exist: here language is, in its very essence, creator of reality. This absolutely creative dimension of language cannot have been lost by humanity, and therefore cannot be retrieved either, because it was never possessed. But to the extent that it is anterior to the original language of human beings, it is also the condition that makes possible the very idea of such an original language. This language, the emergence of which Benjamin locates in the episode of the biblical narrative where Adam names the animals (Gen. 2:18–24), is the "paradisaic language" characterized by the perfect coincidence of the word and the thing it designates. This adequation of the sign and its referent is as distant from the arbitrariness of the sign that defines the present state of language's decay as it is from the primordial unity of word and thing. In the "paradisaic language," language and reality are indeed two different orders, but there exists between them a sort of preestablished harmony: reality is entirely transparent to language, and language joins the very essence of reality with a quasi-miraculous exactitude. This perfect accord between the primordial language of man and the reality of things is due to the fact that they issue from the same source: the original divine word, creative of all natural reality, is also that by means of which man was created. Divine language, forever deprived of its creative dimension, finds itself reinvested, as it were, in Adamic language; to be sure, the latter does not engender reality, but it knows it with a perfect knowledge: an unsurpassable matching of sign and referent such as poetic language may still attest to today.

It is Adamic language, invested with a magic power of "nomination," that was lost when language became a simple instrument of communication. Benjamin, who here interprets the narrative of original sin (Gen. 2:25–3:24) in light of the episode of the Tower of Babel (Gen. 11:1–9), sees in the communicative function of language the sign of its decay. From absolute precision of denomination, language falls into "the abyss of chatter." Once the original accord of word and thing is lost, language is condemned to a perpetual approximation that Benjamin defines as "overnaming." The bankruptcy of communicative language derives not from its being too poor, but from the fact that it is too rich. Correlatively, nature, because not understood by man, sinks into muteness and desolation. Only the presence, even today, of a symbolic dimension of language testifies to the fact that Adamic language is not irrevocably lost, and that the origin survives in some way at the depths of our decay.

In "The Task of the Translator," Benjamin takes his point of departure from this present decay of language, where the corruption of the human condition after the Fall is expressed, in order to sketch a movement of return to the lost perfection. Just as the declining phase of history is linked to the degradation of language, so its ascendant phase coincides with the latter's progressive purification—in other words, with the process of restoring Adamic language. Benjamin here takes up again the distinction between the communicative and symbolic aspects of language, but while combining it with another opposition, that of the act of signifying ("das Meinen") on the one hand and the mode of signifying ("die Art des Meinens") on the other. In communicative language the interlocutor's intention is centered on the act of signifying, and more precisely on the content of the message that he or she attempts to transmit. In the symbolic use of language, by contrast, the accent is placed on the "mode of signifying," that is, on what today we would call the signifier. The more human discourse abstains from aiming at communicable contents, the more it will become absorbed in attending to the mode of signifying, and the more language will reappear in its original purity. This process of purification operates across history through the labor of poets but also—and this is Benjamin's central thesis—through that of translators. True translation, which ought to attempt far less the transmission of a content than the creation of a new system of signs—not mimetic but complementary with respect to that of the original—contributes, in its measure as a great work of literature, to advancing language toward its utopian end, toward that "language of truth" which is nothing other than the language of origins. This itinerary, which Benjamin qualifies as "messianic" and for which the end signifies at the same time the return to the origin, evokes the conception of history proper to Jewish mysticism. The latter has always conceived of the messianic end of history as the fulfillment of the ideal project implied in Creation. In this sense, fulfillment for this mysticism is less a simple restoration of the origin than the realization, across the avatars of human time, of all the utopian virtualities encoded, so to speak, in the original program of the human adventure. This is a vision of history that, while certainly not linear, is not exactly cyclical either, since its end does not coincide purely and simply with its origin. On the other hand, if at the origin of history the presence of a system of invariable givens (in the case of Benjamin's theological paradigm, it is a matter of the primordial "names" that constitute Adamic language) confers on that history a certain measure of determinism, it is no less the case that these givens are pure virtualities, the realization or nonrealization of which depends perhaps on chance, perhaps on human freedom. In "The Task of the Translator" the restoration of paradisaic language comes about by the very movement of poetic invention, by the always unforeseeable emergence of forms and works, so that the return to the original operates in truth by way of the creation of the new.

In the preface to the *Origin of the German Trauerspiel*, Benjamin develops a theory of knowledge at the horizon of which there appears once again the vision of a primordial language of humanity as the original landscape of truth. At first, the "names" that constitute the Adamic language seem to be replaced here by "ideas" of a Platonic type: truth would be made up of a multiplicity of fundamental intuitions that would represent so many categories of apprehension of the real. Since the origin, then, truth presents itself as multiple and discontinuous; in contrast to the Hegelian theory of universal *Geist,* which, after being incarnated in innumerable concrete forms, identifies once again, at the end of its adventures, with its own essential unity, Benjamin constructs the model of a truth exploded from the start, one that no synthesis could ever succeed in totalizing. In this respect, the task of philosophy consists, as with Plato, in contemplating the ideas in their plurality and diversity. Yet if the ideas are multiple, their number is not infinite; the history of philosophy proves that human knowledge obsessively turns around a limited number of questions, always the same, that each generation confronts in its turn. This collection of questions, which it is a matter less of resolving than of reposing anew each time, marks off the original domain of knowledge, the primordial horizon of all thought. As with Rosenzweig, Benjamin opposes to the metaphysical tradition of the unified Logos the vision of a truth originally plural but appearing at the same time as a given, as the unchanging background of knowledge. Each idea defines, in some manner, a particular semantic space, the original place from which there arises one of the fundamental questions to which humanity ceaselessly returns. In this sense there is indeed an ontology of truth in Benjamin: the collection of ideas constitutes a system, a primary landscape always present even when human beings have forgotten it, and to which it is a matter of returning.

The irreducible multiplicity of ideas, their coexistence in the interior of a system, and the fact that this system remains unalterable even when it ceases to appear, together suggest, almost of necessity, the astronomical metaphor of the heavens and their constellations. And this is indeed the image that will dominate the exposition of Benjamin's theory of knowledge, at first explicitly in the *Origin of the German Trauerspiel,* then in an increasingly coded manner, all the way to his very last works. In the book on the baroque *Trauerspiel,* it is by way of the cosmological metaphor that the primordial world of the truth is described:

Just as the harmony of the spheres proceeds from the orbits of stars that never touch one another, so the existence of the intelligible world rests upon the insurmountable distance that separates the pure essences. Each idea is a sun and behaves with respect to other suns in the characteristic manner in which suns behave with respect to one another. The relationship of such essences in the realm of sounds is truth. (I, 217–18)

But it seems that the recourse to "ideas" is only a first approximation in the theory of truth that Benjamin is here developing. In fact, the doctrine of ideas is for Benjamin only a veil behind which is silhouetted the theological vision of his early writings on the philosophy of language: quoting Hermann Güntert, he writes, "The Platonic 'ideas' are at bottom . . . only divinized words and verbal concepts."[1] Benjamin continues: "The idea is part of language, and designates, in the essence of the word, that which is symbolic in it" (I, 216). The "ideas" thus refer back, in truth, to the primitive "names" that constitute Adamic language. These latter designate, as one knows, the symbolic aspect of words, their noncommunicative or still purely poetic aspect by which they accord "magically" with the very essence of reality. It is this miraculous coincidence of the word and the thing that has been lost, and it is what philosophy ought to try to recover. A movement of anamnesis that nonetheless does not lead back to "a sensible representation of images": in contradistinction to Platonic reminiscence, which is essentially visual in nature, the anamnesis to which Benjamin makes allusion is acoustic in nature. As in biblical revelation, it is not by way of vision (the "form of external sense" according to Kant) that the truth gives itself to human perception, but by way of hearing, as the "form of internal sense." Understanding ought to be understood here in the physical sense of the term, as the faculty of perceiving by the ear the sonorous harmonies of the word. In this sense, to know the original means to recover a first hearing, to understand anew the original signification of language on the far side of the loss of acuteness to which repetition and habit have made it submit.[2] "In this renewing," writes Benjamin, "the original perception of words finds itself anew": a movement always resumed from out of forgetting and remembering, the history of philosophy—far from sketching an ascendant curve wherein the regular acts of the progress of reason inscribe themselves— "is nothing other than struggle to represent a very few words—always the same—of ideas" (I, 217). But "in philosophic contemplation the idea most profoundly detaches itself from reality and does so in the form of the word; the word reclaims anew the right to name things. From this point of view, it is not Plato but Adam, father of humankind, who is the father of philosophy" (I, 217).

In the first version of his introduction (a version left unpublished during his lifetime), Benjamin underlines more clearly than in the definitive version the theological connotations of this return to the origin. Indeed, the original is there defined as the "unfinished restoration of Revelation" (I, 935), which latter term is to be understood as the order of Adamic language. Nonetheless, it is not a matter here of a return to a temporal beginning, but rather, at each instant, of a regeneration of the original meaning of words. The original is in effect marked by a "double determination": "[A]s such, it does not show itself unless one recognizes at once the restoration of Revelation and the necessarily unfinished character of such a restoration." To understand anew the original meaning of a word means at one and the same time to return to its initial truth and to discover it as if for the first time. The origin is that which is at once absolutely primordial and radically new. Its occurrence opens up at once toward what was always there and toward what has never yet been known. This is what distinguishes philosophic anamnesis as Benjamin understands it from simple repetition. Each time that reminiscence puts us in renewed contact with the original "names," we have an experience previously unknown, and what reveals itself to us is of the order of the absolutely unknown. To be sure, the void that separates each of these experiences from the following one (these are the voids—or ruptures— that, for Benjamin, constitute the history of philosophy) designates a period of forgetting the original truth. But philosophic anamnesis—like victory over forgetting—does not return us to the anterior stage of reminiscence (nor to any of those that preceded it); in the history of philosophy there is not an accumulation of acquired acts of knowledge, which, were it to exist, would effectively render unthinkable the very idea of a radical innovation. No, to return to the original means, for Benjamin, to rebegin at zero, to undertake as if for the first time the foundational labor of thought. But at the same time this rebeginning models itself, each time, upon the immemorial presence of the primordial "names." It is this contradiction that inspires from the inside the act of reminiscence and confers upon it its unique mystery (cf. I, 936). The original is at once that which reveals itself as absolutely new and that which is re-cognized as having existed at all times: "Recognition of the unheard-of as something that comes forth from the depths of an immemorial order. Discovery of the actuality of a phenomenon as representing the forgotten order of Revelation" (I, 936).

From this point of view, each great historical epoch will appear as an absolute rebeginning, as a new effort to return to one of the primordial ideas, or to one of the primitive names, the set of which formed the original landscape of truth. Philosophy's realm of thought will thus not constitute itself, in the manner of induction and deduction, by "reducing ideas to concepts and projecting them into a pseudological continuum" (I, 223); it will, rather, discontinuously juxtapose moments independent of one another. The phenomenon of origin will thus be that by way of which a certain epoch aims at a certain idea, or, inversely, a certain idea incarnates itself in historical reality (thus, for example, the baroque *Trauerspiel* is a phenomenon of origin). "In every phenomenon of origin," writes Benjamin, "there is determined the form in which an idea ceaselessly reconfronts the historical world, until it attains its completion in the totality of its history" (I, 226). By this one must understand that a primordial idea, such as, for example, that of the baroque, may incarnate and reincarnate itself repeatedly across history, until all the virtualities that it implies are realized. From this one may understand how Benjamin could write that "the origin, being all the while an absolutely historical category, nonetheless has nothing in common with genesis" (I, 226).

In the introduction to the *Origin of the German Trauerspiel,* the two models of original truth—Platonic and biblical—are, however, transposed in their turn upon a language perhaps still more essential: that of the metaphorics of stars. The ideas are names, but both the one and the other shimmer like stars in the heavens of the origin. The theory of knowledge that Benjamin develops in his introduction articulates itself around the play of four notions: idea, concept, element, and phenomenon. The phenomena are the basic givens of empirical reality; to be understood, they have to be decomposed into their elements, and this may be done thanks to the analytic labor provided by the concepts. But these dispersed elements would dissipate into an unintelligible chaos if they were not regrouped into new figures; it is these figures that Benjamin names "ideas."[3] But these figures are also called "configurations" or "constellations": "The ideas are eternal constellations, and to the extent that the elements may be conceived as points within these constellations, the phenomena are separated and rescued at the same time" (I, 215). It is because the elements are initially parts of empirical realities that Benjamin can write, "The ideas are to things as the constellations are to stars" (I, 214).

Two years before the writing of the book on the baroque *Trauerspiel,* the theme of stars had already appeared in Benjamin's study of Goethe's

Elective Affinities (Die Wahlverwandtschaften), not, to be sure, as an element of its visible architecture, but as a half-hidden figure of its secret texture. At the end of his study, Benjamin evokes a stroll by Goethe across the German countryside, during the course of which the writer, already quite old, confides to one of his companions the degree to which the writing of *Elective Affinities* had shaken him, and the passion that he felt for the novel's heroine, Ottilie. "The stars had risen" ([Die] Sterne waren aufgegangen [I, 199]), reports one of the witnesses to this conversation. For Benjamin, this detail recalls the passage in the novel where the two lovers, Eduard and Ottilie, dare—for the first and the last time—to hold each other in their arms; at that point, the narrator commented, "Hope shot by above their heads like a star falling from the sky" [Die Hoffnung fuhr wie ein Stern, der vom Himmel fällt, über ihre Häupter weg (I, 200)]. And Benjamin adds:

> The most paradoxical, the most fleeting hope is born, at the end of the novel, of the appearance of a reconciliation, in the way that, when the sun has disappeared, dusk witnesses the rise of the evening star that lasts longer than the night. . . . the symbol of the shooting star that falls above the heads of the lovers is the appropriate expression of those elements of mystery—in its most precise meaning—that inhabit this work. . . . [This mystery] promises more than reconciliation, it promises redemption. (I, 201)

In the context of the essay on *Elective Affinities,* the metaphor of the stars leads back, it seems, to the idea of an intelligible world (perhaps of Kantian inspiration) that, at very rare moments, stands forth in the background of a novel otherwise, and for the most part, dominated by the Goethean belief in the omnipotence of nature. The presence of the stars, distant signs that point toward the existence of an ethical sphere transcending the obscure fatality of the passions, would thus be the only light of hope within the tragic world of the novel. But at the same time it is clear that the stars here allude to the sphere of astrology. Benjamin suggests that Goethe himself may have believed in astrology: in *Poetry and Truth* (Dichtung und Wahrheit) Goethe begins the story of his life with a presentation—ironic or not?—of his horoscope, just as, in his Orphic poem "Urworte" (Original words), he evokes "the decree of the stars"; the two passages, writes Benjamin, "lead back to astrology as the canon of mythic thought" (I, 150). Admittedly, these two interpretations of the metaphor of the stars—the one Kantian, the other Goethean—are, in a certain sense, the contraries of one another: ethical transcendence is opposed to mythic fatality as liberty is to necessity. But this opposition recalls at the same time the tension that already characterized Adamic language: each of the primordial "names" represents at once an unalterable given, an invariant original that predetermines in some way the history of thought, and the source of a permanent renewal of meaning. Empty forms, deprived of all semantic content, the names that constitute the "language of truth" signify nothing but sketch out the ineluctable horizon within which truth may unfold. In the same way, the contemplation of the starry heavens invites humanity to remember its vocation as the subject of ethics but at the same time recalls to mind the necessary laws that govern human destiny. Names and stars, as metaphors of the origin, open at once upon the presence—always on the near side of ourselves—of an immemorial given, and upon the ceaseless manifestation of the new. Two experiences of the original that, according to Benjamin, correspond to two possible figures of happiness:

> There exists a double will to happiness, a dialectic of happiness. A hymnic figure and an elegiac figure of happiness. The one: the unheard-of, that which has never been, the summit of bliss. The other: the eternal once-again, the eternal restoration of the original, the first happiness. (II, 313).

The connection between the image of the shooting star and the idea of happiness will be underlined again, many years later, in the essay "On Some Motifs in Baudelaire," one of the last texts Benjamin wrote:

> The shooting star that falls into the depths of space has become the very symbol of the fulfilled wish. . . . The instant when the flashing of a falling star dazzles us is made up of a kind of time that Joubert has evoked with the precision peculiar to him: "There is time in eternity itself," he writes, "but it is not a terrestrial or mundane time; . . . it destroys nothing, it only completes." (I, 635)

The view of a star covering, in a flash, thousands of light-years symbolizes the illumination in which the present suddenly rejoins the most distant past, or rather, inversely, where the most ancient hope is unexpectedly incarnated in the present instant. This manifestation of the immemorial at the heart of the present, this epiphany of the most distant in the nearest features, precisely describes the experience of the *aura*. One recalls the definition of the aura that Benjamin gave in his essay "The Work of Art in the Age of Mechanical Reproduction" (1936): "A singular weave of time and space: the unique appearance of distance, however close it might be" (I, 712). The depths of space here metaphorically translate the infinitude of time, but these two dimensions of distance both lead back to the incommensurability of the original. When the original incarnates itself, as in a flash, we undergo, in a present instant, an auratic experience. The aura yields itself to us as the radiance of the original, just as the light of a star reveals to us the brilliance of a star long since disappeared.

In the last text of the collection *One-Way Street (Einbahnstraße),* titled "Toward the Planetarium," Benjamin links the sight of the starry heavens to "the ecstatic experience of the cosmos" that, according to him, characterized the prescientific worldview—an essentially collective experience, comparable, on the individual scale, to that of drugs, "in which we take possession of the nearest and the farthest, and never one without the other" (IV, 146). It is clear that, for Benjamin, the auratic moments of life represent, in our secularized world, the equivalents of the ancient "ecstatic experience of the cosmos."

From another perspective, the experience of the aura, as a manifestation of the original, also lives on by way of our rapport to the universe of names. In a brief aphoristic text dating from the same period, and bearing the title "Platonic Love"—a coded text through and through, demanding the deciphering of its hidden meaning—Benjamin, playing on the two senses of the term *platonic,* interprets the experience of "platonic" love as the desire for the name of the beloved, or for the idea that this name incarnates, that is to say, as a return to the Adamic language that is equivalent to the original order of the truth: "Platonic love [is that] which loves the beloved in its very name." In opposition to physical possession, love "in the name and by the name" is nostalgia for distance, that is, for auratic experience:

That [love] preserves and protects the name, the first name of the beloved, in its integrity—this alone truly expresses the tension, the inclination toward distance that makes of it a platonic love. . . . For this love the existence of the beloved issues from his or her name like heat radiating from a glowing core. . . . Thus *The Divine Comedy* is nothing but the aura around the name of Beatrice. (IV, 368–69)

The idea according to which the being of a person reveals itself, from the origin, in the name that it bears, appears very early in Benjamin's work, and it will return, like a secret theme, up through his last texts. Already in the essay "On Language as Such" (1916) Benjamin affirms that the name the parents give to the child—a name to which no objective knowledge corresponds—is the only trace still remaining of the divine language at the heart of human language. In effect, this name, to which no object corresponds, leads back to a state anterior to that of Adamic language, namely to that primary stage (which the first verses of Genesis evoke) where divine language is presented as the creator of reality. In the same way, human beings borrow from God the faculty of forging their own destinies from the names that they bear. The name of the person, as a mediating instance between divine language and human language, is at once a given received at birth and the source of a permanent invention: "His name guarantees to each man his creation by God, and in this sense it is itself creative, which is what mythological wisdom expresses in the by no means rare intuition that name is destiny" (II, 149–50). An empty form without definite semantic content, the name preexists the man, but the latter engenders, from this pure structure, an infinity of new significations. Whence, in a pseudoautobiographical text written in 1933, the fiction of a "secret name" that his parents were supposed to have given him at birth and that, even since, had governed his life. This name, Agesileus Santander, which Gershom Scholem deciphered as an anagram of "Angelus Satanas," refers to the watercolor by Paul Klee titled *Angelus Novus* that Benjamin acquired in 1921 and that became for him the figure emblematic of his own destiny.[4] The two metaphors of the angel and the name here echo one another as two representations of the manifestation, or rather the irruption, of the original in the heart of the present. "In the room that I occupied in Berlin," writes Benjamin, "this other name . . . had fastened its portrait on my wall: New Angel."[5] But this angel symbolizes as well the central intuition of Benjamin's philosophy of history: "The Kabala," he adds, "recounts that God creates a host of new angels at each second, and that each of them has but a single and unique function: to sing for one instant the praise of God before his throne before dissolving into nothingness. It was as one of them that 'the New One' presented itself to me, before consenting to reveal its name to me."[6] The meaning of history does not reveal itself, for Benjamin, in the process of its evolution, but in the ruptures of its apparent continuity, in its gaps and its accidents, there where the sudden emergence of the unforeseen comes to interrupt the course of things and thus reveals, in a flash, a fragment of original truth. At the heart of the present, the most radically new experience thus transports us, at the same time, all the way toward the most immemorial origin. An experience of flashes where time disintegrates and fulfills itself at once: "What the Angel wants, is happiness: a tension opposing the ecstasy of the unique, of the new, of the not-yet-lived, and that other felicity, that of beginning anew, of finding anew, of the already-lived."[7] This singular rupture of the tissue of the temporal is felt at once as an anamnesis, as a recognition of the original harmonics of language, and as the vertiginous experience of an auratic love: "That is why the only novelty that [the Angel] can hope for passes by way of the path of return when, once again, he entangles a human being with himself. Thus it was for me: no sooner had I seen you for the first time than I returned with you toward the place whence I'd come."[8]

In the unfinished book on the Paris arcades, the auratic connotations of the origin are once again associated with the theme of stars. But this time, the destruction of the aura in the age of industrial revolution, the triumph of technology, and mass civilization are symbolized by the absence of stars from the nocturnal sky of the great cities:

> The great city does not experience a true dusk. In every case, artificial lighting deprives it of the transition into night. This is also the reason why, in the sky of the great city, the stars disappear; what one notices the least is the moment when they appear. Kant's metaphor of the sublime—"the moral law within myself and the starry heavens above my head"—could not have been conceived by a resident of the great cities. (V, 433)

Benjamin notes several times that in Baudelaire, who represents for him the archetype of the poet of modernity, the stars never appear. To be sure, he writes at the end of his essay "On Some Motifs in Baudelaire," the author of *Les Fleurs du mal* was fascinated by the magic of distances; but these took on the ironic form of landscapes smeared on the backdrops of outdoor theaters. Baudelaire was for him "the melancholic whose star calls him toward the distance. But he didn't follow it" (V, 402). For "the renouncing of the magic of distance is a decisive moment in [his] poetry" (V, 417). Baudelaire announces the sensibility of modern man, who experiences sensation only at the price of "the collapse of the aura in the experience of shock" (I, 653). Baudelaire's sky, writes Benjamin, is "a secularized space" (V, 348); but is not the disappearance of the stars in the skies of the great cities, brought about by the reflection of urban lighting, ironically compensated for by the very brilliance of these artificial lights? A paradoxical full circle, in which the industrial civilization that destroys the aura engenders, on the rebound, a "modern beauty" founded precisely on the aesthetics of shock. In this sense the "overturning of tradition" (that is, the forgetting of the origin) would be nothing other than "the flip side of the contemporary crisis and renewal of humanity" (I, 711). This optimistic thesis, which Benjamin develops in his study "The Work of Art in the Age of Mechanical Reproduction" and in his second essay on Brecht (1939), underwrites as well a note in the *Arcades Project,* where Benjamin reinvests in the toponymy of the Paris streets—that is to say, in an entirely secularized space—the lost powers of Adamic language:

> The city gave to all the words (or at least to the great majority of them) a possibility that previously had existed only for the most privileged ones: that of being elevated to the nobility of the name. This revolution of language was accomplished by the most humble of realities—by the street. Thanks to the names of streets, the city became a cosmos of language. (V, 650)

But to the notion of a "modern beauty" belonging to the forms of art produced by the new techniques of reproduction, Benjamin constantly opposes the ideal of the auratic beauty that has disappeared. In Baudelaire, the "Tableaux parisiens," marked by an aesthetics of rupture and dissonance, contrast violently with the incantatory poems such as "La vie antérieure" or "Correspondances," which express the nostalgia for a return to archaic forms of experience, to magical modes of perception of reality. To be sure, when Benjamin, in his essay "On Some Motifs in Baudelaire," analyzes these "auratic" poems, he no longer evokes—at least not explicitly—the idea of a first origin of language that ought to be retrieved. The lost origin is rather thought (as in the text on "The

Mimetic Faculty" from 1933) in terms of historical anthropology: as a very ancient stage of civilization, where humanity was capable of deciphering cosmic analogies, and of perceiving the synesthetic unity of all the sensations. This magical vision of reality continues to stand out, in Baudelaire, in the background of our modern sensibility, and against this very background, as the almost already unconscious memory of a lost happiness. Auratic poetry would thus be, at the heart of our civilization of writing and reading, like the last trace of an archaic cultural model, to the extent that the experience of reading itself, felt as "profane illumination," might have preserved up to this very day something of its original magic. In the same way, the philosopher who goes against the grain of history, or who reads the book of history "in reverse," retrieves at the heart of our most profane experiences a trace of the magic that inhabited them at the origin. This image of a rider riding backward on the road of time was inspired in Benjamin by Kafka's tale "The Next Village," for which he proposed (in his conversations with Brecht) the following interpretation:

> The true measure of life is memory. It traverses life in a flash, the gaze turned back. In as little time as it takes to flip backward through a few pages of a book, it returns from the nearest village to the spot where the horseman decided to set out on his way. Those for whom, like the ancients, life is transformed into writing, can only read this writing in reverse. It is only thus that they encounter themselves, and it is only thus—in fleeing the present—that they can understand that life. (VI, 529–30)

To the young horseman in Kafka's tale, who never will reach the nearest village, Benjamin opposes the grandfather's point of view, for whom the retrospective gaze embraces, in a blink of the eye, the duration of an entire life. It is not only a matter, as in the essay on Proust, of rediscovering a personal past, of restoring a primordial happiness, that of childhood, but of a return, at the heart of the present, of the origin of history itself.

These allusions—most often encoded—to the scattered traces of auratic experience in the depths of modernity bear witness beyond any doubt to the persistence in Benjamin of a theological model of history. Flashes of original truth subsist even today, hidden here and there in the depths of our profane world; the task of the "historical materialist," he will say in the "Theses on the Philosophy of History," consists precisely in collecting these "sparks of hope" (I, 695) buried in the past and giving them new life—like citations of ancient texts retrieving their youth in the new context into which they are integrated—in the very heart of the present (I, 694). But these "splinters of messianic time" (I, 704) are lost in a reality hopelessly emptied of all auratic magic. In a world irrevocably deprived of the depth of distances, the poetry of Baudelaire itself "shines in the sky of the Second Empire like 'a star without atmosphere'" (I, 653).[9]

Translated by Timothy Bahti

NOTES

1. Benjamin cites Hermann Güntert, *Von der Sprache der Götter und Geister* . . . (Halle a.d.S., 1921), 49.
2. "I should like you to pay close attention to the exact words you used," says Freud to Dora, and he adds in a footnote: "I laid stress on those words because they took me aback." The Pelican Freud Library, *Case Histories 1, "Dora" and "Little Hans,"* tr. Alix Strachey and James Strachey, ed. Angela Richards (London: Pelican, 1977), 100.
3. If one wants an example of this method, one will find it in Benjamin's literary criticism: the work that he studies has the status of a phenomenon; the conceptual analysis releases its motifs, which appear as so many elements; these latter are then regrouped into a series of key notions that correspond to the ideas and constitute a critical metalanguage or even a sort of metatext where the truth of the empirical text is expressed.
4. Gershom Scholem, "Walter Benjamin und sein Engel," in *Zur Aktualität Walter Benjamins,* ed. Siegfried Unseld (Frankfurt am Main: Suhrkamp, 1972), 87–138.
5. Scholem, "Walter Benjamin," 100.
6. Scholem, "Walter Benjamin," 100–101.
7. Scholem, "Walter Benjamin," 102.
8. Scholem, "Walter Benjamin," 102.
9. Benjamin is quoting here from Friedrich Nietzsche, *Unzeitgemäße Betrachtungen,* 2d ed. (Leipzig, 1893), 1:164.

Chapter 9

Walter Benjamin's Variations of Imagelessness

Winfried Menninghaus

Walter Benjamin's early philosophy is marked by a "category" of "antithesis" (I, 194) to the beautiful and indeed to the aesthetic altogether. Its enigmatic name is "das Ausdruckslose"—the expressionless (I, 181). At first one is inclined to compare the expressionless with related words such as *ausdrucksarm* or *ausdrucksschwach,* which signify a poverty or weakness of expression; and it is only in this sense that Schiller, for example, speaks of a "flachen und ausdruckslosen" *Gesichts*-"Bildung," of flat and expressionless features of the face.[1] But Benjamin's concept of the expressionless refers to neither a subjective deficiency in expression nor a counterweight to expressive styles. Rather, it modifies a series of prominent concepts that also end with the syllable *los* but invest the lack indicated therein with a positive meaning: the *Zweck-lose, Interesse-lose, Begriffs-lose*—the purposeless, disinterested, unconceptualizable character of the beautiful in Kant, and the *Bilder-losigkeit,* the imagelessness of God. Semantically, it stands in closest affinity only to one of these versions of *-losigkeit,* of "-lessness": to the Jewish prohibition of the image. This commandment of imagelessness informs almost all areas of Benjaminian thought: the theories of art and of language, moral philosophy, and anthropology.

Since Kant and Hegel, God's imagelessness has counted as a paradigm of the aesthetics of the sublime. "Perhaps"—so it reads in the *Critique of Judgment*—"there is no passage in the scriptures of the Jews more sublime than the commandment: Thou shalt not make unto thee any graven image, or any likeness of anything that is in heaven or on earth, or under the earth. This commandment . . . also holds for our presentation of the moral law, and for the predisposition within us for morality."[2] Benjamin actualized this commandment in a double manner: beyond God and morality, he related it to much else of what "is on earth," and especially to art, language, and the human body as well as to fantasy and color. And he reformulated it not only as a commandment of passive respect before divinity, but also of the active production of imagelessness, indeed, as the *action* of breaking with aesthetic phenomenality. I wish to show that in its multiple and often striking metamorphoses of imagelessness, Benjamin's doctrine of the expressionless carries on the tradition of reflection about the sublime. My exposition will refer above all to his essay on Goethe's *Wahlverwandtschaften* (Elective affinities) as well as to an abundance of fragments and paralipomena that have been published in volume 6 of the *Gesammelte Schriften* and have thus far received little attention.

Semblance/Absence of Semblance; Life/Death; Motion/Motionlessness

In Plato's *Symposium,* the image of the beloved—"bodily living beauty" (I, 194)—figures as the first model for the beautiful. Benjamin held to this model more strictly than Plato himself. It represents, for him, as for Kant,[3] the "ideal of beauty" (VI, 129). His essay on Goethe's *Wahlverwandtschaften* turns into a general theory of the beautiful[4] only because he defines "Ottilie's beauty" as the "fundamental condition for an affective engagement with the novel" (I, 179) and indeed as "the center of the literary work" (I, 186). Benjamin sees two aspects of everything beautiful represented to "the greatest intensity" in the beautiful body of the beloved: aliveness and semblance (*Lebendigkeit* and *Schein,* I, 194). Both are, for him, inextricably bound up with one another: the semblance of the beautiful is essentially the semblance of its aliveness, of its *Lebendigkeit.* "In infinitely differentiated degrees," Benjamin's theory holds, a semblance of aliveness remains "maintained even in the least alive *(im Unlebendigsten),* just in case it is essentially beautiful. . . . Accordingly, that semblance—which is to say that touching and bordering upon life—continues to reside in all beauty of art, and such beauty is impossible without this" (I, 194).

This semantics of the concepts beauty, semblance, and life reformulates in the language of philosophical aesthetics a position that has long had a place in the theory of art and poetics as the "enlivening" quality of beauty; its literary model is the Pygmalion myth, the bringing of stone to life in a beautiful creation. Yet Benjamin's philosophy of art only begins where the Pygmalionist discourse of the aliveness of the beautiful precisely ends. It also subverts Schiller's idealist discourse of a "beautiful life,"[5] to which the *Wahlverwandtschaften* essay alludes with the formula: "beautiful life, the essentially beautiful, and the semblantly beautiful *(scheinhafte Schönheit)*, these three are identical" (I, 194). Both the alive and the beautiful become the object of a definite critique. That is, while the illusion of the alive represents, under the sign of Pygmalion, the positive telos of the beautiful, Benjamin sees the essence of art precisely in a counteractive process of petrification and critical demolition of living beauty. He robs Pygmalion once again of his living beloved. The moment of death—and all that is related to it—drives the moments of illusionistic animation out of the center of art. By virtue of the "jagged line of demarcation" that death engraves between sensuous "physis" and supersensuous "significance" (I, 343—the formulation is from Benjamin's *Ursprung des deutschen Trauerspiels* [Origin of the German Trauerspiel]), it destroys the harmonizing ideologeme of a "beautiful life," in which—in Schiller's words—"all . . . dividing borderlines have disappeared" in favor of a "harmony" of reason and sensuousness.[6] After taking the position that the beauty of art is impossible without that touching and bordering upon life, Benjamin then immediately draws a limitation: "But [this semblance] does not altogether make up [beauty's] essence. Rather, every work of art must stage a conflict between beautiful semblance and its mortification, so that the life surging within it . . . becomes motionless, and, as if in an instant, appear[s] captivated" (cf. I, 181). Precisely this intervention in the beautiful semblance is what Benjamin calls the expressionless:

> What commands a halt to this semblance, checks its motion and interrupts the harmony, is the expressionless. That [semblance of] life founds the mystery of the work; this petrification *(Erstarren)* founds its content. (I, 181)

I shall comment on this difficult and often-quoted "key passage" in Benjamin's philosophy of art on several levels and by way of several approaches. I begin with the most direct form of petrification, of the opposite to the aliveness of beautiful semblance: death. As the alive body is the model of beautiful semblance, so is the corpse that of the "decline of semblance" (I, 193). This accounts for the prominent, indeed leitmotif-like role of the corpse in all of Benjamin's more extended works. As various modes of the "production of the corpse" (I, 392) Benjamin reads ancient tragedy, the baroque *Trauerspiel,* Goethe's *Wahlverwandtschaften,* and Baudelaire's lyrics. Of the ancient hero it is said that he "shrinks before the power of death as before a power familiar, personal, and inherent in him. Indeed, his life unfolds out of death, which is not its end but its form" (I, 293). In the baroque *Trauerspiel* Benjamin diagnoses the power of death not as that "unique" to a heroic self, but as one befalling the characters of the *Trauerspiel* by virtue of the "allegorical intention":

> The characters of the *Trauerspiel* die because it is only thus, as corpses, that they may enter the homeland of allegory. Not for the sake of immortality, but for the sake of the corpse do they meet their end. . . . For the seventeenth-century *Trauerspiel* the corpse becomes quite simply the preeminent emblematic stage-property. (I, 391–92)

Even where allegory does not directly lead to the "production of the corpse," it lets "life . . . flow out" of whatever it takes possession of (I, 359). For just this reason, Benjamin claims, allegory drives every transfiguring semblance out of [art]works, and indeed is an art of "the absence of semblance" [Scheinlosigkeit] (I, 356) and "acknowledges itself beyond beauty" (I, 353, 354).

In Goethe's *Wahlverwandtschaften,* Benjamin discovers a threefold critique of the beautiful semblance that is so effectively invoked in the figure of Ottilie. Two of these critical determinations once again have directly to do with death.[7] The first is the novella, in which Benjamin reads the "antithesis" to the mystical "thesis" of the novel (I, 171). The girl's "furious attack . . . against the eyesight of the beloved" already hints at a "disposition . . . that is averse to all semblance" (I, 186)—provided that the beautiful semblance, as already with Plato, is preeminently linked to the *ópsis,* to the visibility and phenomenality of light. But above all the love of the odd neighbor children "risks . . . life" (I, 184), and it transforms the loving girl into a near-corpse, in whose "veilless *(hüllenlose)* nakedness" for Benjamin "the essentially beautiful [has] given way, and a being beyond all beauty [has been] achieved—the sublime" (I, 196). What connects the sublime with the naked body—the negation of semblance—is meanwhile seen by Benjamin to be accomplished not only in the novella's antithesis to the novel's action, but equally in the beautiful main figure of Ottilie herself. For her semblance is, in contrast to the triumphant Luciane's (I, 193, 194), one that "passes away," and its "decline" [Untergang], described in several stages, is at once the "transition *(Übergang)* . . . to the sublime" (I, 193). The sublime in turn thus arises in the critical decline of the beautiful, and indeed as the transformation of the living body into a corpse: "The more life fades," Benjamin writes, "the more all semblant beauty—which can cling only to what is living—also fades, until in the total end of what is living, beauty, too, must pass away" (I, 197).

For Benjamin's theory of the sublime as a critique of the beautiful, death and the corpse have yet a further general significance besides that of the destruction of the semblance of living beauty: they isolate, and as a consequence of this isolation they disavow every aesthetic figure of totality as ideological. "The body," Benjamin says, "is for man the seal of his solitude, and this seal will not break—even in death" (VI, 80); rather, the relation to death is the strongest form of isolation. The "expressionless," in its double relation to deadly petrification as well as to *physis* without semblance, is therefore for Benjamin a manifestation of "singularity" (VI, 128). Here, too, it stands in polar opposition to the beautiful, which comes forward with claims to aesthetic wholeness, "totality" (VI, 128). Benjamin goes even further: man's own body is altogether inaccessible to him in an aesthetic totalization in an image, in a figuration of its wholeness. But more on this later; here, first, a remark on the imagelessness of man's moral essence. To negate such imagelessness, and to claim an intuition, an *Anschauung* of beautiful morality that would harmonize reason and sensuousness, was a major ideologeme of eighteenth-century aesthetics, the cipher for which was the concept of moral beauty. Benjamin draws a blunt line through the middle of this compound concept and splits morality off from every mode of imagistic portrayal *(Abbildbarkeit)*: " 'Thou shalt make thee no image'—this holds not only for the defense against idolatry. With incomparable emphasis, the prohibition of the body's representation prevents the appearance that the sphere may be portrayed in which the moral essence of man might be perceptible" (I, 284). In Goethe's *Wahlverwandtschaften* it says analogously: "The highest, the most excellent in man, is shapeless, without shape *(gestaltlos)*"[8]—a phrase to which Benjamin already refers in one of his earliest writings (II, 51). The "expressionless," then, in its allusion to the imagelessness of God and human morality, at the same time reformulates the Goethean shapeless—consequently an element of that text, the immanent "critique" of which concerns Benjamin's "category."

If one places the preceding remarks in the larger context of the tradition of the sublime, six comparative determinations may be formulated.

First, in almost the entire tradition—in Longinus, Addison, Dubos, Burke, Klopstock, Kant, and so on—the aesthetics of the sublime is connected to the concept of motion, in many authors even to mystical intensifications of the concept of motion such as ecstasy and enthusiasm. The sublime, says Burke, "is productive of the strongest (e)motion that the mind is capable of feeling."[9] Benjamin's expressionless sublime is by contrast a "power" of "petrification": it precisely "checks" "motion," interrupts it (I, 181). The rhetoric of *movere* is critically limited in it. A sober, decidedly antienthusiastic gesture of protest altogether opposes ecstatic intoxication or enthusiastic soaring. This idea, consistently invoked throughout Benjamin's works, of a kind of *Läuterung durch Erstarrung* (purification through petrification) has its antecedents in mystical forms of being struck by a divine power. German romanticism has reenacted this model of a finally salvational petrification several times; the perhaps best known of it is the "Golden Pot" of E. T. A. Hoffmann, in which the hero, Anselmus, undergoes an *Erstarrung* in a crystal glass before he is able to enter the realm of Atlantis.

Second, as the power of petrification, the sublime in Benjamin is related to death in a privileged manner, and indeed quite literally to the "production of the corpse"; to this stands opposed the beautiful as the semblance of aliveness. As widespread as is the discourse of an aliveness of the beautiful—for Kant, too, "the beautiful carries with it directly a feeling of life's being furthered"[10]—there is also a formidable tradition that associates death and the sublime. The sublime heroes of the *Iliad* look death fearlessly in the eye, and Burke enthrones death—even in the form of public execution—as the essential content of the sublime. But death plays this role in Burke and other writers above all, if not exclusively, as the "king of terrors."[11] Benjamin, on the other hand, while retaining the privileged role of death, releases it from a restriction to the genre of the terrible sublime. The "flowing away of life" and active "mortification" (I, 357) are promoted to being the essential content of a critical process, a critical labor that differentiates "semblance" and "essence"—or, more exactly, that "forbids [the two] to blend together," without nonetheless being able to "separate" them (I, 181). In Benjamin's sublime, death turns from a tribunal of terror into a moment of critique, the theological paradigm of which is the Last Judgment. In a way, for Benjamin every work of art enacts an analogy to the Last Judgment by criticizing its own aesthetic appearance via the antiaesthetic interruption brought forth by a sublime counterweight.

Third, Longinus repeatedly characterizes the sublime with a metaphorics of light *(phos):* as light's radiant intensification, as an all-surpassing oratorical brilliance.[12] Benjamin opposes to the sublime maximum of shining semblance its equally sublime minimum.[13] The sublime truth does not appear positively in the "world of perception" (cf. VI, 85; I, 215), and the naked body, deprived of all semblance, is nonphenomenal and inaccessible to any intuition of a symbolic meaning. Sublime truth and the naked body both abandon the symbolic space of the sensuous-spiritual, of the phenomenal and the shape endowed, and they abandon it on behalf of two opposed extremes: one of expressionless spirituality and another of expressionless corporeality. As the expressionless, Benjamin's sublime continues the nonphenomenality already diagnosed by Kant, which compels a negative mode of representation. Hegel formulated it as follows: the sublime is "whatever is sublimated . . . above all expression."[14] What is probably Benjamin's best-known example of sublime expressionlessness goes back behind Kant to Longinus's famous passage on Ajax's sublime silence. The "speechlessness" of the tragic hero, his "being struck dumb," is said to be "the sublime of the tragedy," indeed "probably the ground of the sublime altogether" (II, 175; cf. also I, 182). The silence of the tragic hero distinguishes itself from simple silence as the mere absence of words through the fact that, for its part, it is strikingly audible within a context of speech—as its very interruption—and indeed represents the maximum of a communication. It is an articulation of nonarticulation.

Fourth, the theory of the sublime is to a large extent a rhetoric and poetics of deception and illusion. With Longinus it inherits Gorgias's poetics of *apáte:*[15] the sublime figures of speech allow their own artificiality to appear as nature.[16] They disguise and outshine their content;[17] indeed they mislead to false conclusions (paralogisms).[18] They confuse the boundaries between production and reception[19] as well as those between representation and the real presence of what is represented.[20] Burke as well connects the sublime to deception and illusion: "No work of art can be great, but as it deceives."[21] Kant tries to get rid of this deceptive-illusionistic heritage of the sublime,[22] but with little unequivocal success: everywhere in Kant's text we continue to encounter figures of deception. Benjamin pursues Kant's strategy more consequently than Kant himself does. He opposes the sublime to all illusion and all semblance as their determinate negation: as the nakedness of the body on the one hand, as "truth" transcendent of consciousness on the other.

Fifth, for Longinus, the sublime was the highest degree of the beautiful rather than its opposite. Only in the eighteenth century, mainly in Burke and Kant, do the beautiful and the sublime tend to be regarded as two separate and virtually polar modes of the aesthetic, each of which has its own typical "objects." Benjamin, too, claims an "opposition" between the beautiful and the sublime, but he intertwines them so inextricably that neither is independent of the other. Instead, each work of art has to enact the conflict of both moments, and it is only the preponderance of one moment or the other that differs. The paradigm of such an irreducible interplay of two opposite powers is to be found neither in Longinus nor in Kant or Burke, but in Nietzsche's theory of art as offering various interplays of the Apollonian and the Dionysian. Also, Nietzsche's semantics of the two interplaying poles to a certain extent anticipate Benjamin's theory of the beautiful and the sublime. For already Nietzsche opposes to the semblance of the Apollonian its negation or destruction through a power of truth, which is "beyond all semblance."[23] But, contrary to Benjamin, the negation of semblance in the Nietzschean Dionysian is brought about not by the "fading" of life, but by its exuberance, and it is marked exactly by those features of intoxication, enthusiasm, and ecstatic dance that find their direct opposite in Benjamin's antimotionalist pathos of interruption, petrification, and sobriety.

Finally, the Kantian sublime is a mode of the "representation" of "totality" and "infinity."[24] Benjamin, by contrast, links the categories of "totality" and "unity" precisely with the ideological or "false" semblance of the beautiful. He diagnoses them already in his earliest writings as a "phenomenon of aesthetic reaction," in which "the classics" [die Klassik] sought to balance the "cutting consciousness" of torn unity and impossible totality in a momentary reconciliation, and he opposes to this the sublime as an instance of "singularity" (VI, 128) that rather has to do with the "particular" in its "solitariness" and finiteness (I, 184, 287; VI, 80).

Beautiful Mystery and Sublime Unveiling, Ambiguity, and Univocality

In order to be able to formulate an irreducible principle of the beautiful in the aesthetic-metaphysical terminology of semblance and essence, Benjamin breaks apart their dualism and hierarchy: the semblance of the beautiful is "not appearance," "not a veil for an other"—for example, for a "truth" becoming visible in it (I, 194, 195); it rather defines the essence of the beautiful itself and constitutes its irreducible mystery. Only a strictly antidecoding intuition or a similarly hermeneutic-critical reading may do justice to this structure of the beautiful, locked in upon itself:

> Thus, in relation to everything beautiful, the idea of unveiling turns into that of the impossibility of being unveiled. This is the ideal of the critique of art. (I, 195)

With this "idea" Benjamin not only complied with the contemporary search for an autochthonous essence of literature, its so-called literariness, he also anticipated the most recent theories of reading, which define reading essentially as the reading of an unreadability. All the more remarkable, then, that Benjamin did not leave the matter at that. Neither the mystery nor the impossibility of being unveiled has the last word. This last word rather goes to the sublime, in which the semblance of the beautiful together with its mystery gives way to an expressionless and veilless "being above all beauty." The theological model of sublime unveiling is the "revelation" that "undoes the mysteries" (I, 195); its physical model is the naked body, in which "the duality of nakedness and the veiled" (I, 196) is opposed to the unity of the veil and the veiled. By virtue of its mortality, no beautiful *physis* is "incapable of being unveiled": "death, like love, has the power to denude" (I, 197). For Benjamin, in love as well as in the "corpse," Goethe's "profound saying" that "beauty can never become lucid about itself"[25] reaches its limit at the same time that it is confirmed: for its unveiling, its becoming lucid about itself, succeeds only at the cost of its semblance and thus at the cost of itself.

The opposition between beauty's impossibility of being unveiled and a sublime unveiling has superimposed upon it a further opposition: to the "ambiguity" (I, 175) of myth as well as of beauty, their incapacity for lucidity about themselves, are opposed "univocality" (I, 162, 174), "clarity" (I, 177, 185), decidedness (I, 176), and self-lucidity. The verbally articulated resolution represents their common model. In it above all Benjamin sees a further dimension of the sublime: the "moral word" (I, 181). "For if anywhere," Benjamin writes, "then it is in resolution that the moral world shows itself illuminated by the spirit of language" (I,

176). A word of "decision" is moral not because it conveys moral max-
ims or even pleads for them, but rather because and to the extent that it
produces univocality, clarity, self-lucidity. Benjamin, it is well known,
criticizes the lack of this kind of "morality" in the muteness and death of
the beautiful Ottilie (I, 176). She could be moral as an adulteress as well
as a renouncer—if both were only an "object of communication," a "res-
olution" clearly uttered before others.[26] At least according to Benjamin,
it is all the same what she might have resolved upon; were it communi-
cated, her resolution would already be moral, precisely because it would
produce univocality, clarity, lucidity. On the other hand, "the inner" [das
Innere] of one who acts speechlessly could at best be brought to a "seem-
ing clarity" and would remain "in truth . . . obscure to himself no less
than to others" (I, 177). This variation of decisionism aims not, like Carl
Schmitt's version, at the foundation of order in general or at a theocratic-
representative form of the immediate exercise of power over others, but
rather solely at the reflexive moment of verbally articulated decision for
the deciding one himself: it aims, that is, at its retroactive effect upon the
agent's "inner" aspect, which thereby undergoes a clarification otherwise
unattainable.[27]

On this basis two further comparative determinations may be formu-
lated:

First, Kant writes: "Perhaps nothing more sublime has ever been said,
or a thought ever been expressed more sublimely, than in that inscription
above the temple of Isis (Mother Nature): 'I am all that is, that was, and
that will be, and no mortal has lifted my veil.'"[28] Similarly Schiller:
"Everything that is *veiled,* everything *mysterious,* . . . is . . . capable of
sublimity."[29] For Benjamin, on the other hand, it is precisely the pulling
aside of the veil that is the operation of the sublime.

Second, in Burke and Kant, and to some extent already in Longinus,
the semantics of the term sublime is associated with confusion, uncer-
tainty, indefiniteness, and lack of clarity. "A clear idea," Burke observes
laconically, "is therefore another name for a little idea."[30] Benjamin takes
another view, at least the early Benjamin: sublime is for him precisely the
bringing about of unequivocalness, clarity, and lucidity; sublime is the
"pure" and clear communication. However, if Benjamin propagates uni-
vocality, clarity, and decisiveness as imperatives, he only does so against
the background of an insight into some unsublatable moments of unde-
cidability (I, 156; II, 196, 203).[31]

Morality and Language

The *Wahlverwandtschaften* essay says that the expressionless has its "critical power . . . as the moral word" (I, 181). But what is the linguistic particularity of an expressionless word? First of all, it has nothing to do with the "immediate expression" (II, 141) that Benjamin sometimes called "magic" (II, 143), sometimes the "mimetic aspect" of language. For while the magic of language knows "no object . . . of communication" (II, 144), exactly the reverse goes for the moral "resolution," of which it is said that it cannot "come to life without linguistic form and, strictly speaking, without having become an object of communication" (I, 176). The resolution is expressionless because it "switches off" every magical immediacy of linguistic "expression" in favor of a nakedness of signifying and unequivocal communicating.[32]

The "moral word" is expressionless in yet a further respect that directly approximates it to silence. The clarity and univocality of utterance that Benjamin demands of a resolution are, according to him, at the same time impossible and indeed misplaced with regard to the resolution's possible motives. The word of "decision" not only is involved in the "undecidable aspect of morality" (I, 156), such that—whatever it may decide—it never decides anything about "morality." It is also the case that, despite all its clarity, it cannot prove its motives. It is instead always "transcendent" (I, 189) and cannot be established through cognition *(Erkenntnis)*. As forms of "action-determining knowledge *(Wissen)*" (VI, 48) Benjamin considered "conviction" [Überzeugung] and "hope" in particular. They share the feature of working "against the intention of cognition" (VI, 62). For as much as they admittedly "determine the agent," they nonetheless may not—Benjamin says—"motivate the action" (VI, 49). It is much more the case that they escape objectification as "motive" (VI, 48, 61) and cannot be established by any "argumentation" (VI, 61). Benjamin's philosophy of hope in the *Wahlverwandtschaften* essay, just as in the *Arcades Project,* lives directly from this positively appointed transcendence vis-à-vis cognition. Hope, like truth, thus itself implies a moment of "death," of mortification: a "death," that is, of the cognizing "intention" (I, 216).

The early text *Der Moralunterricht* defines this as a general structure of the "moral will": "it is 'free of motive,'" because the moral law wants to be obeyed not on the grounds of whatever motives but for its own sake and because furthermore "the empirical accomplishment of morality is never indicated in the moral norm" (II, 48). Therefore, the "process of moral education on principle resists every rationalization and schematization." This means at the same time the "renunciation of a theory of moral education deduced on scientific and scholarly *(wissenschaftliche)* grounds" (II, 49, 50). Instead of establishing its "bankruptcy," this renunciation, and the moment of "irrationalism" recognized as unsublatable in it, saves moral education from its "deepest danger," namely the danger of leading by way of the "motivation . . . of the pure will" to a "suppression of freedom" (II, 51). The argumentative limitation of the theory of morality is thus established altogether positively by Benjamin: "freedom" of the will and of action exist at all only insofar as they are free of motives, irrational, and rest upon transcendent decisions.

Already in Kant, practical philosophy maintained strained relations with the theoretical concept of cognition. Practical reason cannot argumentatively deduce its highest imperative, the moral law, but rather must decree it as an undeducible "fact of pure reason."[33] Benjamin took radically seriously this insolubility of practical, action-determining knowledge in cognition. Indeed, he considered it not as a danger, as pointing toward a lack, but rather as a proof of the knowledge's critical value. For thanks to its inaccessibility to and unavailability for intentionality, which features for Benjamin—as for some of his contemporaries—contained an opaque potential for resistance to a world of universal instrumentality, the action-determining knowledge is, Benjamin writes, "only expressionlessly, not expressly . . . determining" [nur ausdruckslos nicht ausdrücklich . . . bestimmen(d) (VI, 61)]. From this there follows for Benjamin a tendency toward remaining "mute," indeed, toward "silence" (VI, 62): "It is clear that this action-determining knowledge leads to silence. As such it is therefore not teachable" (VI, 49). The clear and univocal "moral word" of "decision" thus implies that the deeper it is grounded in a conviction that "determines the agent," the greater is the expressionlessness of that which "motivates the action" (VI, 49). On the one hand it transforms the "moral resolution" into an "object of communication" and is without semblance thanks to the "nakedness" of its intention of signification; on the other hand it refers to an action or decision-determining knowledge, which precisely withdraws from objectification and thus maintains "a constitutive relation . . . to silence" (VI, 64). This is its twofold expressionlessness.

Body

The body—as "expression of the sublime" (VI, 129)—shares with the moral word not only the semblanceless "nakedness" of its "communication" but also its unavailability to itself. The most direct mode of appearance of this is the body's visual inaccessibility to itself. "It is very significant," Benjamin writes,

> that our own bodies are in so many respects inaccessible to us. We cannot see our faces, our backs, nor our entire heads—in other words, the noblest parts of our bodies; we cannot lift ourselves up with our own hands, cannot embrace ourselves, and so on. We plunge into the world of perception feet first, as it were, not headfirst. (VI, 67)

In another fragment the inaccessibility of the body is formulated such that we can have a "perception" of its "shape" only insofar as we transform it into a symbolic "body" [Leib] that is no longer a "substratum" but rather "only a function . . . of our being" (VI, 79). This symbolic body, in contrast to the body otherwise designated with the word *Körper*, is always simultaneously "spirit and body." Both are, according to Benjamin,

> identical, only different in terms of perspective. The term "shape" *(Gestalt)* denotes the zone of their identity. The spiritual-bodily is in every stage of its existence the shape of the historical, spiritual-bodiliness, thus in some way the category of its "*Nu*," its nowness, its instantaneous appearance as at once transient and intransient. . . . Everything of himself of which man somehow has a perception of shape—the whole of his shape as well as his limbs and organs insofar as they appear to him as shaped—belongs to his symbolic body *(Leib)*. All boundaries that he sensuously perceives as belonging to himself likewise belong as shape to this symbolic body. It follows from this that the sensuously perceived individual existence of man is the perception of a relation in which he finds himself, but not the perception of a substratum, of a substance of himself such as the body *(Körper)* sensuously represents. (VI, 78, 79)

As the appearance of a shape in a *Nu*, a "nowness," Benjamin defines the spirit-body in strict analogy with the symbol (I, 342). The body *(Körper)*, on the other hand, is not always already the body of a soul or of a spirit. It is inaccessible to symbolic intention, and, Benjamin writes, "[T]he optical perception shows the body, if not unbounded, then nonetheless with wavering, shapeless boundaries. Thus in general one may say," Benjamin continues, "that insofar as we know of perception, we know of our body *(Körper)*, which in contrast to our symbolic body *(Leib)* extends without definite, shaped boundaries" (VI, 79). Our body is thus, philosophically considered, monstrous for self-perception. It disfigures every possible image of itself as a figured whole and to that extent is as imageless as the moral being of humanity. The body never achieves for direct self-perception the imaginary totality of a mirror image; it remains to a certain extent in a mirror stage without the mirror, incapable of an integrative appropriation of itself. It is only for this shapeless, virtually unbounded and visually inaccessible body that the category of "singularity" (VI, 81) is fitting, which for its part correlates with the sublime expressionless (VI, 128–29). The individual existence of the symbolic body *(Leib)*, on the other hand, is "only function" and the "perception of a relation in which it finds itself."

This leads to a ninth comparative assertion: With the description of the body as something shapeless and virtually unbounded, Benjamin reactualizes a canonical Kantian definition of the sublime. For Kant, "[T]he beautiful . . . concerns the form of the object, which consists in [the object's] being bounded. But the sublime can also be found in a formless object, insofar as we present *unboundedness* in it."[34] Surprisingly, Benjamin discovers these characteristics in an "object" that Kant regarded as neither formless and unbounded nor sublime: in the body as "expression of the sublime" (VI, 129). As great as is Benjamin's proximity to Kant's relevant definition, its extension and employment by him are radically novel.

Precisely by virtue of its antisymbolic shapelessness, its unboundedness, its unavailability, singularity, and "solitude," Benjamin calls the body *(Körper)* "a moral instrument" (VI, 82). On the one hand, this definition reflects the fact that what Benjamin calls the "verbal structure" of "morality" (VI, 48) is being described with the same or at least similar categories. On the other hand, it refers once again to the cardinal motif of the corpse as the flowing away of life and beautiful semblance from the dead "body *(Körper)* . . . that steps denuded before God" (I, 197). It is to this antisymbolic and semblanceless body that Benjamin links, in a privileged way, "hope" as a "moral phenomenon": "the symbolically-bodily *(leibliche)* nature moves toward its dissolution, the bodily *(körperliche)* toward its resurrection" (VI, 80).

Benjamin's reflections on the body have in the field of the sublime a double effect: on the one hand they conflict with a directly metaphysical investment in the sublime; on the other hand they nonetheless lead to charging the body itself with an allegorical meaning. However, except for the dismembered bodies and corpses in the scenarios of the baroque *Trauerspiel*, Benjamin avoids designating the nonsymbolic body positively as allegorical. Yet his "theory" of the body participates clearly enough in that "leaping over" from the sorrowful, death-subjected, fragmented temporality "of human existence" (I, 343) into an "awakening in God's world" that makes allegorical "transience" itself again readable as an allegory, and indeed in Quintilian's[35] sense as an allegorical inversion of itself: "as the allegory of resurrection" (I, 405). In Benjamin the naked body's lack of all semblance is an allegory of that protest, that caesura, whose nondialectical simultaneity of destruction and salvation, annihilation and reconciliation (I, 184), bears the as it were blind name of the "expressionless."

The Beauty of Color

In Benjamin's thought, the critique of the beautiful through the sublime undergoes a significant exception. This is the beauty of color and indeed of children's colors. To the creating, shaping power of art (VII, 20) Benjamin contrasts these colors as a medium of "deshaping" [Entstaltung], as a "dissolving play" (VI, 114, 115). In them "contours [are] everywhere effaced in a rainbowlike play . . . soap bubbles, tea games, the moist colorfulness of magic lanterns, painting in watercolors, transfer pictures. The color is always as hazy and dissolving as possible. . . . Woolly sometimes, like the many-colored wool used in needlework" (VII, 25). By virtue of this woolly, cloudy, rainbowlike dissolution of contours, color represents the "purest expression" (VII, 22) of fantasy—of fantasy, that is, as a faculty of "deshaping" or disfiguring. With this definition, Benjamin also places fantasy in opposition to the realm of "shape," to the shaped unity of spirit and body *(Leib)*. And next to the category of shapelessness is assigned that of expressionlessness as well. To the extent that in the colors of fantasy "a being appears without being the expression of something inner," they constitute "expressionlessly signifying appearance" (VI, 71). The general connection of the expressionless to the category of singularity recurs as well in the realm of color: in color Benjamin sees a "rejection of every synthetic principle" and the tendency toward "the most intense separation" (VI, 125).

Benjamin formulated the essential characteristics of colorful and all analogous deshaping in a fragment on "phantasy":

> Phantasy's deshaping of creations distinguishes itself from all destructive decay of the empirical through two aspects: it is, first of all, uncoerced, comes from within, is free and thus painless, indeed, is lightly beatifying; and secondly, it never leads to death but rather eternalizes the decline that it performs in an endless series of transitions. As for the first of these aspects, it means that to the subjective conception of phantasy through pure reception there corresponds the objective realm of its deshaping as a world of painless birth. All deshaping of the world will thus phantasize in its meaning a world without pain that nonetheless would have the richest sense of eventfulness flowing through it. This deshaping further indicates—as the second aspect shows—the world conceived in endless dissolution, which means, however, in eternal transience. It is as it were the sunset behind the abandoned stage of the world with its deciphered ruins. It is the endless dissolution of the cleansed beautiful semblance, that is, of the beautiful semblance discharged of all its seduction. (VI, 115)

With the last sentences even Benjamin's theory of fantasy appears to add up to the unavoidable ruins, the transience, and the dissolution of beautiful semblance. The preceding sentences, however, mark a sharp difference from the expressionless petrification in the *Wahlverwandtschaften* essay or the allegorical representation of transience in the *Trauerspiel* book. The deshaping that displays the world of fantasy as grasped in dissolution does not befall it as a "violence" of protest and of mortification, but rather occurs "uncoerced," "painlessly" from within. The beautiful semblance of fantasy feels itself in nonviolent "dissolution" from within, and not because of the intervention of a power that stands "in opposition" to it. While the model for the latter is death, "phantasy's deshaping . . . never leads to death." It is "lightly beatifying," a "world of painless birth" precisely in its dissolving play. In this it represents a "memory of paradise"—just as Benjamin frequently mentions the "light" of paradise in this connection (VI, 116, 120, 121, 125).

The sublime, however, is, at least in aesthetics, a category of the fallen

world, the world driven from paradise. Only because we are so pro-
foundly fallen do we need to raise ourselves up, to sub-limate ourselves at
all. This accounts for the exemplary sublimity precisely of Satan and the
fallen world in Milton's *Paradise Lost* as well as for Hegel's sentence:
"Precisely this is the grandeur of man, to eat amid the sweat of the
brow."[36] For happiness provides no aesthetic of the sublime, which is
always bound up with effort, negativity, and resistance to be overcome.
Paradise was beautiful and not sublime. Thus the sublime, even as a
"critical power," is out of a job as soon as a beauty is at stake that
reminds Benjamin of paradise as well as of Elysium and the Seraphim
(VI, 120, 121). Power and violence in general give way to the "light" of
this beauty. To the ideal of salvation through "critical power," this beauty
opposes that of nonviolent "blissfulness" (cf. VI, 99). Benjamin's critique
of the beautiful through the sublime has its counterpart in his interpreta-
tion of fantasy and children's color as a critique of the sublime through
the beautiful.

Translated by Timothy Bahti and David C. Hensley. Original language ver-
sion copyright © 1992 by Winfried Menninghaus.

NOTES

1. Friedrich Schiller, "Über Anmuth und Würde," in *Schillers Werke,* Na-
tionalausgabe, ed. Benno v. Wiese (Weimar: Böhlaus Nachfolger, 1962), 20:274.
2. Immanuel Kant, *Critique of Judgment,* trans. Werner S. Pluhar (Indi-
anapolis: Hackett Publishing Company, 1987), 135.
3. Cf. Kant, *Critique of Judgment,* 81.
4. Cf. Gary Smith, "Walter Benjamin's Idea of Beauty," Ph.D. diss., Boston
University, 1989.
5. Schiller, "Über Anmuth und Würde," 287.
6. Schiller, "Über Anmuth und Würde," 287.
7. I do not here go into the third determination, that of the "falling star" and
"hope."
8. Johann Wolfgang von Goethe, *Die Wahlverwandtschaften,* in *Goethes*
Werke, Hamburger Ausgabe, ed. Erich Trunz, 10th ed. (Munich: C. H. Beck,
1981), 6:407.
9. Edmund Burke, *A Philosophical Enquiry into the Origin of Our Ideas of*
the Sublime and Beautiful, ed. J. T. Boulton (London: Routledge and Kegan Paul,
1958), 39.
10. Kant, *Critique of Judgment,* 98.

11. Burke, *Philosophical Enquiry,* 59.

12. Cf. Longinus, *On the Sublime,* in Aristotle, *The Poetics,* Longinus, *On the Sublime,* Demetrius, *On Style,* Loeb Classical Library (London: W. Heinemann, 1927), 15, 11; 17, 2, 3; 30, 1.

13. Longinus had already discovered that both could cross over into one another. The great volcanic explosions are "fire of the heavens that nonetheless often plunges into the dark" (35, 4). And just as the light of the sun blinds and allows nothing more to be seen, it is precisely the splendor of sublime figures of speech that leaves them "no longer visible" but rather "overshadows their artificial arrangement and keeps them hidden beneath a veil" (17, 2, 3; author's translations).

14. G. W. F. Hegel, *Vorlesungen über die Ästhetik I,* in *Werke* (Frankfurt am Main: Suhrkamp, 1969–), 13:467.

15. On this, cf. Max Pohlenz, "Die Anfänge der griechischen Poetik," in *Kleine Schriften,* ed. Heinrich Dörrie (Hildesheim: Olms, 1965), 2:436–72.

16. Longinus, *On the Sublime,* 17, 2, 3; 22, 1.

17. Longinus, *On the Sublime,* 15, 11.

18. Longinus, *On the Sublime,* 18, 2.

19. Longinus, *On the Sublime,* 7.

20. Longinus, *On the Sublime,* 15, 1.

21. Burke, *Philosophical Enquiry,* 76.

22. Cf. Kant, *Critique of Judgment,* 197.

23. Cf. Friedrich Nietzsche, *Die Geburt der Tragödie,* in *Sämtliche Werke,* Kritische Studienausgabe (Munich: Deutscher Taschenbuchverlag, 1980), 1:38, 39, 51, 104, 141.

24. Nietzsche, *Die Geburt der Tragödie,* 254–55.

25. "Die Schönheit kann nie über sich selbst deutlich werden" (*Goethes Werke,* 12:468).

26. The category of the resolution is, like several others in Benjamin's interpretation, drawn from the novel itself, and indeed specifically from Ottilie's representation and her own discourse. In chapter 9 of book 2 of the work, it first reads: "But she was altogether decided for herself, never to belong to another" (*Die Wahlverwandtschaften,* 6:425). This decision to want to belong to no one other than Eduard leaves the "actual" question of decision regarding Eduard itself still altogether open. Ironically enough, the narrator entangles his main character in a commonplace and in a condition of impossibility: "She wished only happiness for her friend, she believed herself capable of renouncing him, even of never seeing him again, if she only knew him to be happy." Disregarding the conspicuous altruism of her wish and the dubious belief in her capabilities, the if-clause immediately relieves itself of any serious testing, for Eduard is unambiguous, if anywhere, at least in his precisely *not* being able to be "known happy" without Ottilie. But to Charlotte, then, Ottilie altogether intensifies her condi-

tioned inner decision into the clear linguistic communication demanded by Benjamin: "I am resolved, and how I was, and to what I am resolved, you must also learn. I will never be Eduard's!" (463) This utterance of decision nonetheless—and thus it does not refute Benjamin's critique—is retransformed into mute nonunivocality in a twofold manner. First and above all through being struck dumb vis-à-vis Eduard: instead of clear information about his vain hopes he receives an imploring gesture of defense, the heartrending nature of which testifies to Ottilie's by-no-means-conquered inclination at least as much as to her will to renunciation. In her writing to the friend—"finally a resolution seemed to ripen in her," it says just beforehand (476)—Ottilie then transforms her earlier resolution as well into a preterit to which no fulfillment was assigned: "Altogether pure *was* my plan to renounce Eduard" (emphasis added); through the meeting with him, however, everything "became otherwise." Not only is the resolution retroactively weakened into a mere "plan" and its "purity" into a past and failed one, now no longer valid. It is also already for the past transformed into an "impure" and highly conditioned one, for it now appears to have been bound to the condition "of not meeting him again." In the place of this former resolution that really was not one at all, Ottilie's writing puts not a new one, but rather the refusal of further words: "[N]ow I have nothing more to say" (477).

27. For a comparative definition of Benjamin's version of decisionism, cf. Norbert Bolz, *Auszug aus der entzauberten Welt: Philosophischer Extremismus zwischen den Weltkriegen* (Munich: Fink, 1989) 47–95, esp. 85–94.

28. Kant, *Critique of Judgment,* 185.

29. Schiller, "Vom Erhabenen," in *Schillers Werke,* 20:191.

30. Burke, *Philosophical Enquiry,* 63.

31. On this cf. Jacques Derrida, "Force de Loi: Le 'Fondement mystique de l'Autorité'/Force of Law: The 'Mystical Foundation of Authority,'" *Cardozo Law Review,* 11 (1990): 1030–35.

32. Cf. II, 957 and Gershom Scholem, *Walter Benjamin-die Geschichte einer Freundschaft* (Frankfurt am Main: Suhrkamp, 1975), 258–59.

33. Kant, *Kritik der praktischen Vernunft,* in *Kants gesammelte Schriften,* ed. Königlich Preußische Akademie der Wissenschaften (Berlin: Reimer, 1913), 5:47.

34. Kant, *Critique of Judgment,* 98.

35. Quintilian, *Institutio Oratoria,* VII 6, 44.

36. G. W. F. Hegel, *Vorlesungen über die Philosophie der Religion,* in *Werke* (Frankfurt am Main: Suhrkamp, 1969–), 17:77.

Chapter 10

In Citing Violence: Gestus in Benjamin, Brecht, and Kafka

Patricia Anne Simpson

Gestus . . . die Art, wie man sich trägt oder hält; die körperliche Stellung, Bewegung oder Gebärde eines Redners, bes. die Handbewegung.
[*Gestus:* The way one carries or holds oneself; the physical position, movement, or bearing, gesture of a speaker, esp. the movement of the hand.]
—Dr. Joh[ann] Christ[ian] Aug[ust]

Secular and sacred texts are sources of citation, with the double meaning the word implies. Citation intends to invoke authority, both textual and judicial, as an entering into language and linguistic circulation, or as a summons before the court. In the triangular constellation of Benjamin, Brecht, and Kafka, citation specifically calls into question both metaphysics and Marxism, the relationship between the text and the Law or Doctrine. Benjamin, poised in the delicate balance between metaphysics and materialism, between Kafka and Brecht, relies on the significative force of the citable *Gestus* for mediation between the two, even if the mediation turns out to be a disjuncture that cannot be bridged. In the spirit of Brecht's epic theater, the role of theater aligns with the Marxist injunction to change the world; in Benjamin's essay on Kafka, we hear the variation of this citation at the end of the section "The Little Hunchback" (Das bucklicht Männlein) in the example of a great rabbi who says of the Messiah ". . . that he did not wish to change the world by force, but would only make a slight adjustment in it" [daß er nicht mit Gewalt die Welt verändern wolle, sondern nur um ein Geringes sie zurechtstellen werde (II, 432)].[1] There are, then, similarities between Brecht's materialism and Kafka's mysticism that Benjamin mediates, although the avoidance of violence belongs to the realm of his "messianic" politics.[2] These two positions reflect the tension in his own work between ideology and theology, for his readings of Brecht and Kafka place Benjamin in a double, biographical bind.[3]

There are clear differences in Benjamin's relationship to Brecht and Kafka respectively. Brecht occupies a position of both direct influence and interference, according to some. Asja Lacis introduced Benjamin to Brecht and his Marxism.[4] Kafka occupies another space altogether, although the Kafka essay remains a point of connection between Benjamin and Gershom Scholem, as well as Benjamin and Adorno and by extension the Institute for Social Research. Yet several of Benjamin's contemporaries despaired of the friendship between Benjamin and Brecht. As Hannah Arendt points out in her introduction to *Illuminations,* the reasons for this dismay lie in the "undialectic usage of Marxian categories and [Benjamin's] determined break with all metaphysics" (15).[5] Brecht's "plumpes Denken," or "crude thinking," was necessary for thought to be translated into action. Arendt quotes Benjamin in her introduction: "[A] thought must be crude to come into its own in action" (*Illuminations,* 15). Further, Gershom Scholem called Brecht's influence "baleful, and in some respects disastrous."[6] Adorno's student (and one editor of the standard Benjamin edition) Rolf Tiedemann believes the relationship should be understood less in intellectual than psychological terms: that Benjamin was afraid of Brecht.[7] Adorno himself questions Brecht's influence on Benjamin, especially in the latter's reading of Kafka. Again, Adorno's objections rely on the operation of the dialectic, with an undialectical, crudely thinking Brecht hovering in the background: Adorno sets up two models of interpretation that oppose "illumination" with "dialectic."[8] On one point there was consensus: "Especially baleful, they all agreed, was Benjamin's acceptance of Brecht's crude, even vulgar, materialism."[9] Here vulgar materialism can be understood as the failure of dialectical thought. Yet it seems that the critics rely precisely on the means of analysis they criticize. Adorno uses the gesture as an arrested dialectical moment, figured by the visualization (or phenomenalization) of the narrative text. The reading of images in Kafka effectively transforms allegory (with the implicit abstract referent) into symbol, attributing motivated meaning where none necessarily exists.[10] Whereas the dialectic relies on the totalizing capacity of symbolic discourse, allegory, in the form of parable in both Brecht and Kafka, operates according to principles of radical discontinuity.[11] Thus crude thinking allows Benjamin to read Brecht and Kafka allegorically and in the same light, according to gestus, but with attention to the use of "daily" speech. This form of cognition is specifically associated with a certain type of language, as Arendt remarks: "Well, what attracted Benjamin to crude thinking was probably not so much a referral to practice as to reality, and to him this reality manifested itself most directly in the proverbs and idioms of everyday language" (*Illuminations*, 15). This observation is common to Brecht and Kafka. Brecht plays with the literalization of figurative language; Kafka takes proverbs and idioms of everyday speech literally.[12] What, then, is the relationship between gestus and language in its literal and figurative modes?

One thing is immediately clear: the central place of gestus in Benjamin's work on Kafka and Brecht indicates more than a biographical instance of influence or a psychological relationship between Brecht and Benjamin. While Brecht praises Kafka as a "true Bolshevist writer" (II, 1155), he elsewhere expresses (through Benjamin's indirect citation) a disparaging view of Kafka's and by extension, Benjamin's "Jewish fascism," which can be traced precisely to the cloudy, obscure use of allegory from which his own dramaturgical work derives its considerable force.

My Kafka essay, for example—it was concerned with Kafka merely from the phenomenal point of view, Brecht said—took the work as something that had grown by itself—the man, too—severed all its connections—even that with its author. It was always the question of *essence* that finally interested me, said Brecht. (*Reflections*, 207)[13]

[Mein Kafkaaufsatz zum Beispiel—er beschäftige sich mit Kafka lediglich von der phänomenalen Seite—nehme das Werk als etwas für sich Gewachsenes—den Mann auch—löse es aus allen Zusammenhängen—ja sogar aus dem mit dem Verfasser. Es sei eben wieder die Frage nach dem *Wesen*, auf die es bei mir herauskomme. (II, 1164)]

Brecht, as reported by Benjamin, sets up an opposition between the phenomenal and the essential. Benjamin's concern with "essence" would have to be related dialectically to the phenomena (Brecht, for example, highlights Kafka's life as a city dweller [*Reflections*, 208–9]) to clarify the author and determine what he is and does—in other words, Brecht contextualizes Kafka in his material surroundings. In another discussion, Brecht sharpens the critique. Benjamin reports:

The day before yesterday we had a long and heated debate on my Kafka. Its basis: the charge that it advanced Jewish fascism. It increased and propagated the obscurity surrounding this author instead of dispersing it. Whereas it was of crucial importance to clarify Kafka, that is, to formulate practicable proposals that can be derived from his stories. (*Reflections,* 208)

[Vorgestern (i.e. am 29. August) eine lange und erregte Debatte über meinen Kafka. Ihr Fundament: die Anschuldigung, daß er dem jüdischen Faschismus Vorschub leiste. Er vermehre und breite das Dunkel um diese Figur aus statt es zu zerteilen. Demgegenüber komme alles darauf an, Kafka zu lichten, das heißt, die praktikablen Vorschläge zu formulieren, welche sich seinen Geschichten entnehmen ließen. (II, 1165)]

Brecht's strange formulation about the dark spots in Kafka and Benjamin respectively sets up a marked contrast between the "Jewish fascism" associated with darkness, and the Marxist light of formulating practicable proposals from the stories. Benjamin faces the tenets of Marxist criticism in Brecht's comments: the connection between literature and social context, the reliance upon clear illustration of difficult passages, and the practical program for political progress. The implicit goal of this critique would amount to asking Kafka to be more like Brecht. How, under these conditions of criticism, does Benjamin bring together textual elements of Brecht and Kafka?

The gestus provides the common ground. Benjamin's own theory of gestus as citation corresponds to Brecht's practice of epic theater, the point of which is precisely to politicize the stage and the audience by changing thought patterns. In contrast, the cloud of Kafka's parables is the source of exemplary failure, the unreadable in his work that prompted him, in his testament, to have the manuscripts destroyed. Benjamin offers this failure of understanding and intelligibility as an explanation of Kafka's testament. Benjamin writes:

Kafka could understand things only in the form of a *gestus,* and this *gestus* which he did not understand constitutes the cloudy part of the parables. Kafka's writings emanate from it. The way he withheld them is well known. His testament orders their destruction. . . . He did fail in his grandiose attempt to convert poetry into doctrine, to turn it into a parable and restore to it that stability and unpretentiousness which, in the face of reason, seemed to him to be the only appropriate thing for it. (*Illuminations*, 129)

[Etwas war immer nur im Gestus für Kafka faßbar. Und dieser Gestus, den er nicht verstand, bildet die wolkige Stelle der Parabeln. Aus ihm geht Kafkas Dichtung hervor. Es ist bekannt, wie er mit ihr zurück-hielt. Sein Testament befiehlt sie der Vernichtung an. . . . Gescheitert ist sein großartiger Versuch, die Dichtung in die Lehre zu überführen und als Parabel ihr die Haltbarkeit und die Unscheinbarkeit zurück-zugeben, die im Angesicht der Vernunft ihm als die einzig geziemende erschienen ist. (II, 427–28)]

There is a veiled response to Brecht in this excerpt; where Kafka fails, Brecht succeeds (at least theoretically) in converting literature into doc-trine. The gestus, then, figures the locus of unreadability in Kafka's work. Yet for Brecht's epic theater, it marks precisely the place of intelligibility, of citationality, and of a persuasion that thinks into the heads of the audi-ence.[14] How can the gestus be central to both Brecht and Kafka in Ben-jamin's estimation? Why does epic theater reach the "real" world Kafka could not see? And why does it signify that Kafka's world amounts to a "world theater" (*Illuminations*; II, 422; 124)?

Benjamin specifies this meaning of gestus in Kafka in relation to the world of facts:

Max Brod has said: "The world of those realities that were important for him was invisible." What Kafka could see least of all was the *ges-tus*. (*Illuminations*, 121)

[Wenn Max Brod sagt: "Unabsehbar war die Welt der für ihn wichti-gen Tatsachen," so war für Kafka sicher am unabsehbarsten der Ges-tus. (II, 419)]

In this context, the place of translation is crucial. The failure of transla-tion is inscribed in the task itself. It is impossible, as we learn from essays on Benjamin's theory of translation, to acknowledge the materiality of signifiers when moving them across linguistic borders.[15] This difficulty becomes evident in the translations of *Gestus* in Benjamin's essays on Brecht and Kafka. Where Benjamin uses *Gestus* in the essay on Brecht, Harry Zohn translates with "gesture" (*Illuminations*, 151).[16] However, when Benjamin uses the same signifier in the essay on Kafka, Zohn retains the foreign borrowing: *gestus*. The task of translation from one medium of expression to another is precisely the issue. *Unabsehbar* is conventionally translated as "limitless," "boundless," and perhaps, in that sense, "invisible." But the signifier also carries the meaning of its opposite: *absehen,* to look away from: *unabsehbar* would then literally be that from which you cannot turn away, but which is boundless, immense, incalculable, like the Kantian sublime. It is that which you cannot see, but from which you cannot look away. I would like to offer another translation: "When Max Brod says, 'For him, the world of important facts was immense, incalculable,' then that which was most boundless, from which Kafka could least turn away, was the gestus." The gestus for Kafka figures the cloudy place beyond signification: it marks the unreadable place in his work, and is, in this sense, "invisible." Benjamin goes on to specify his meaning:

> Each gesture is an event—one might even say, a drama—in itself. The stage on which this drama takes place is the World Theater which opens up toward heaven. On the other hand, this heaven is only background; to explore it according to its own laws would be like framing the painted backdrop of the stage and hanging it in a picture gallery. (*Illuminations,* 121)

> [Jeder *(Gestus)* ist ein Vorgang, ja man könnte sagen ein Drama, für sich. Die Bühne, auf der dieses Drama sich abspielt, ist das Welttheater, dessen Prospekt der Himmel darstellt. Andererseits ist dieser Himmel nur Hintergrund; nach seinem eigenen Gesetz ihn zu durchforschen, hieße den gemalten Hintergrund der Bühne gerahmt in eine Bildergalerie hängen. (II, 419)]

The English translation erases the persistence of the theatrical metaphor of the sky: *Prospekt* is not only perspective view, but also, in the technical language of the stage, the backcloth that represents the heavens. The metaphor of the world theater, the stage of gestus, is both backcloth and background: "Hintergrund," a strange designation, the heavens as both sky and ground. To ask for the law of the divine background is like the act of framing a prop, limiting and marking that which is unknowable. Can we, like the subject of Kant's *Critique of Judgment,* just frame a piece of the limitless and rely on the negative capacity of the imagination to totalize the rest?[17] The blind spot of our understanding of divine law is passed on to and through the gestus. Gestus, then, for Benjamin reading Kafka, becomes a deconstructive metaphor for the inability to cognize that which we cannot see as a totality. He reinforces this conclusion when he suggests that Kafka writes a complement to a world whose shape he cannot know.[18]

Adorno read this passage as evidence of Brecht's influence: in a letter to Benjamin from 17 December 1934, he complains about the metaphor of the theater and suggests the place to look for the gesture is in modernity, in the "Absterben der Sprache" (II, 1177):

> In Kafkaesque gestures the creature for whom the words have been taken from the things is born and set free . . . and the only thing I think is foreign to the work is the bringing in of categories from epic theater.

> [In den Kafkaschen Gesten entbindet sich die Kreatur, der die Worte von den Dingen genommen worden sind . . . und das einzige, was mir an der Arbeit materialfremd dünkt ist die Hereinnahme von Kategorien des epischen Theaters. (II, 1177)]

Adorno recognizes the silence in Kafka's prose; the birth of a creature for the model of signification, in which the words are taken away from the things, has shifted. This, he argues, is the crux of Kafka's work, not the gestural aspects of the theater Benjamin introduces, presumably, "under the influence" of Brecht. The loss of language's capacity to refer to things signals Adorno's modernity: for Benjamin, this loss is supplemented by gestus, both as body language and as allegory. For Kafka's parables and Brecht's fables intersect at the point of linguistic displacement: of materiality of signifiers inscribed without necessary reference. The reliance on the tropological operation of allegory, the ability to sign without referent, to abstract without the concrete, is resolved in the gesture of gestus. For, as Benjamin wrote about Kafka: "In other words, everything he describes makes assertions about something other than itself" [Mit anderen Worten, alles, was er beschreibt, macht Aussagen über etwas anderes als sich selbst (II, 678; II, 1204, here; in the diary entry, the sentence ends with "selber")].

Handhabe, die: Möglichkeit, Anlaß zum Handeln, zum Einschreiten [the possibility or motivation to act, to intervene]

handhaben: a) <etwas h.> *richtig gebrauchen:* eine Waffe, ein Instrument h.; das Gerät ist leicht zu h. [to use something correctly: to manipulate a weapon, an instrument; the machine is easy to operate]

—*Duden*

The resolution of the gesture of thought, the dialectic at work, is figured by the persistent use of the verb *handhaben* with various objects. The gesture is something you have in your hand; and it is given in the form of citation.[19] One formulation recurs in Benjamin's readings of Brecht and Kafka. In both Brecht's theoretical work and Benjamin's reading of it, the dialectic is at a standstill. If, as Scholem and Adorno suggest, Benjamin derives his vulgar Marxism from Brecht, then that vulgarity must be defined simultaneously as the failure and the success of dialectical thought. There are echoes of Hegel's reading of his contemporary Solger, in which the former accuses the latter of undialectical thought: Solger's dialogues, according to Hegel, never progressed to the dialectic. They remained trapped in the subjective mysticism Hegel and Hotho opposed.[20] What is it about the theory of gestus as undialectical, undigested thought in Benjamin that elicits a similar response from his contemporaries? One articulation is repeatedly cited: one must have the dialectic "at hand" [die Dialektik handhaben]. Benjamin applies the same operative verb to Kafka's parables (II, 420–22), the meaning of which lies "on the palm of his hand" [auf der flachen Hand liegt] (*Illuminations,* 122; II, 420). And again, the point is to have something at hand: "One must keep in mind Kafka's way of reading as exemplified in his interpretation of the above-mentioned parable" (*Illuminations,* 124) [Man muß sich Kafkas Eigenart zu lesen vor Augen halten, wie er sie in der Auslegung der genannten Parabel handhabt" (II, 422)]. Further, Benjamin asserts, the parables unfold, not as a paper ship to a blank page, but as buds to blossoms:

> This does not mean that his prose pieces belong entirely in the tradition of Western prose forms; they have, rather, a similar relationship to doctrine as Haggadah does to the Halakah. They are not parables, and yet they do not want to be taken at their face value; they lend themselves to quotation and can be told for purposes of clarification. (*Illuminations,* 122)

[Das hindert nicht, daß seine Stücke nicht gänzlich in die Prosaformen des Abendlandes eingehen und zur Lehre ähnlich wie die Haggadah zur Halacha stehen. Sie sind nicht Gleichnisse und wollen doch auch nicht für sich genommen sein; sie sind derart beschaffen, daß man sie zitieren, zur Erläuterung erzählen kann. (II, 420)]

Benjamin specifies his understanding of the parables by comparing their mode of representation to the relationship between "Haggadah," which in Hebrew means "that which is narrated," and "Halaka," the law code.[21] Yet, Benjamin continues in a sublime mode, Kafka offers us interpretations of a text that does not exist. Benjamin explains Kafka's use of allegory in terms of a Jewish tradition of interpreting texts, but elsewhere, he distinguishes between the two in rhetorical terms:

While the doctrine in Kafka's pieces appears in the form of the parable, their symbolic content is expressed in the gesture. The actual antinomy of Kafka's work lies locked up in the relationship between fable and symbol.

[Während der Lehrgehalt von Kafkas Stücken in der Form der Parabel zum Vorschein kommt, bekundet ihr symbolischer Gehalt sich im Gestus. Die eigentliche Antinomie von Kafkas Werk liegt im Verhältnis von Gleichnis und Symbol beschlossen. (II, 1255)]

Benjamin's own debt to two traditions is carried here as well. What is the rhetorical relationship between allegory, symbol, and the transmissibility of thought? What is the nature of a comparison that is not something other, yet not just itself, but designed for citation? In other words, something similar is happening in this reading of rhetoric capable of passing from a tropological model of language to a performative.[22] If doctrine is made available to cognition through allegory (parables, examples), why is the gestural symbol required? What "knowledge" does it convey? For if the symbolic content is expressed in the gestus, then it is a dialectical instrument that implies a partial relationship to a totality. And precisely that totality is questioned in the use of allegory. If this is so, then the use of the gestus constitutes a dialectical gesture of recuperation. This relationship is crucial to an understanding of the place of Benjamin between Brecht and Kafka.

I will suggest what it means to "employ" the dialectic through a reading of references to Benjamin's essays on Brecht, then of Brecht's theoretical work, specifically *Der Messingkauf* and the essay "Die Dialektik auf dem Theater," and finally, of Benjamin's "Franz Kafka."[23] In Brecht's stage, the burden of deferral is shifted from the spoken word to the gesture and ultimately to *Schrift*. In Kafka's work, the deferral to oral narration signals a capitulation to meaning for the sake of transmissibility.[24] The gesture is the vehicle for both; its dialectical stillness is crucial to both. Benjamin's understanding of Brecht's work on citationality and its relationship to gestus is projected onto Kafka's prose, which earns Adorno's critical reproach. At the center of the issue is the pedagogical potential of reading, of the stage or of the page, which Brecht advocates as essential to art, but which he himself finds missing in Kafka. The two superstructural realms of reference are a concept of the law and a theory of history: the stakes in this debate are high.

In his dramaturgical deliberations, Brecht retreats from his own theory of epic theater to accommodate the practice of performance; this retreat, though it is evident throughout his work, is focused in the essay "Die Dialektik auf dem Theater." This essay, in which Brecht revises the "too formal" designation of epic theater to one of a dialectic of performance, is underestimated in criticism. His radical revision of the stage, his theory of epic theater, remains firmly in the foreground of Brecht interpretation, though Brecht himself displaces the model with the dialectic. A consideration of the relationship between the dialectic in motion and the dialectic in a frozen frame is figured by the gestus, which derives its considerable authority from quotation. The violent interruption that forces the literarization of the figurality of the stage points to a theory of performance that foregrounds the gestus as an aspect of performance. The rhetoric of gestus is finally the means of persuasion that in Brecht connects the performance to the politics of spectacle; in Kafka, it marks the unreadability of the parables. The political poetics of Brecht's dramaturgy rests on the dialectical relationship of the street and the stage: he brings the street into the theater in order to stage politics in the street. The stage incites the violence required for the revolution, echoing Benjamin's essay "Zur Kritik der Gewalt" (Critique of violence) in which he reserves the right to strike for organized labor (*Reflections*, 281). In order to "mobilize" the audience, a persuasion must take place. How does Brecht recognize the disjuncture between the performance and the politics of persuasion and thereby (he hopes) exceed the boundaries of representation? The answer lies in the enacted theory of cognition at work in his dramaturgy.

The political deliberations at work in Brecht's plays and Benjamin's commentary point to the larger problem of the place of the theater in the history of philosophy. In a variety of textual sites, Brecht posits the stage as the proper place of philosophy and politics, suggesting a larger contextual relationship between aesthetics and ethics. At this point, the dialectical moment of the performative *Aufhebung* constitutes an incision into the temporal continuum of the performance, crucial to the understanding of setting the dialectic "at rest" and "in motion." What does it mean for the body to interpret the consciousness of the performing actor? Gestus itself extends the corporeal interpretation of language to a generalized notion of performance. The gesture becomes the visible, external sign of the words it accompanies. Put differently, the gesture functions as a kind of literalization of the figurality of the text. The body must be read. There is, however, a degree of slippage between the versions of Benjamin's interpretation of the Brechtian concept and practice. This slippage warrants further examination.

In "From the Brecht commentary" (*Understanding Brecht,* 21f.) [Kommentare zu Werken von Brecht], Benjamin writes of Brecht's own dictum, "Gesten zitierbar zu machen" (II, 507). He adds with regard to Brecht's Keuner and Fatzer:

In each case what is quotable is not just the attitude but also the words which accompany it. These words, like gestures, must be practised, which is to say first noticed and later understood. They have their pedagogical effect first, their political effect second and their poetic effect last of all. (*Understanding Brecht,* 28)

[(W)as an ihnen zitierbar ist, das ist nicht nur Haltung, genauso sind es die Worte, die sie begleiten. Auch diese Worte wollen geübt, das heißt erst gemerkt, später verstanden sein. Ihre pädagogische Wirkung haben sie zuerst, ihre politische sodann, ihre poetische ganz zuletzt. (II, 507)]

The citationality of the text is here crucial to an understanding of its mediating function. Words "want" to be practiced, a statement that Benjamin glosses with a sequential priority: first internalized, later understood. Similarly he assigns a priority to the process of mediation by citation: words have three functions, a pedagogical, a political, and a poetic, in that order.

In "What Is Epic Theater?" [Was ist das epische Theater? (1)] Benjamin, in an act of self-citation with incremental repetition, alters and specifies the location of the citable gesture. This phase of his own work is itself marked by citation, his of Brecht:

> "The actor must show an event, and he must show himself. He naturally shows the event by showing himself, and he shows himself by showing the event. Although these two tasks coincide, they must not coincide to such a point that the contrast (difference) between them disappears." . . . "To make gestures quotable" is the actor's most important achievement; he must be able to space his gestures as the compositor produces spaced type. (*Understanding Brecht*, 22, with reference to *Illuminations*, 151, 153)

> ["Der Schauspieler muß eine Sache zeigen, und er muß sich zeigen. Er zeigt die Sache natürlich, indem er sich zeigt, und er zeigt sich, indem er die Sache zeigt. Obwohl dies zusammenfällt, darf es doch nicht so zusammenfallen, daß der Gegensatz (Unterschied) zwischen diesen beiden Aufgaben verschwindet." "Gesten zitierbar zu machen" ist die wichtigste Leistung des Schauspielers; seine Gebärden muß er sperren können wie ein Setzer die Worte. (II, 529)]

In this passage, the citationality of the text is shifted to a dramatic context in which the actor is primary in his role as living quotation of a text. The comparison Benjamin adds turns on a simile, which itself invites a close reading. The actor must be able to space or spread out certain gestures as a typesetter spaces out certain words. The gestures provide a kind of corporeal syntax capable of marshaling the inner meaning. Again, there is a resonance in the choice of figurative explanations: the typesetter makes a text available, for example, for citation. The act of *setzen,* too, invokes the philosophical act of positing, and this moment connects the cognitive activities of making a text available and using words to posit. The actor's position is that of positing the larger cognitive work and word of the text. The gestus, then, bears the burden of interpretation and political persuasion, for the actor's gesture "[d]emonstrates the social significance and applicability of dialectics" (*Understanding Brecht,* 12) [Die Geste demonstriert die soziale Bedeutung und Anwendbarkeit der Dialektik (II, 530)].

In "Was ist das epische Theater? [2]," Benjamin further specifies the role of gestus with regard to theater, texts, and the act of citation:

To quote a text involves the interruption of its context. It is therefore understandable that the epic theater, being based on interruption, is, in a specific sense, a quotable one. There is nothing special about the quotability of its texts. It is different with the gestures which fit into the course of the play.

"Making gestures quotable" is one of the substantial achievements of the epic theater. An actor must be able to space his gestures the way a typesetter produces spaced type. . . . Epic theater is by definition gestic theater. For the more frequently we interrupt someone in the act of acting, the more gestures result. (*Illuminations*, 151)

[Einen Text zitieren, schließt ein: seinen Zusammenhang unterbrechen. Es ist daher wohl verständlich, daß das epische Theater, das auf die Unterbrechung gestellt ist, ein in spezifischem Sinne zitierbares ist. Die Zitierbarkeit seiner Texte hätte nichts Besonderes. Anders steht es mit den Gesten, die im Verlaufe des Spiels am Platze sind.

"Gesten zitierbar zu machen" ist eine der wesentlichen Leistungen des epischen Theaters. Seine Gebärden muß der Schauspieler sperren können wie ein Setzer die Worte. . . . Im übrigen ist das epische Theater per definitionem ein gestisches. Denn Gesten erhalten wir um so mehr, je häufiger wir einen Handelnden unterbrechen. (II, 536)]

Benjamin revises or reassigns the priority of gestus to that of epic theater in general. In addition to the *Leistung* of the actor, the quotability of gestures is here ranked among the more essential achievements of epic theater. The function of the theater turns on interruption of the context. However, the nature of interruption is contingent upon a temporal, linear continuum of the performance. A dialectical understanding of the interruption is no longer optional, for, in order to experience interruption, a context, a *Zusammenhang* must be present as a criterion for a *Zusammenfallen*. The production of interruption is therefore dependent on the uninterrupted activity of the *Handelnden*, the actor. The introductory example, the citing of a text as constitutive of interruption of a context, raises the question: to what extent does the stage ask to be "read"? What is the relationship between the stage and the text? How does the performance, rather, the interruption of the dialectic performed, persuade the public present? And why, finally, is it important that Benjamin understands Kafka's works in terms of the theater and Brecht's in terms of the typeset page/stage?

Benjamin, in referring to epic theater, does not distinguish theoretically between the text and the performance;[25] or more accurately, between a viewing and a reading public. In fact, if we recall his description of gestus in Kafka, Benjamin sets up a metaphorical equivalence between the stage and the world and then dismisses the metaphor. However, if one takes seriously the violent lessons of the *Lehrstücke* or the often cruel corporeality needed to achieve "interruption" of audience consciousness, then the difference is one toward which an actor cannot be indifferent. As Nägele points out, the political content of the *Lehrstücke* obscures their tendencies toward cruelty.[26] The relationship between the stage and the world, in modernity no longer connected by words and things, turns on the capacity to think in gestures. The contingency here is thought prompted by watching the theory behind the practice open up to the audience. Benjamin, in "A Family Drama in the Epic Theater" (*Understanding Brecht*, 33f.) [Ein Familiendrama auf dem epischen Theater], regarding the premiere of Brecht's *Die Mutter*, writes:

> It is in the nature of epic theatre to replace the undialectical opposition between the form and content of consciousness (which means that a character can only refer to his own actions by reflexions) by the dialectical one between theory and praxis (which means that any action that makes a breakthrough opens up a clearer view of theory). Epic theatre, therefore, is the theatre of the hero who is beaten. A hero who is not beaten never makes a thinker. (*Understanding Brecht*, 35)

> [Es entspricht nämlich der Natur des epischen Theaters, daß der undialektische Gegensatz zwischen Form und Inhalt des Bewußtseins (der dahin führte, daß die dramatische Person sich nur in Reflexionen auf ihr Handeln beziehen konnte) abgelöst wird durch den dialektischen zwischen Theorie und Praxis (der dahin führt, daß das Handeln an seinen Einbruchsstellen den Ausblick auf die Theorie freigibt). Daher ist das epische Theater das Theater des geprügelten Helden. Der nicht geprügelte Held wird kein Denker. (II, 512)]

Crucial to Benjamin's distinction between the undialectical opposition between form and content of consciousness is that it is superseded by the dialectical relationship between theory and practice, with presumed reference to Brecht's epic theater. The moments of collapse, the interruptions, the breaks make theory behind the *Handeln* visible. What opens up, or sets our view of theory free, is the spectacle of the battered hero. The relationship between the old and the epic is mediated by the peda- gogical norms of crime and punishment, visible, readable on the body, for violence staged leads to thought about the nature of the lesson. If Kafka's gestures are obscure, Brecht's allegedly set free vision of theory "behind" the action.

Brecht's dramaturgy attempts to overcome, or incorporate, the other- wise "restlose Verwandlung" or "remainderless transformation" of the actor into the character portrayed.[27] The transformation without remainder known from conventional dramaturgy endangers the resis- tance to *Einfühlung,* or identification between the thought process of the performance and the public. The nature of this mediation is crucial, as is the role of the actor as actor, who is not self-same and identical with the part played. The nature of the persuasion lies therefore not in perfect, but imperfect identity, that is, in the recognition of difference that constitutes the political moment of consciousness. In the second essay on epic the- ater, specifically, in the subsection on the actor, Benjamin writes:

> In other words: an actor should reserve for himself the possibility of stepping out of character artistically. At the proper moment he should insist on portraying a man who reflects about his part. It would be erroneous to think at such a moment of Romantic Irony, as employed by Tieck in his *Puss in Boots.* This irony has no didactic aim. Basically, it demonstrates only the philosophic sophistication of the author who, in writing his plays, always remembers that in the end the world may turn out to be a theater. (*Illuminations,* 153)

> [Mit andern Worten: Der Schauspieler soll sich die Möglichkeit vorbe- halten, mit Kunst aus der Rolle zu fallen. Er soll es sich, im gegebenen Moment, nicht nehmen lassen, das (über seinen Part) Nachdenkenden vorzumachen. Mit Unrecht würde man sich an die romantische Ironie erinnert fühlen, wie zum Beispiel Tieck sie im "Gestiefelten Kater" handhabt. Diese hat kein Lehrziel; sie weist im Grunde nur die philosophische Informiertheit des Autors aus, dem beim Stück- eschreiben immer gegenwärtig bleibt: Die Welt mag am Ende wohl auch ein Theater sein. (II, 538)]

Benjamin again makes the equation, albeit speculatively, that the world may be a theater even for the Romantic ironist Tieck. What is the difference between Benjamin's use of world theater in the Kafka essay, in which the stage is elevated to ontological status, and the world theater he disparages in Tieck? Or, to ask the question in another way: how is the performance of the dialectic in Brecht performing more than itself? The remainder of the quotient between the actor who is conscious of acting a role and the audience that falls into the consciousness of the artificiality of the performance leads to self-consciousness on both parts. If we look beyond the pedagogical and ideological persuasion of Benjamin, how can we distinguish between epic theater and the Romantic stage? If we go beyond the doctrinaire concerns of consistence within Marxist theory, what is left in the above passage to maintain a firm dividing line between the sustained irony of Tieck's *Gestiefelter Kater* and the interruptive moments of the literarized, epic stage?

The answer lies in the meaning of the verb *handhaben*. In the above quotation, Benjamin describes Tieck's use of irony in these terms. Brecht associates this verbal designation—not accidentally—with the dialectic in his own theoretical work. It is necessary to look closely at Brecht's descriptions of how the stage initiates and enacts cognition. This imperative mediation implies both production and citation.

In the dialogue play *Der Messingkauf* (1937–51), Brecht posits an allegorical cast of characters—the Philosopher, the Actor, the Actress, the Dramaturg, and the Electrician—who, over a series of four nights, philosophize together about the theater.[28] The play takes its name from the example, offered by the Philosopher to describe himself, about a dealer in scrap metal who goes to a band to buy brass, not instruments. In this odd example, the Philosopher is interested in the material, not the trumpets.[29] The characters describe the theory of theater from a historical perspective, debating specific constants, such as the role of imitation, the relationship between the play and the public, as well as the relationship between politics and theater, and the production of imitation. The polysemy of gestus sets the dialectic "in motion" and stops it in its tracks. What does it mean in this context to have the dialectic at hand?

This is theory staged, theater philosophized, language performed. The ability to cognize difference between the stage and society calls attention to the theater, the stage, as a model. The comparison drawn in this play is to that of the natural scientist conducting an experiment. The play is a "position," in the sense of a model. The performance posits a relationship between itself and the audience, mediated not only by words, but by gestures, and ultimately by actors. The question persists: how is the mediation achieved? The Actor in the play—about actors in plays—explains the effect with a violent vocabulary: What the Philosopher describes as the "art of inspiring belief"[30] [Kunst des Glaubenmachens], the Actor supplements: "Because we want to fill people with sensations and passions, to take them out of their everyday life and its events" [Um die Menschen mit Leidenschaften und Gefühlen zu erfüllen, um sie aus ihrem Alltag und ihren Vorfällen herauszureißen (to rip out)].[31] The Actor offers a metaphor by way of explanation: "The events are simply the framework on which we deploy our art, the springboard for us to take off from" [Die Vorfälle sind da sozusagen das Gerüst, an dem wir unsere Kunst ausüben, das Sprungbrett, das wir benützen].[32] The imitated incidents provide the scaffolding, the springboard for the art of acting. These two figures seem to represent the dialectic "at rest" and "in motion" respectively. There is a tension between the two examples, if one considers the intended stability of scaffolding and the mobile force of a springboard. Such is the function of the stage: to be a stable frame on which to hang the experiential world, and to provide a trajectory of thought between the staged events and the everyday. The purpose, in any case, with the implied violence of displacement, is to rip the spectator out of life. In order to achieve this end, the Actor confesses to the specific need of "mobilizing our feelings and passions" [unsere Gefühle und Leidenschaften (zu) mobilisieren].[33] The military mobilization of feelings and passions belongs to the Actor's repertoire of persuasion. This amounts to a figurative declaration of war between the actor and the public.

The key to cognition in the phenomenal art of the stage is controlling the view. The "limited scope" of the figure also limits the range of the audience. The lack of total vision is crucial to realistic realism. The gesture bears the burden of this partial vision. The "real" realism must be recognized as artificial realism, that is, a trope of representation that relies on the apparent resemblance to the referential, experiential world. The Philosopher expects, through a cognitive process, the invisible to become visible, that the laws of life be "seen."

The cognitive process, then, relies on the capacity not to empathize, but to see and think a certain way. Specifically, the Philosopher outlines the necessity of abstract thought in the transference of the performed model to the activated spectator. In an explanation of *abstrahieren,* the allegorizing of the self into a staged character, the spectator is presumed to ask:

The more concretely a case is put before him, the easier it is for a spectator to abstract ("Lear behaves like that." "Do I behave the same way?") One special father can be fathers in general. The specialness is a mark of generality. It's general to find something special.

[Der Zuschauer kann um so leichter abstrahieren (Lear handelt so, handle ich so?), je konkreter ein Fall ihm vorgestellt wird. Ein ganz besonderer Vater kann der allgemeinste Vater sein. Die Besonderheit ist ein Merkmal des Allgemeinen. Man trifft ganz allgemein Besonderes.][34]

This assertion would be unthinkable without the dialectical relationship between the specific and the general, and the cognitive process is one based on the allegorical imperative of abstraction. The comparison of the *Zuschauer* to Lear must pass through the linguistic process of interpretation. The epistemology of this particular trope, allegory, constitutes the mediation between the performance of the play and the audience, transformed by thought, by interpreting figurative language, into social players. The hermeneutic of the spectacle is thus set in motion, and cognition performed in the comparison between the individual and the *Vorbild,* in this example, Lear. In the larger context of my argument, Marxist persuasion is contingent upon the reading of the critical principle within language that leads to the disarticulation of the text from the context. The theory of citation, of quotability, becomes the common ground of the political and philosophical critiques of identity and transcendence respectively.

The Philosopher, again, articulates the comparison between the actor's art and the representational mode of theater. By way of comparison, by way of tropology, he redefines the play of the play as its own means of representation:

The art of acting is one of society's elementary capacities; it is based on a direct social asset, one of humanity's pleasures in society; it is like language itself; it's really a language of its own.

[Die Schauspielkunst gehört zu den elementaren gesellschaftlichen Kräften, sie beruht auf einem unmittelbaren gesellschaftlichen Vermögen, einer Lust der Menschen in Gesellschaft, sie ist wie die Sprache selber, sie ist eine Sprache für sich.][35]

The shift from simile to metaphor marks a larger shift from figural to literal reading. The basis, of course, of the actor's trade is grounded in society. First, acting is "like" language itself, and in sequence, it *is* language for itself. This shift radically revises the relationship between the stage and society. However, the *Sprache* here that acting constitutes is used metaphorically. Language, then, is the only adequate metaphor to "perform" the displacement of language (text) by acting/quoting (gestus). The shift is away from the foregrounded language of the text to the performance. Still, language continues to perform by inhabiting the spectator, prompting a political, public *Handlung*. Brecht hereby realigns the relationship between figurative language, a substitutive economy without end, and shifts to a performative model that performs cognition. Brecht's thoughts on theater forbid the actor to portray a character as "ethical substance," or self-same and identical. The residual self, the remainder of the interpersonal quotient of actor and character sets the dialectic in motion. If we invoke Benjamin's view of Kafka's "world theater" at this juncture, we reach an impasse. For the epic stage projects itself through gestus onto the "world," which is itself a stage, the text of which remains unwritten and therefore unknown to the actors of Kafka's "Nature Theater" (*Illuminations,* 137).

Überall, wo es auf das Erkennen der Realität ankommt, müssen wir lernen, die Dialektik zu handhaben.

[Wherever things depend on the recognition of reality, we must learn to have the dialectic at hand.]
    (—*Notizen über die Dialektik auf dem Theater* [GW 16, 868])

What does it mean for the stage, "die Dialektik zu handhaben"? From the "Dialektik im Stillstand,"[36] as tableau, to the re-cognition of reality, the dialectic is the cognitive tool of viewing theater. The difference, emphasized in *Der Messingkauf,* between reading as a solitary activity and the stage as collective cognition, is the "visibility" of the gesture, the materiality of the hand. *Hand* is present in the materiality of the related terms: *Handlung, handeln, handhaben.* It is the agent of activity: the hand that writes, the hand that gestures, the hand that seduces, the hand that works, the hand that is raised in violence, and the hand that takes its own life. The dialectic is the cutting tool that makes incisions and decisions. The final example of having a "hand" on the dialectic occurs in *Der Messingkauf* in a passage put in the mouth of the Philosopher:

> We're working with a very fine balance, making calculations, elegantly, without caring how the ground is crumbling under our feet. . . . The more haste, the less speed. The surgeon who has heavy responsibilities needs the little scalpel to lie lightly and easily in his hand. The world is out of joint, certainly, and it will take powerful movements to manipulate it all back again. But among the various relevant instruments there can be one that is slight and delicate and needs to be handled with ease.

> [Wir hantieren hier mit einer Goldwaage, in abgemessenen Bewegungen, mit Eleganz, gleichgültig, wie sehr uns der Boden unter den Füßen brennen mag. . . . Hast hilft ja nicht, wo Eile not tut. Dem Chirurgen, dem schwere Verantwortung aufgebürdet ist, muß das kleine Messer doch leicht in der Hand liegen. Die Welt ist gewiß aus den Fugen, nur durch gewaltige Bewegungen kann alles eingerenkt werden. Aber es kann unter manchen Instrumenten, die dem dienen, ein dünnes, zerbrechliches sein, das leichte Handhabung beansprucht.][37]

Theater and art in general are forms of production. In this excerpt from the Philosopher's conclusions about the relationship between political context and text, he produces two metaphors of production. The gold balance represents the activity of artistic production, specifically, the theater; and the surgeon, who must exercise "leichte Handhabung" in order to cut with a delicate knife. The Philosopher sets up a figural equivalence between the theater, the act of judgment implied by the allegory of the scale, and the delicate operation of the surgeon. Like the surgeon with his instrument, so must the theater producer "operate" with the dialectic. The means of the production of meaning, finally, relies exclusively on having the dialectic at hand. The cognitive capacity to "read" body language, to allegorize the concrete detail to the abstract condition, to produce as a process of witnessing production—each turns on the capacity to literalize the figural pedagogy both posited and positioned on stage. The gestus is quotable only in the act of quotation. This final act of quotation implies a history, conscious of the act of quoting, as well as the act of reading. The latter calibrates the relationship between the dialectic of the stage and society, the text in a collective context.

Whereas Brecht's work mobilizes the parables of the past to politicize his own present, he reads Kafka's work as prophetic. In his "Conversations with Brecht," Benjamin notes the crucial point of difference in the use of parables: "In Kafka," Benjamin writes, citing Brecht, "therefore, parable is in conflict with vision. But as a visionary, Brecht says, Kafka saw what was to come without seeing what is" (*Reflections,* 205). Further, Kafka's "images are good," according to Brecht, "but the rest is obscurantism" (*Reflections,* 207). This obscurity constitutes a serious violation of the pedagogical imperative. Benjamin refuses to clarify Kafka, and Brecht refuses to see that which is not clear, not "visible." Benjamin marks the unreadability of Kafka's texts, passing on the enscripted secrets. Benjamin refutes Brecht's reading: "For my part, I give the following interpretation: the true measure of life is remembrance" (*Reflections,* 209–10), where life is here understood as writing read backward. If we recall for a moment the point of Brecht's epic theater, to make the invisible visible, to make the interpretation available to spectator cognition by the citable gesture, then the problematic of reading is suspended in his political pedagogy. Benjamin finds a message in Kafka that Brecht failed to see, that Brecht failed to read. For Kafka's message is only citable in that it is not sightable: it can only be endlessly deferred, perhaps a border imposed, as in the framed background of the sky from the opening example. Kafka offers allegories for which the concept, the original abstraction, has been erased: only the material signifier remains. There is no justice, only the scale by which we figure the invisible abstraction in the first place. This is precisely what Benjamin saw in Kafka: the hands that applaud "are 'really steam hammers'" (*Illuminations,* 113). While his gestures rip open the view of the sky, the ground is that of language, specifically, the German language. In his section on "The Little Hunchback," Benjamin writes: "In his depth Kafka touches the ground which neither 'mythical divination' nor 'existential theology' supplied him with. It is the core of folk tradition, the German as well as the Jewish" (*Illuminations,* 134). In language, then, the two traditions meet on common ground.

If the instrumentality of "concrete" images is at issue here, then the significative system of the brass purchased by the Philosopher is transformed into a tool *(Werkzeug)* not in Brecht, but in Kafka. In the haunting story "In the Penal Colony,"[38] the brass returns, perhaps purchased by the Philosopher, as part of the hideous writing machine that is also the instrument of punishment.

By now the voyager was beginning to feel some stirring of interest in the apparatus; with one hand raised to protect himself against the sun he gazed up at it. It was a large structure. The bed and the designer were of the same size and looked like two dark chests. The designer was mounted some two metres above the bed; both were joined at the corners by four brass rods that almost flashed in the sunlight. Between the two chests, suspended on a steel belt, was the harrow.[39]

[Der Reisende war schon ein wenig für den Apparat gewonnen; die Hand zum Schutz gegen die Sonne über den Augen, sah er an dem Apparat in die Höhe. Es war ein großer Aufbau. Das Bett und der Zeichner hatten gleichen Umfang und sahen wie zwei dunkle Truhen aus. Der Zeichner war etwa zwei Meter über dem Bett angebracht; beide waren in den Ecken durch vier Messingstangen verbunden, die in der Sonne fast Strahlen warfen. Zwischen den Truhen schwebte an einem Stahlband die Egge.][40]

The voyager's hand covers his eye against the sun, in which the brass rods almost gleam. The brass rods hold the machine together; the machine operates without the touch of human hands, and suffices as spectacle to affect a change in the voyager/voyeur. The voyager is transformed by the spectacle from an impartial observer, as in Brecht's theater, to an accessory to execution: "The voyager, inclining an ear to the officer, was watching the machine at work with his hands in his pockets" [Der Reisende hatte das Ohr zum Offizier geneigt und sah, die Hände in den Rocktaschen, der Arbeit der Maschine zu];[41] and further, "The voyager wanted to avert his face from the officer and looked aimlessly about him. The officer thought he was contemplating the desolate state of the valley; he therefore seized him by the hands, moved round to look him in the eyes and asked: 'Can't you just see the shame of it?'" [Der Reisende wollte sein Gesicht dem Offizier entziehen und blickte ziellos herum. Der Offizier glaubte, er betrachte die Öde des Tales; er ergriff deshalb seine Hände, drehte sich um ihn, um seine Blicke zu fassen, und fragte: "Merken Sie die Schande?"][42] This shame Benjamin describes as Kafka's central gesture with regard to *Der Prozeß* (The trial), although it extends to a reading of the situation of the penal colony:

Corresponding as it does to his "elemental purity of feeling," shame is Kafka's strongest gesture. It has a dual aspect, however. Shame is an

intimate human reaction, but at the same time it has social preten-
sions. Shame is not only shame in the presence of others, but can also
be shame one feels for them. (*Illuminations,* 129–30)

[Die Scham, die seiner "elementaren Reinheit des Gefühls" entspricht,
ist die stärkste Gebärde Kafkas. Sie hat aber ein doppeltes Gesicht. Die
Scham, die eine intime Reaktion des Menschen ist, ist zugleich eine
gesellschaftlich anspruchsvolle. Scham ist nicht nur Scham vor den
andern, sondern kann auch Scham für sie sein. (II, 428)]

In the penal colony, the hands freed by the brass rods of the machine hold
the spectator: that from which he can not look away, avert his gaze, is the
self-operating machine of justice. The machine, like the scales, is the
material remains of an invisible concept.

In the end, the officer does not even have to touch the machine: "He
only had to stretch out a hand towards the harrow for it to raise and
lower itself several times" [Er hatte die Hand der Egge nur genähert, und
sie hob und senkte sich mehrmals].[43] The instrument of death and justice
is capable of operating without hands. In this story, the officer uses his
hands to direct the gaze of the voyager, who wants to look away. Hands
must be kept clean. Execution is elevated to an aesthetic event, a specta-
cle one observes *gleichgültig,* with hands tucked in pockets and the gaze
held by the hands of power. This, perhaps, constitutes one of Kafka's
"prophetic" moments.

It seems fitting to close with a quotation from Brecht's poem on Ben-
jamin's suicide, perhaps the most acute violation of belief in the future:
"I'm told you raised a hand against yourself . . . Then at last, brought up
against an impassable frontier / You passed, they say, a passable one . . .
So the future lies in darkness . . . All this was plain to you / When you
destroyed a torturable body"[44] [Ich höre, daß du die Hand gegen dich
erhoben hast   / . . . / Zuletzt an eine unüberschreitbare Grenze
getrieben / Hast du, heißt es, eine überschreitbare überschritten / . . . / So
liegt die Zukunft in Finsternis / . . . / . . . All das sahst du / Als du den quäl-
baren Leib zerstörtest (qtd. in II, 1366)]. Benjamin saw the secrets in the
darkness and kept them in the destruction of his body. In citing this act of
self-inflicted violence, I acknowledge yet again the imperative of passing
on words: " 'To read what was never written' " (*Reflections,* 336) ["Was
nie geschrieben wurde, lesen" (II, 213)]. That which was not written con-
stitutes a separate act of violence: of fate, history, of accident. While Ben-

jamin is referring to a place *before* language, the language of the stars and that of the dance—a language he shares with Nelly Sachs[45]—I reroute his intention in closing. Benjamin's work, like Sachs's poetry, takes the reader to a place *after* language. To read what was never written amounts to obeying the "ungeschriebene Gesetze" [unwritten laws] that Kafka's figures constantly violate because the law is kept secret, because the border was not violated. In death, the best secrets are kept and kept best.

NOTES

This essay is based in part on my "Theater of Consciousness: The Language of Brecht's Body Politic" in *Brecht Yearbook* 17 (1992): 214–32. I am grateful for permission to reprint portions of this earlier essay.

1. Translations, unless otherwise noted, are taken from Walter Benjamin, *Illuminations* and *Reflections;* see "Editors' Notes" and "Works Cited" for complete information. When necessary for my reading, I modify the translations. I also quote from the English version of the essays in *Versuche über Brecht: Understanding Brecht,* translated by Anna Bostock (London: NLB, 1973) (henceforth cited in text as *Understanding Brecht*). "Conversations with Brecht," translated by Anna Bostock, is reprinted in the volume *Aesthetics and Politics,* afterword by Frederic Jameson, translation edited by Ronald Taylor (London and New York: Verso, 1980), 86–99.

2. For a reading of the ambivalent relationship between Benjamin's own practice and theory of history, see Alina Clej, "Walter Benjamin's Messianic Politics: Angelus Novus and the End of History," *Cross Currents* 11 (1992): 23–40. See also Susan Buck-Morss, *The Origin of Negative Dialectics: Theodor W. Adorno's Debt to Walter Benjamin* (New York: Free Press, 1977), 169, on the relationship between revolution and the Messiah.

3. Buck-Morss treats this constellation briefly (*Origin of Negative Dialectics,* 141ff.). She describes this tension in Benjamin as his "Janus-Face" (141), which applies to the biographical as well as to the ideological tensions in his work. Benjamin himself recognized the extremes at work in the Kafka essay as the two ends of the political and the mystical (141). See also Benjamin II, 1158ff. For the reaction of Benjamin's contemporaries, particularly of Adorno, to the Kafka essay, see Buck-Morss, 143ff. Stéphane Mosès presents a brief summary of the biographical complications of the Kafka essay, then a careful comparison of Brecht's and Benjamin's respective readings of "Das nächste Dorf," in "Brecht und Benjamin als Kafka-Interpreten," in *Juden in der deutschen Literatur: Ein deutsch-israelisches Symposion,* ed. Stéphane Mosès and Albrecht Schöne (Frankfurt am Main:

Suhrkamp, 1986), 237–56. For a reading of this constellation that exceeds the biographical, see Rainer Nägele, *Theater, Theory, Speculation* (Baltimore: Johns Hopkins University Press, 1991), esp. 135–66. He locates this discussion of the imperative relationship among the elements of his title in Benjamin's early work on the baroque tragedy, and specifically on the role of *Haltung* and gestus. His analysis is particularly persuasive with regard to his larger argument about the caesura, with gestus as a constitutive, performative moment in a specific syntax (159). My own reading relies on Nägele's insightful discussion of gestus, though the points of difference with his overall argument will become clear. I am indebted to Nägele's reading of Brecht's attention to gestus first in poetry, then in drama.

4. See II, 1363ff. for biographical information.

5. See also Arendt, *Walter Benjamin, Bertolt Brecht: Zwei Essays* (Munich: R. Piper, 1971), for a more sustained reading of the two authors and their relationship.

6. Quoted in Martin Jay, *The Dialectical Imagination: A History of the Frankfurt School and the Institute of Social Research 1923–1950* (Boston: Little, Brown, 1973), 338.

7. Jay, *Dialectical Imagination,* 201.

8. II, 1176ff. In their notes to Walter Benjamin's *Gesammelte Schriften,* specifically on Benjamin's correspondence with Adorno about Benjamin's "Franz Kafka," the editors quote Adorno, who writes, "Hier ist mehr als 'Wolke' [s. Text, 420], nämlich Dialektik und die Wolkengestalt gewiß nicht 'aufzuklären' aber durchzudialektisieren—gewissermaßen die Parabel regnen zu lassen—das bleibt das innerste Anliegen einer Kafkainterpretation; dasselbe wie die theoretische Durcharchartikulation des 'dialektischen Bildes'" (II, 1176). Adorno's own reading of Kafka also foregrounds the gestural and "visual" elements in his work. See Theodor W. Adorno, "Aufzeichnungen zu Kafka," in *Prismen: Kulturkritik und Gesellschaft* (Berlin: Suhrkamp, 1955), 302–42, esp. 314. Here Adorno writes: "Verewigte Gesten bei Kafka sind ein erstarrt Momentanes." I quote the English translation: "Eternalized gestures in Kafka are the momentaneous brought to a standstill," from "Notes on Kafka," *Prisms,* trans. Samuel Weber and Shierry Weber (Cambridge: MIT Press, 1982), 252–53. Adorno adds a telling footnote about the relationship between the visual elements in Kafka's work and the possibility of dramatization. He argues that Kafka's characters act as if caught in a magnetic field, not of their own volition: "Das verurteilt alle Dramatisierungen. Drama ist nur so weit möglich, wie Freiheit, wäre es auch als sich entringende, vor Augen steht; alle andere Aktion bliebe nichtig" (*Prismen,* 329) [This dooms all dramatizations. Drama is possible only in so far as freedom—even in its painful birth-pangs—is visible; all other action is futile (*Prisms,* 262)]. See also Buck-Morss, *Origin of Negative Dialectics,* 143, and, more generally on the illumination of cloudy places, Werner Hamacher, "The Word *Wolke*—If It Is One,"

in *Benjamin's Ground: New Readings of Walter Benjamin,* ed. Rainer Nägele (Detroit: Wayne State University Press, 1988), 147–75, esp. 174.

9. Jay, *Dialectical Imagination,* 201.

10. Scholars have relied on the "visual" elements in Kafka's texts and transposed them into the scenic. See for example James Rolleston, *Kafka's Narrative Theater* (University Park: Pennsylvania State University Press, 1974). For a more figurative reading of the relationship between spatial metaphors and language, see Henry Sussman, *Franz Kafka: Geometrician of Metaphor* (Madison, Wisc.: Coda Press, 1979). Clayton Koelb notes the theatrical setting of some narratives in *Kafka's Rhetoric: The Passion of Reading* (Ithaca, N.Y.: Cornell University Press, 1989), 68. He understands reading as an act of violence with regard to Kafka (43).

11. My general discussion of allegory relies on Paul de Man, "The Rhetoric of Temporality," in *Blindness and Insight: Essays in the Rhetoric of Contemporary Criticism,* 2d ed. (Minneapolis: University of Minnesota Press, 1983), 187–228. For a discussion of genre in this context, see Heinz Hillmann, "Fabel und Parabel im 20. Jahrhundert—Kafka und Brecht," in *Die Fabel: Theorie, Geschichte und Rezeption einer Gattung,* ed. Peter Hasubek (Berlin: Erich Schmidt, 1982), 215–35. Scholem, in a letter to Benjamin, at one point notices a similarity between the end of Brecht's *Dreigroschenroman* and Kafka's *Der Prozeß*. See *The Correspondence of Walter Benjamin and Gershom Scholem 1932–1940,* trans. Gary Smith and André Lefevre (New York: Schocken Books, 1989), 237, 243, and 247 (henceforth cited in notes as *Correspondence*). "We (my wife and I)," writes Scholem, "think that the end of *Threepenny Novel* is a materialistic imitation of the chapter 'In the Cathedral' from *The Trial.* Doesn't this suggest itself quite naturally?" (247). Benjamin does not have occasion to respond to this observation.

12. Arendt, *Illuminations,* 15. For a sustained rhetorical reading of Kafka's prose, see Koelb, *Kafka's Rhetoric,* esp. 15 on Kafka's use of literal and figural language. I rely on Koelb's general construction of the problem of reading and writing in Kafka's work, as closer reading of the texts exceed the limits of this essay.

13. Jephcott's translation here modified by editors.

14. I allude to the title of an enlightening essay by Rolf Tiedemann, "Brecht oder Die Kunst, in anderer Leute Köpfe zu denken," in *Dialektik im Stillstand: Versuche zum Spätwerk Walter Benjamins* (Frankfurt am Main: Suhrkamp, 1983), 42–73.

15. Paul de Man, "Conclusions: Walter Benjamin's 'The Task of the Translator,'" *Yale French Studies* 69 (1985): 25–46. De Man points to the rhetorical basis of history and the poetics of politics (46). Note also the relationship between politics and "minor literature" put forth in Gilles Deleuze and Félix Guattari, *Kafka: Toward a Minor Literature,* trans. Dana Polan, foreword by

Réda Bensmaïa (Minneapolis: University of Minnesota Press, 1986). Bensmaïa highlights the importance of gestus and suggests that the Deleuze and Guattari reading departs from Benjamin's, though they displace a consideration of language (specifically, rhetoric, allegory, etc.) with "machine of expression" (xvii) and law with a "continuum of desire" (51). While their reading of the political nature of all minor literature will certainly alter the course of Kafka scholarship, they dismiss too quickly the relationship between rhetoric and their own definition of the political. In this context, I would like to acknowledge a general scholarly debt to the work of Timothy Bahti, Winfried Menninghaus, and Irving Wohlfarth on Benjamin's theory of history and language, and that on the Jewish tradition.

16. This is a minor complaint, for the word *Gebärde* is used often interchangably with *Gestus,* and Benjamin employs the former to illustrate the latter. However, it is telling that the use of the English term *gesture* would be more easily associated with the visible and physical art of acting.

17. For a reading of some Kantian elements in Benjamin, see Winfried Menninghaus's contribution to this volume.

18. "Kafka lives in a *complementary* world. . . . Kafka offered the complement without being aware of what surrounded him" (*Illuminations,* 143).

19. See Rainer Nägele, "Augenblicke: Eingriffe. Brechts Ästhetik der Wahrnehmung," *Brecht Yearbook* 17 (1992): 29–51, for a reading of the place of the hand in relation to the eye.

20. See my "'Wo die Ironie erscheint': Tieck als Herausgeber in den 'Jahrbücher'-Rezensionen," in *Die "Jahrbücher für wissenschaftliche Kritik":* *Hegels Berliner Gegenakademie,* ed. Christoph Jamme (Stuttgart: Frommann-Holzboog, 1994), 301–20.

21. For the relationship between the two, see Benjamin, "Some Reflections on Kafka," *Illuminations,* 144. It is clear from his correspondence with Scholem that his attention to Jewish tradition in his work on Kafka can be accounted for in part by the circumstances of its production, in particular for *Die Jüdische Rundschau,* and that he relied on Scholem's expertise in this matter (*Correspondence,* 111).

22. I borrow this argument from Paul de Man.

23. Along the way, I make hasty reference to three quite extensive scholarly traditions, without doing justice to any. The point of this essay is to calibrate the balancing act Benjamin does between Brecht and Kafka, and the significance to his work, not an extended reading of the individual authors.

24. Benjamin, "Some Reflections on Kafka." "It is this consistency of truth that has been lost. Kafka was far from being the first to face this situation. Many had accommodated themselves to it, clinging to truth or whatever they happened to regard as truth and, with a more or less heavy heart, forgoing its transmissibility. Kafka's real genius was that he tried something entirely new: he sacrificed

truth for the sake of clinging to its transmissibility, its haggadic element" (*Illuminations*, 143–44).

25. He does, however, offer examples from performances of Brecht's plays to illustrate his argument.

26. Rainer Nägele, "Brecht's Theater of Cruelty," in *Reading after Freud: Essays on Goethe, Hölderlin, Habermas, Nietzsche, Brecht, Celan, and Freud* (New York: Columbia University Press, 1987), 113.

27. See Bertolt Brecht, *Gesammelte Werke,* ed. Suhrkamp Verlag in cooperation with Elisabeth Hauptmann (Frankfurt am Main: Suhrkamp, 1967), 16:622–23 (henceforth cited in notes as *GW*).

28. For a reading of the ideological critique inscribed in this piece, see Klaus-Detlev Müller, "Der Philosoph auf dem Theater: Ideologiekritik und 'Linksabweichung' in Bertolt Brechts 'Messingkauf,' " in *Bertolt Brecht,* Sonderband aus der Reihe Text und Kritik, ed. Heinz Ludwig Arnold (Munich: Boorberg, 1972), 45–71.

29. See Müller, "Der Philosoph," 49. Here Müller interprets the Philosopher's use of the brass-buying image: "The Philosopher, however, is not interested in the pure 'material value' of the theater, but rather in its new duties. To stay with the image, it would be necessary to offer the new application of the brass as the motivation for buying the brass, that some sort of tool would be made from the trumpet" [Der Philosoph ist aber nicht am reinen "Materialwert" des Theaters interessiert, sondern an seiner neuen Aufgabe. Um im Bild zu bleiben, wäre es notwendig, daß die neue Verwendung des Messings als Motivation des Kaufes angegeben würde, daß also etwa aus der Trompete ein Werkzeug angefertigt werden sollte]. The refashioning of brass into a tool has resonance for my reading of Kafka's "In der Strafkolonie."

30. Bertolt Brecht, *The Messingkauf Dialogues,* trans. John Willett (London: Methuen, 1965) 14, henceforth cited in notes as *Messingkauf*. German from *GW*, 16:505.

31. Brecht, *Messingkauf,* 14; *GW*, 16:505–6.

32. Brecht, *Messingkauf,* 14; *GW*, 16:506.

33. My translation. Willett uses "calling on" (15), which obscures the military metaphor; *GW*, 16:506.

34. Brecht, *Messingkauf,* 79; *GW*, 16:614.

35. Brecht, *Messingkauf,* 98; *GW*, 16:648.

36. Brecht, *GW*, 16:530.

37. Brecht, *Messingkauf,* 94; *GW*, 16:643.

38. See Ehrhard Bahr's contribution to this volume for a further reference to Kafka.

39. Franz Kafka, "In the Penal Colony," in *The Transformation and Other Stories: Works Published during Kafka's Lifetime,* trans. and ed. Malcolm Pasley (London: Penguin Books, 1992), 130.

40. Franz Kafka, "In der Strafkolonie," in *Gesammelte Schriften,* ed. Max Brod (New York: Schocken Books, 1946; Lizenzausgabe, Berlin: Schocken, 1935), 1:203.

41. Kafka, "In the Penal Colony," 137; "In der Strafkolonie," 213. For a reading of the position of the reader as voyager, the concept of reading as an act of violence, and the significance of the machine that runs itself, see Koelb, *Kafka's Rhetoric,* 66–67.

42. Kafka, "In the Penal Colony," 141; "In der Strafkolonie," 219.

43. Kafka, "In the Penal Colony," 150; "In der Strafkolonie," 231.

44. Bertolt Brecht, "On the Suicide of the Refugee W. B.," in *Poems 1913–1956,* ed. John Willett and Ralph Manheim, with Erich Fried, trans. Edith Anderson et al. (New York: Methuen, 1976), 363.

45. See Elisabeth Strenger's and Dorothee Ostmeier's contributions to this volume. Benjamin's essay "On the Mimetic Faculty" (*Reflections,* 333–36) (Über das mimetische Vermögen [II, 210–13]) ends with a brief history of mimesis and reading. His characterization of the language of dance gestures toward the poetics of Nelly Sachs.

Works Cited

Adler, H. G. *Versuch einer Charakterisierung des Jüdischen: Juden-Christen-Deutsche.* Ed. Hans Jürgen Schultz. 3d ed. Stuttgart: Kreuz Verlag/Olten, Freiburg: Walter-Verlag, 1961.

Adorno, Theodor W. "Aufzeichnungen zu Kakfa." In *Prismen: Kulturkritik und Gesellschaft.* Berlin: Suhrkamp, 1955. 302–42.

———. *Gesammelte Schriften.* 20 vols. Frankfurt am Main: Suhrkamp, 1973–84.

———. *Minima Moralia: Reflexionen aus dem beschädigten Leben.* Frankfurt am Main: Suhrkamp, 1976.

———. "Notes on Kafka." *Prisms.* Trans. Samuel and Shierry Weber. Cambridge: MIT Press, 1982. 243–71.

Allemann, Beda. "Hinweis auf einen Gedichtraum." In *Das Buch der Nelly Sachs,* ed. Bengt Holmqvist, 291–308. 2d ed. Frankfurt am Main: Suhrkamp, 1977.

Arendt, Hannah. *Walter Benjamin, Bertolt Brecht: Zwei Essays.* Munich: Piper, 1971.

Assmann, Jan. *Stein und Zeit: Mensch und Gesellschaft im alten Ägypten.* Munich: Fink, 1991.

Atlas: Zusammengestellt von deutschen Autoren. Berlin: Wagenbach, 1965.

Bahr, Ehrhard. *Nelly Sachs.* Munich: Beck, 1980.

Baumgart, Reinhart. "Unmenschlichkeit beschreiben." In *Literatur für Zeitgenossen: Essays.* Frankfurt am Main: Suhrkamp, 1966. 12–36.

Benjamin, Walter. *Briefe.* Ed. Gershom Scholem and Theodor W. Adorno. 2 vols. Frankfurt am Main: Suhrkamp, 1966.

———. *Gesammelte Schriften.* Ed. Rolf Tiedemann and Hermann Schweppenhäuser. 7 vols. Frankfurt am Main: Suhrkamp, 1972–89.

———. *Illuminations.* Trans. Harry Zohn. Ed. Hannah Arendt. New York: Schocken, 1968.

———. *The Origin of German Tragic Drama.* Trans. John Osborne. London: New Left Books, 1977.

———. *Reflections: Essays, Aphorisms, Autobiographical Writings.* Trans. Edmund Jephcott. Ed. and intro. Peter Demetz. New York: Schocken, 1978.

Berendsohn, Walter A. *Nelly Sachs: Einführung in das Werk der Dichterin jüdischen Schicksals*. Darmstadt: Agora, 1974.

Blomster, W. V. "Theosophy of the Creative Word: The Zohar-Cycle of Nelly Sachs." *Germanic Review* 44 (1969): 211–27.

Böhme, Jacob. *Mysterium Magnum, oder Erklärung über Das Erste Buch Mosis* (1623). Vols. 7 and 8 of *Sämtliche Schriften*. Stuttgart: Fr. Frommanns Verlag, 1955–60.

Bolz, Norbert. *Auszug aus der entzauberten Welt: Philosophischer Extremismus zwischen den Weltkriegen*. Munich: Fink, 1989.

Bossinade, Johanna. "Fürstinnen der Trauer: Die Gedichte von Nelly Sachs." *Jahrbuch für Internationale Germanistik* 16, no. 1 (1984): 133–57.

Brecht, Bertolt. "An die Nachgeborenen." In *Gedichte und Lieder*. Frankfurt am Main: Suhrkamp, 1979.

———. *Ausgewählte Gedichte*. Frankfurt am Main: Suhrkamp, 1964.

———. *Gesammelte Werke*. 20 vols. Ed. Suhrkamp Verlag in cooperation with Elisabeth Hauptmann. Frankfurt am Main: Suhrkamp, 1967.

Buber, Martin. *Die chassidischen Bücher*. Hellerau: Hegner, 1928.

———. *Die Legende des Baalschem*. Rev. ed. Zürich: Manesse, 1955.

———, ed. *Tales of the Hasidim*. Trans. Olga Marx. New York: Schocken Books, 1947.

Buck-Morss, Susan. *The Origin of Negative Dialectics: Theodor W. Adorno's Debt to Walter Benjamin*. New York: Free Press, 1977.

Burke, Edmund. *A Philosophical Enquiry into the Origin of Our Ideas of the Sublime and Beautiful*. Ed. J. T. Boulton. London: Routledge and Kegan Paul, 1958.

Campbell, David A. *Greek Lyric Poetry*. London: Macmillan, 1967.

Celan, Paul. *Gesammelte Werke*. Ed. Beda Allemann and Stefan Reichert. 5 vols. Frankfurt am Main: Suhrkamp, 1983.

———. *Poems of Paul Celan*. Trans. Michael Hamburger. New York: Persea, 1988.

Cicero, [Marcus Tullius]. *De oratore*. Trans. E. W. Sutton and Horace Rackham. 2 vols. Loeb Classical Library. Cambridge: Harvard University Press, 1988.

Clej, Alina. "Walter Benjamin's Messianic Politics. Angelus Novus and the End of History." *Cross Currents* 11 (1992): 23–40.

The Correspondence of Walter Benjamin and Gershom Scholem 1932–1940. Trans. Gary Smith and André Lefevre. New York: Schocken, 1989.

Cuddon, John Anthony. *A Dictionary of Literary Terms and Literary Theory*. 3d ed. Oxford: Blackwell, 1991.

de Man, Paul. "Autobiography as De-facement." *Modern Language Notes* 94 (1979): 919–30.

———. "Conclusions: Walter Benjamin's 'The Task of the Translator.'" *Yale French Studies* 69. *The Lesson of Paul de Man* (1985): 25–46.

———. "The Rhetoric of Temporality." In *Blindness and Insight: Essays in the Rhetoric of Contemporary Criticism*. 2d ed. Minneapolis: University of Minnesota Press, 1983.

Deleuze, Gilles, and Félix Guattari. *Kafka: Toward a Minor Literature*. Trans. Dana Polan. Foreword by Réda Bensmaïa. Minneapolis: University of Minnesota Press, 1986.

Derrida, Jacques. "Force de Loi: Le 'Fondement mystique de l'Autorité'/Force of Law: The 'Mystical Foundation of Authority.'" *Cardozo Law Review,* 11 (1990): 1030–35.

———. "Des tours de Babel" (1980). In *Psyché: Inventions de l'autre*. Paris: Galilée, 1987. 203–35.

Dinesen, Ruth. *"Und Leben hat immer wie Abschied geschmeckt": Frühe Gedichte und Prosa der Nelly Sachs*. Stuttgart: Heinz Akademischer Verlag, 1987.

———. *Nelly Sachs: Eine Biographie*. Trans. Gabriele Gerecke. Frankfurt am Main: Suhrkamp, 1992.

———. "Verehrung und Verwerfung: Nelly Sachs—Kontroverse um eine Dichterin." In *Kontroversen, alte und neue: Akten des VII. Internationalen Germanisten-Kongresses Göttingen 1985,* ed. Albrecht Schöne, 10:130–37. Tübingen: Niemeyer, 1986.

Domin, Hilde. Afterword to *Gedichte,* by Nelly Sachs, 105–37. Frankfurt am Main: Suhrkamp, 1977.

Duncan, Isadora. "Dancing in Relation to Religion and Love." *Theatre Arts Monthly* 11, 8 (1927): 584–93.

Ecker, Ute. *Grabmal und Epigramm: Studien zur frühgriechischen Sepulkraldichtung*. Palingenesia, vol. 29. Stuttgart: Franz Steiner, 1990.

Frenz, Horst, ed. *Literature 1901–1967: Nobel Lectures, Including Presentation Speeches and Laureates' Biographies*. Amsterdam: Elsevier, 1969.

Freud, Sigmund. *Case Histories 1, "Dora" and "Little Hans."* The Pelican Freud Library. Ed. Angela Richards. Tr. Alix Strachey and James Strachey. London: Pelican, 1977.

Friedländer, Saul, ed. *Probing the Limits of Representation: Nazism and the "Final Solution."* Cambridge: Harvard University Press, 1992.

Geißner, Hellmut. "Sprache und Tanz." In *Das Buch der Nelly Sachs,* ed. Bengt Holmqvist, 363–80. Frankfurt am Main: Suhrkamp, 1968.

Goethe, Johann Wolfgang. *Die Wahlverwandtschaften*. Vol. 6 of *Goethes Werke*. Hamburger Ausgabe. Ed. Erich Trunz. 10th ed. Munich: C. H. Beck, 1981.

———. *Werke*. Hamburger Ausgabe. 14 vols. Ed. Erich Trunz. Hamburg: Wegner, 1949.

Hamacher, Werner. "The Second of Inversion: Movements of a Figure through Celan's Poetry." *Yale French Studies* 69 (1985): 276–311.

———. "The Word *Wolke*—If It Is One." In *Benjamin's Ground: New Readings of Walter Benjamin,* ed. Rainer Nägele, 147–76. Detroit: Wayne State University Press, 1988.

Hardegger, Luzia. *Nelly Sachs und die Verwandlungen der Welt.* Bern: Herbert Lang, 1975.

Hart Nibbrig, Christiaan, ed. *Ubersetzung: Walter Benjamin.* Frankfurt am Main: Suhrkamp, forthcoming 1996.

Hartman, Geoffrey. *Beyond Formalism: Literary Essays 1958–1970.* New Haven: Yale University Press, 1970.

———. *Wordsworth's Poetry 1787–1814.* New Haven: Yale University Press, 1964.

Hegel, Georg Wilhelm Friedrich. *Vorlesungen über die Ästhetik I.* Vol. 13 of *Werke.* Frankfurt am Main: Suhrkamp, 1969–71.

———. *Vorlesungen über die Philosophie der Religion. Werke.* Vol. 17 of *Werke.*

Herder, Johann Gottfried. *Blätter der Vorzeit: Dichtungen aus der morgenländischen Sage (Jüdische Dichtungen und Fabeln).* Berlin: Schocken, 1936.

———. *Sämtliche Werke.* Ed. Bernhard Suphan. Vol. 18. 1883; rpt. Hildesheim: Olms, 1967–68.

Herman, Simon N. *Jewish Identity: A Social Psychological Perspective.* Beverly Hills: Sage, 1977.

Highwater, Jamake. *Dance: Rituals of Experience.* New York: Alfred von der Marck, 1985.

Hillmann, Heinz. In "Fabel und Parabel im 20. Jahrhundert—Kafka und Brecht." *Die Fabel: Theorie, Geschichte und Rezeption einer Gattung,* ed. Peter Hasubek, 215–35. Berlin: Schmidt, 1982.

Hirsch, Leo. "Die Kehrseite der Konjunktur." *Der Morgen* (Berlin) 5, no. 14 (1938): 163–68.

Holmqvist, Bengt. "Die Sprache der Sehnsucht." In *Das Buch der Nelly Sachs,* ed. Bengt Holmqvist. 7–70. 2d ed. Frankfurt am Main: Suhrkamp, 1977.

———, ed. *Das Buch der Nelly Sachs.*

Horch, Hans Otto, ed. *Conditio Judaica.* Tübingen: Niemeyer, 1988–.

Jäckel, Eberhard. "Die elende Praxis der Untersteller." In *"Historikerstreit,"* ed. Piper Verlag, 115–22. Munich: Piper, 1987.

Jakobson, Roman. *Kindersprache, Aphasie und allgemeine Lautgesetze.* Frankfurt am Main: Suhrkamp, 1969.

Jay, Martin. *The Dialectical Imagination. A History of the Frankfurt School and the Institute of Social Research 1923–1950.* Boston: Little, Brown, 1973.

Kafka, Franz. "In der Strafkolonie." In *Gesammelte Schriften,* ed. Max Brod, 199–237, vol. 1. New York: Schocken, 1946; Lizenzausgabe, Berlin: Schocken, 1935.

———. "In the Penal Colony." In *The Transformation and Other Stories. Works*

Published During Kafka's Lifetime, trans. and ed. Malcolm Pasley. 127–53. London: Penguin, 1992.

———. *Tagebücher 1910–1923.* Ed. Max Brod. Frankfurt am Main: Fischer, 1967.

Kant, Immanuel. *Critique of Judgment.* Trans. and intro. by Werner S. Pluhar. Indianapolis: Hackett, 1987.

———. *Kritik der praktischen Vernunft.* In *Kants gesammelte Schriften,* ed. Königlich Preußische Akademie der Wissenschaften. Berlin: Reimer, 1913.

Kersten, Paul. *Die Metaphorik in der Lyrik von Nelly Sachs. Mit einer Wort-Konkordanz und einer Nelly Sachs-Bibliographie.* Hamburg: Lüdke, 1970.

Kippax, John R. *Churchyard Literature: A Choice Collection of American Epitaphs.* 1876; rpt. Williamstown: Corner House, 1978.

Kleist, Heinrich. *Werke in einem Band.* Munich: Hanser, 1966.

Klingmann, Ulrich. *Religion und Religiosität in der Lyrik von Nelly Sachs.* Frankfurt am Main: Peter Lang, 1980.

Koelb, Clayton. *Kafka's Rhetoric: The Passion of Reading.* Ithaca: Cornell University Press, 1989.

Krieg, Matthias. *Schmetterlingsweisheit: Die Todesbilder der Nelly Sachs.* Berlin: Selbstverlag Institut Kirche und Judentum, 1983.

Lagercrantz, Olof. *Versuch über die Lyrik der Nelly Sachs.* Trans. Helene Ritzerfeld. Frankfurt am Main: Suhrkamp, 1967.

Lakoff, George, and Mark Johnson. *Metaphors We Live By.* Chicago: University of Chicago Press, 1980.

Lang, Berel. *Act and Idea in the Nazi Genocide.* Chicago: University of Chicago Press, 1990.

Langer, Lawrence L. *The Holocaust and the Literary Imagination.* New Haven: Yale University Press, 1975.

Lattimore, Richmond. *Themes in Greek and Latin Epitaphs.* University of Illinois Studies in Language and Literature 28, nos. 1–2. Urbana: University of Illinois Press, 1942.

Longinus. *On the sublime.* In Aristotle, *The Poetics,* Longinus, *On the Sublime,* Demetrius, *On Style.* Loeb Classical Library. London: W. Heinemann, 1927.

Masters, Edgar Lee. *The New Spoon River.* New York: Macmillan, 1968.

———. *Spoon River Anthology.* New York: Macmillan, 1919.

Menke, Bettine. *Sprachfiguren: Name, Allegorie, Bild nach Benjamin.* Munich: Fink, 1991.

Miller, J. Hillis. *The Ethics of Reading: Kant, de Man, Eliot, Trollope, James, and Benjamin.* New York: Columbia University Press, 1987.

Mills-Courts, Karen. *Poetry as Epitaph: Representation and Poetic Language.* Baton Rouge: Louisiana State University Press, 1990.

Missac, Pierre. *Passage de Walter Benjamin.* Paris: Seuil, 1987.

Moore, Carol-Lynne, and Kaoru Yamamoto. *Beyond Words: Movement Observation and Analysis.* New York: Gordon and Breach, 1988.

Mosès, Stéphane. "Brecht und Benjamin als Kafka-Interpreten." In *Juden in der deutschen Literatur: Ein deutsch-israelisches Symposion,* ed. Stéphane Mosès and Albrecht Schöne, 237–56. Frankfurt am Main: Suhrkamp, 1986.

Müller, Ernst. *Der Sohar und seine Lehre.* Vienna: R. Löwit, 1920.

Müller, Klaus-Detlev. "Der Philosoph auf dem Theater: Ideologiekritik und 'Linksabweichung' in Bertolt Brechts 'Messingkauf.'" In *Bertolt Brecht,* Sonderband aus der Reihe Text und Kritik, ed. Heinz Ludwig Arnold, 45–71. Munich: Boorberg, 1972.

Nägele, Rainer. "Augenblicke: Eingriffe. Brechts Ästhetik der Wahrnehmung." *Brecht Yearbook* 17 (1992): 29–51.

———. "Brecht's Theater of Cruelty." In *Reading after Freud. Essays on Goethe, Hölderlin, Habermas, Nietzsche, Brecht, Celan, and Freud.* New York: Columbia University Press, 1987.

———. *Theater, Theory, Speculation: Walter Benjamin and the Scenes of Modernity.* Baltimore, London: Johns Hopkins University Press, 1991.

———, ed. *Benjamin's Ground: New Readings of Walter Benjamin.* Detroit: Wayne State University Press, 1988. First published as a special issue of *Studies in Twentieth Century Literature* 11, no. 1 (fall 1986).

Nelly Sachs zu Ehren: Zum 75. Geburtstag am 10. Dezember 1966: Gedichte, Beiträge, Bibliographie. Ed. Suhrkamp Verlag. Frankfurt am Main: Suhrkamp, 1966.

Neruda, Pablo. *Tercera Residencia (1935–1945).* 3d ed. Buenos Aires: Editorial Losada, 1961.

Nietzsche, Friedrich. *Die Geburt der Tragödie.* Vol. 1 of *Sämtliche Werke.* Kritische Studienausgabe. Munich: Deutscher Taschenbuchverlag, 1980.

Pinthus, Kurt. "Jüdische Lyrik der Zeit." *C.-V.-Zeitung* (Berlin) 15 (2d supplement), 9 April 1936.

———. "Rilkes 'Briefe aus Muzot': Zu Rilkes 60. Geburtstag: 4. Dezember 1935." *C.-V.-Zeitung* (Berlin) 49 (3d supplement), 5 December 1935.

Pohlenz, Max. "Die Anfänge der griechischen Poetik." In *Kleine Schriften,* ed. Heinrich Dörrie, 436–72, vol. 2. Hildesheim: Olms, 1965.

Quintilian, *Institutio Oratoria,* trans. H. E. Butler. 4 vols. Loeb Classical Library. Cambridge: Harvard University Press, 1969.

Raddatz, Fritz J. *Verwerfungen: Sechs literarische Essays.* Frankfurt am Main: Suhrkamp, 1972.

Redfield, James. "Herodotus the Tourist." *Classical Philology* 80 (1985): 97–118.

Rickels, Laurence A. *Aberrations of Mourning: Writing on German Crypts.* Detroit: Wayne State University Press, 1988.

Rilke, Rainer Maria. *Sämtliche Werke.* 12 vols. Frankfurt am Main: Insel, 1976.

Rolleston, James. *Kafka's Narrative Theater.* University Park: Pennsylvania State University Press, 1974.

Rosenfeld, Alvin. *A Double Dying: Reflections on Holocaust Literature.* Bloomington: Indiana University Press, 1980.

Rosenzweig, Franz. *Der Stern der Erlösung.* Frankfurt am Main: Suhrkamp, 1988.

Sachs, Nelly. *Briefe der Nelly Sachs.* Ed. Ruth Dinesen and Helmut Müssener. Frankfurt am Main: Suhrkamp, 1984.

———. *Fahrt ins Staublose: Die Gedichte der Nelly Sachs.* Frankfurt am Main: Suhrkamp, 1961.

———. *Gedichte.* Ed. Hilde Domin. Frankfurt am Main: Suhrkamp, 1977.

———. *In den Wohnungen des Todes.* Berlin: Aufbau, 1947.

———. *O the Chimneys. Selected Poems, Including the Verse Play, Eli.* Trans. Michael Hamburger, Christopher Holme, Ruth Mead, Matthew Mead, and Michael Roloff. New York: Farrar, Straus and Giroux, 1967.

———. *The Seeker and Other Poems.* Trans. Ruth Mead, Matthew Mead, and Michael Hamburger. New York: Farrar, Straus and Giroux, 1970.

———. *Sternverdunkelung: Gedichte.* Amsterdam: Bermann-Fischer, Querido, 1949.

———. *Suche nach Lebenden: Die Gedichte der Nelly Sachs.* Vol. 2. Frankfurt am Main: Suhrkamp, 1971.

———. *Zeichen im Sand: Die szenischen Dichtungen der Nelly Sachs.* Frankfurt am Main: Suhrkamp, 1962.

Schiller, Friedrich. "Über Anmuth und Würde." In *Schillers Werke,* Nationalausgabe, ed. Benno v. Wiese, vol. 20. Weimar: Böhlaus Nachfolger, 1962.

———. "Vom Erhabenen." In *Schillers Werke.* Nationalausgabe, vol. 20.

Scholem, Gershom. *Die Geheimnisse der Schöpfung: Ein Kapitel aus dem Sohar.* Berlin: Schocken, 1935.

———. *Major Trends in Jewish Mysticism.* Jerusalem: Schocken Books, 1941.

———. *Walter Benjamin—die Geschichte einer Freundschaft.* Frankfurt am Main: Suhrkamp, 1975.

———. "Walter Benjamin und sein Engel." In *Zur Aktualität Walter Benjamins,* ed. Siegfried Unseld, 87–138. Frankfurt am Main: Suhrkamp, 1972.

———, ed. *Walter Benjamin/Gershom Scholem: Briefwechsel 1933–1940.* Frankfurt am Main: Suhrkamp, 1980.

Schwarz-Bart, André. *The Last of the Just.* Trans. Stephen Becker. New York: Atheneum, 1960.

Simon, Lili. "Nelly Sachs: Dichterin der großen Trauer." *Neue deutsche Hefte 35,* no. 4 (1988): 687–704.

Simpson, Patricia Anne. "Theater of Consciousness: The Language of Brecht's Body Politic." *Brecht Yearbook 17* (1992): 214–32.

———. "'Wo die Ironie erscheint': Tieck als Herausgeber in den 'Jahrbücher'-Rezensionen." In *Die Jahrbücher für wissenschaftliche Kritik": Hegels*

Berliner Gegenakademie, ed. Christoph Jamme, 301–20. Stuttgart: From-mann-Holzbook, 1994.

Smith, Gary. *Walter Benjamin's Idea of Beauty.* Ph.D. diss., Boston University, 1989.

Sussman, Henry. *Franz Kafka: Geometrician of Metaphor.* Madison, Wisc.: Coda Press, 1979.

Tiedemann, Rolf. "Brecht oder Die Kunst, in anderer Leute Köpfe zu denken." In *Dialektik im Stillstand: Versuche zum Spätwerk Walter Benjamins,* 42–73. Frankfurt am Main: Suhrkamp, 1983.

———. *Studien zur Philosophie Walter Benjamins.* Frankfurt am Main: Europäische Verlagsanstalt, 1965.

Walser, Martin. "Unser Auschwitz." In *Heimatkunde: Aufsätze und Reden.* Frankfurt am Main: Suhrkamp, 1968.

Watt, Roderick H. " 'Wanderer, kommst du nach Sparta?' History through Propaganda into Literary Commonplace." *Modern Language Review* 80, no. 4 (1985): 871–83.

———. " 'Wanderer, kommst du nach Sparta?'—A Postscript." *Forum for Modern Language Studies* 23, no. 3 (1987): 274–79.

Weber, Samuel. "Genealogy of Modernity: History, Myth, and Allegory in Benjamin's *Origin of the German Mourning Play.*" *Modern Language Notes* 106, no. 3 (1991): 465–500.

Weissenberger, Klaus. *Zwischen Stein und Stern: Mystische Formgebung in der Dichtung von Else Lasker-Schüler, Nelly Sachs und Paul Celan.* Bern: Francke, 1976.

Wiedemann-Wolf, Barbara. *Antschel Paul—Paul Celan: Studien zum Frühwerk.* Studien zur deutschen Literatur 86. Tübingen: Niemeyer, 1985.

Wood, Michael. "The Poetry of Pablo Neruda." *New York Review of Books,* 3 October 1974, 8–12.

Wordsworth, William. *The Prose Works.* Vol. 2. Ed. Alexander B. Grosart. London: Edward Moxon, Son, and Co., 1876.

Young, James E. *Writing and Rewriting the Holocaust: Narrative and the Consequences of Interpretation.* Bloomington: Indiana University Press, 1988.

Contributors

Johannes Anderegg, Professor of German, University of St. Gallen, Switzerland, focuses on literary theory, in particular on theories of aesthetics. His publications include *Leseübungen: Kritischer Umgang mit Texten* (1970); *Fiktion und Kommunikation* (1973); *Literaturwissenschaftliche Stiltheorie* (1977); and *Sprache und Verwandlung: Zur literarischen Ästhetik* (1985). Anderegg is former President of the University of St. Gallen.

Ehrhard Bahr, Professor of German, UCLA, specializes in German literature of the eighteenth and early nineteenth centuries, and of the twentieth, with particular attention to exile literature. His books include *Die Ironie im Spätwerk Goethes* (1972); *Georg Lukács* (1970); *Ernst Bloch* (1974); and *Nelly Sachs* (1980). He has also written articles on Thomas Mann, the Frankfurt School, Hofmannsthal, Kafka, Sachs, and exile literature. Bahr is a former president of the German Studies Association and president-elect of the Goethe Society of North America.

Timothy Bahti, Professor of Comparative Literature and German at the University of Michigan, is author of *Allegories of History: Literary Historiography After Hegel* (1992) and *Ends of the Lyric: Direction and Consequence in Western Poetry* (1995), and articles on Walter Benjamin, German philosophy, European poetry, and literary theory.

Ruth Dinesen teaches German Literature in Copenhagen. She is editor of *Briefe der Nelly Sachs* (1984), and of *Und Leben hat immer wie Abschied geschmeckt: Frühe Gedichte und Prosa der Nelly Sachs* (1987), and author of *Nelly Sachs: Eine Biographie* (1992) for which she received the Statens Kunstfonds Litteraere pris in 1994.

Marilyn Sibley Fries, 1945–95, was Associate Professor of German and Women's Studies at the University of Michigan, editor of *Responses to Christa Wolf: Critical Essays* (1989), and author of *The Changing Consciousness of Reality: The Image of Berlin in Selected German Novels from Raabe to Döblin* (1980) as well as of several articles on twentieth-century German literature, with concentration on the postwar period.

Winfried Menninghaus, Professor of General and Comparative Literature, Free University of Berlin, is author of *Walter Benjamins Theorie der Sprachmagie* (1980), *Paul Celan: Magie der Form* (1980), *Artistische Schrift: Studien zur Kompositionskunst Gottfried Kellers* (1982), and *Unendliche Verdopplung: Die frühromantische Grundlegung der Kunsttheorie im Begriff absoluter Selbstreflexion* (1987), and coeditor of *Paul Celan: Materialien* (1986) and *Für Walter Benjamin* (1992).

Stéphane Mosès, Professor and Director at The Franz Rosenzweig Research Center for German-Jewish Literature and Culture, The Hebrew University of Jerusalem, and formerly professor of German at the Sorbonne, is the world's foremost scholar of German-Jewish literary relations. He is author of *Une affinité littéraire: Le Titan de Jean Paul et le Docteur Faustus de Thomas Mann* (1972), *Système et révélation: La Philosophie de Franz Rosenzweig* (1982), and numerous essays on Benjamin, Jabès, and other Jewish writers, as well as co-editor of *Juden in der deutschen Literatur* (1986) and *Franz Kafka und das Judentum* (1987).

Dorothee Ostmeier is Assistant Professor of German at the University of Washington in Seattle. She received her M.A. from the Ruhr University, Bochum and her Ph.D. from The Johns Hopkins University in 1993. Her interest in the borders between poetic and dramatic expression in texts from the eighteenth to the nineteenth century has led to her current focus on the relation between expressionist and postmodern dramatic concepts and their reflections on the crises in and of language. Ostmeier is preparing articles on Samuel Beckett and August Stramm. Her essay on Nelly Sachs and Walter Benjamin in this volume presents a part of a larger project, titled *Sprache des Dramas—Drama der Sprache: Nelly Sachs' Poetik*.

Patricia Anne Simpson is Assistant Professor in the Department of Germanic Languages and Literatures at the University of Michigan, Ann Arbor. She is currently completing a book titled *Irony, Gender, and the Dialectic in German Romanticism*. Simpson has also published articles on a wide range of topics including popular culture in the former GDR, German "marginal" literature, and the poetry of Karoline von Günderrode.

Elisabeth Strenger has taught at Brandeis University, where she was

Assistant Professor of German. In addition to her work on German-Jewish women writers, she has written on Reformation and Baroque drama.

William West is a doctoral candidate in the Program in Comparative Literature at the University of Michigan. He is writing a dissertation on the relations between the encyclopedia and the theater in early modern England.

Index